FRANCE AND THE ALGERIAN CONFLICT

To my family and Doron

France and the Algerian Conflict

Issues in Democracy and Political Stability, 1988–1995

CAMILLE BONORA-WAISMAN

ASHGATE

Published by
Ashgate Publishing Limited
Gower House
Croft Road
Aldershot
Hants GU11 3HR
England

Ashgate Publishing Company
Suite 420
101 Cherry Street
Burlington, VT 05401-4405
USA

Ashgate website: http://www.ashgate.com

British Library Cataloguing in Publication Data
Bonora-Waisman, Camille
 France and the Algerian Conflict : issues in democracy and
 political stability, 1988-1995. - (Leeds studies in
 democratization)
 1. Democratization - Algeria 2. France - Foreign relations -
 Algeria 3. Algeria - Foreign relations, France 4. France -
 Foreign relations - 1981- 5. Algeria - Foreign relations -
 20th century 6. Algeria - Politics and government -
 1962-1990 7. Algeria - Politics and government - 1990-
 I. Title
 327.6'5'044

Library of Congress Control Number: 00-109129

ISBN 1 84014 751 2

Printed and bound by Athenaeum Press, Ltd.,
Gateshead, Tyne & Wear.

Contents

Part Three: Opposing the FIS

List of Tables

List of Tables

Acknowledgments

In its general terms, the subject of this book is the result of a deal dating back to my post-graduate studies. It was defined as part of a give-and-take agreement between the research interests of the Leeds University Politics Department and my own, with, in the background, the prospect of a grant. I must, therefore, thank the Politics Department first among all for its generosity without which this project could not have been mine. The perspicacity and flexibility of my interviewers must also be recognised. Interested in the European Union's policy towards democratization, they suggested Algeria as a case-study. But they also gave me the freedom to define the boundaries of my research so that I was able to specifically focus on France's policy towards Algeria well after the short-lived democratic experience of that country.

In doing this research, I have incurred many debts. Without the testimonies of members of the French political establishment, much of this work would have been beside the point. Jean Audibert, Claude Cheysson, Roland Dumas and Georges Morin helped me a great deal by giving me insights into the foreign policy decision-making process and into the realm of perceptions and feelings about Algeria. I owe them more than they perhaps realise. High civil servants also brought an illuminating contribution to my understanding of the French government's perceptions of Algeria's crisis and of "how things work" between the two states. The time spared by Christophe Bigot and Lucile Schmid was not lost – at any rate not for me!

Jean-Pierre Brevost, from the Total Oil Company, was very helpful in explaining the logics of contemporary oil trade, the scope of Algeria's hydrocarbon reforms and the technical aspects of Franco-Algerian oil trade. He also provided me with a general vision of what may be coined the "business view" of instability in Algeria. On the Algerian side, Sadek Boussena, who spent more hours with me than I could expect, was of a fabulous assistance to the many questions I had about Algeria and Franco-Algerian relations.

In the academic world, I am of course indebted to many scholars through the work they did on Algeria, Islamism, and Franco-Algerian relations. I would like to thank those who personally made a contribution to this work. François Burgat, with his eternal brainstorming effect, was a good mentor in introspection about ready-made presumptions. Throughout my research, Simon Bromley, George Joffé and Hugh Roberts made useful comments and constructive criticisms, thus, helping me to structure my thoughts.

Finally, I must thank my parents for having been so supportive and, not the least, for having borne my obsessions.

List of Abbreviations

AIS	*Armée Islamique du Salut* (Islamic Salvation Army, Algeria)
AMU	Arab Maghreb Union
Bcm	Billions of cubic meters
BDF	*Banque de France* (French Central Bank)
CDS	*Centre des Démocrates Sociaux* (Social Democrats, France)
COFACE	*Compagnie Française d'assurance pour le Commerce Extérieur* (public company for export insurance, France)
DGSE	*Direction Générale de la Sécurité Extérieure* (French intelligence)
DREE	*Direction des Relations Economiques Extérieures* (Department for Foreign Economic Relations, Economic Affairs Ministry, France)
ECU	European Currency Unit
EEC	European Economic Union
EU	European Union
FAF	*Fraternité Algérienne en France* (Algerian Brotherhood in France)
FDI	Foreign direct investment
FFS	*Front des Forces Socialistes* (Socialist Forces Front, Algeria)
FIS	*Front Islamique du Salut* (Islamic Salvation Front, Algeria)
FLN	*Front de Libération Nationale* (National Liberation Front, Algeria)
FN	*Front National* (National Front, France)
GDF	*Gaz de France* (French gas public utility)
GIA	*Groupe Islamique Armé* (Islamic Armed Group, Algeria)
HAMAS	*Mouvement pour la Société Islamique* (Movement for an Islamic Society, Algeria)
HSC	High State Council
IAEA	International Atomic Energy Agency
IBRD	International Bank for Reconstruction and Development
IEA	International Energy Agency
IMF	International Monetary Fund
LNG	Liquefied Natural Gas
MAE	*Ministère des Affaires Etrangères* (Foreign Affairs, France)
MAJD	*Mouvement Algérien pour la Justice et le Développement* (Algerian Movement for Justice and Development)
MCB	*Mouvement Culturel Berbère* (Berber Cultural Movement, Algeria)

MDA	*Mouvement Démocratique Algérien* (Algerian Democratic Movement)
MEED	Middle East Economic Digest
MEI	Middle East International
MIA	*Mouvement Islamique Armé* (Islamic Armed Movement, Algeria)
Mmt	Millions of metric tons
MNI	*Mouvement de la Nahda Islamique* (Movement of the Islamic Renaissance, Algeria)
MRP	*Mouvement pour la République* (Movement for the Republic, Algeria)
OECD	Organisation of Economic Co-operation and Development
OPEC	Organisation of the Petroleum Exporting Countries
PAGS	*Parti de l'avant-guarde Socialiste* (Socialist Vanguard Party, Algeria)
PCF	*Parti Communiste Français* (French Communist Party)
PRA	*Parti du Renouveau Algérien* (Algerian Renewal Party)
PS	*Parti Socialiste* (Socialist Party, France)
PT	*Parti des Travailleurs* (Workers' Party, Algeria)
RCD	*Rassemblement pour la Culture et la Démocratie* (Rally for Culture and Democracy, Algeria)
RNP	*Rassemblement National Patriotique* (Patriotic National Rally, Algeria)
RPR	*Rassemblement pour la République* (Rally for the Republic, France)
SOAS	School of Oriental and African Studies (University of London)
UDF	*Union pour la Démocratie Française* (Union for French Democracy)
UGTA	*Union Générale des Travailleurs Algériens* (Algerian Workers' Union)
UN	United Nations

Introduction:
France and Algeria's
Short-lived Democratization Process

From its Independence from France in 1962 until the beginning of a democratization process in 1989, Algeria was a one-party state. The FLN (National Liberation Front), which co-opted or eliminated the various nationalist movements during the War of Liberation (1954–62) and whose armed wing, the ALN (National Liberation Army), fought the war against French occupation, was established as unique party in 1963. In practice, however, the FLN never ruled Algeria. Its role was limited to the control and mobilization of Algerian society for the implementation of policies designed by the Military, the actual nucleus of power. In 1989, following the out-break of violent popular riots throughout the country (October 1988), the Algerian Administration engaged in a fast-track democratization process which came to parallel a policy of economic liberalization initiated in the early 1980s. Democratization was characterised by the introduction of multi-party politics and, thus, the abolition of the one-party system. The new 1989 Constitution, which was approved by referendum, clearly separated the executive, legislative and judicial functions and waived major principles that had guided the Algerian Revolution such as Socialism, Non-alignment, and Third-Worldism. The Army was entrusted with the sole task of defending the country and was no longer to be viewed as the 'Guardian of the Revolution'. Lastly, civil society was left to organize itself.

The October 1988 revolt and, later, the democratization process allowed the Islamist movement[1] to enter the Algerian political arena. In 1982, following student demonstrations, the Algerian Islamist movement had already manifested its inclination for political activity: it then put forward a platform enjoining the Algerian regime to remain true to its Islamic tradition. However, it was 'Black October' of 1988[2] that allowed the Islamist movement to show itself as a significant political force. Indeed, without sparking off the uprising, the Islamists managed to channel the people's anger. As its leaders were received by President Chadli Benjedid in the wake of the riots, the Islamist movement established itself as a mediator between the regime and the people. As the events were later to demonstrate, the Islamist movement was the major beneficiary of democratization. The Islamic Salvation Front (FIS), which was recognized as a political party in 1989, triumphed in Algeria's first free local and regional elections (June 1990) and in the first round of the December 1991 parliamentary election. The prospect of a FIS-dominated parliament, however, led the Algerian Army to stage a coup d'état, thus, abruptly bringing to an end the democratization process. Since the coup of January 1992, repression and counter-violence have been the major items on Algeria's political agenda. Indeed, the country has been in a virtual state of war between official troops and various Islamist guerrilla forces which have either vied to overthrow the regime by force or have hoped that violence would eventually bring the regime to recognize the banned FIS as a political partner. In its struggle for survival, the Algerian regime, more than ever in the hands of the Army, has again locked the political arena: censorship of the media and violent intimidation measures against the population have been daily occurrences. Although political dialogue between the regime and the outlawed FIS as well as other political parties occurred throughout the conflict, it did not succeed in bringing a lasting solution to Algeria's protracted crisis because the Algerian regime never saw political dialogue as anything else than a tool to legitimise its own rule.

Algiers at the centre of a silent world attention

The Algerian conflict has not generated any uproar on the international diplomatic scene but has paradoxically been at the centre of world attention and this for several reasons. First, because of the ferocity of a conflict which in eight years has reportdely killed 100 000 people. The barbaric methods used both by the Islamist guerrillas and the Army have also been distressing news for believers in the respect of human rights and the respect of the Other.

Second, the Algerian conflict has caused world-wide concern because it has raised questions about the political evolution of the Muslim world. Most states in the Muslim world face opposition movements which draw upon the religious dogma in order to contest the legitimacy of the established regimes. It is often perceived that what has been happening in Algeria could very well occur elsewhere. The 'Algerian case' has been particularly destabilizing in terms of predicting change. Algeria was considered one of the most stable states in the developing world; now political instability has devastated the country. State ideology in Algeria was profoundly progressive and, thus, seen as immune from religious controversy; the Islamist movement has been quite successful in promoting its cause. Algeria's foundering in a conflict that could have turned into a true civil war has, therefore, been alarming news for those states in the Muslim world whose maintenance in power is threatened by Islamist activism. The rise of Islamism in Algeria has also been a source of concern for the West which feels threatened by the anti-Western rhetoric of Islamism and which may have something to lose in changes of regimes throughout the Muslim world.

Lastly, in a context where the fall of the Berlin Wall has generated hopes for global democratization, the Algerian conflict has raised questions anew. How do we deal with a democratization process which, instead of bringing about liberal democracy, favours the access to power of a political party which qualifies the concept of democracy as alien to the Islamic tradition and whose emphasis on moral order threatens to be socially reactionary? Should we trust the political process and the civil society's counterpowers? Or should we favour non-democratic methods today in order to protect democracy tomorrow? These questions were inevitably raised by the January 1992 coup d'état in Algiers and generated debates not only among academics but also among politicians in Algeria and elsewhere. However, even though the theme of democracy has pervaded political discourse both in Algeria and in the West, democracy has been the prime casualty in the Algerian conflict. Democracy has lost its sense in Algeria because, despite a formal concern for a return to democratic life, democracy has been the yardstick neither of policy in Algeria nor of foreign policies towards Algeria. This book is devoted to the study of France's foreign policy towards Algeria once the democratization process was brought to an end there. This choice must be explained.

France and Algeria

Even though the Algerian conflict has aroused world concern, focussing on French foreign policy is justified by the fact that no other state has led as active a policy. The reason for this is quite simple. Particularly in the first years of the Algerian conflict, the international community reacted to political upheavals in Algeria by reference to the French position because Algeria has always been regarded as France's backyard. This state of affairs directly flows from History. In 1830, the French conquered Algeria which was then under Ottoman rule. Colonization lasted for more than a century. In contrast with the Moroccan and Tunisian protectorates, Algeria was made an integral part of France and became a colony of settlement for one million Europeans. Despite the fact that, under colonial rule, Algerians encountered France's 'civilizing mission' only through the plundering of lands and colonial apartheid society and despite the sufferings of a seven year long War of Liberation, political Independence did not bring about a break in the relationship between the states. On the eve of its Independence, Algeria was too weak to walk by itself. But, as its geostrategic location did not bring as many advantages as that of Morocco or Tunisia, neither the USA nor the Soviet Union showed much interest in cultivating a strong influence in Algeria. In contrast, General de Gaulle saw Independent Algeria as a diplomatic asset. By initiating an 'exemplary co-operation' with its ex-colony, France, it was believed, would be absolved of its colonial sin. France's close association with Algeria, whose role as an active promoter of the Third World's claim for international political and economic restructuring was growing, would allow Paris to gain prestige in the Third World and, thus, to assert itself as a 'Third Force' in the bipolar world of the time. In addition to Algeria's function as a 'narrow door to the Third World' in de Gaulle's international policy of 'greatness', there were very pragmatic reasons for the French Administration to keep close ties with Algeria. French property in natural resources, industry, banking and trade needed to be protected. Access to the Algerian market, both as an outlet for French manufactured and capital goods and as a supply of raw materials and agricultural products, needed to be maintained. The Saharan nuclear testing sites had to be kept running if France was ever to dispose of a nuclear 'striking force', allowing it to be independent from the American nuclear umbrella and to be ranked as a great power. The Evian accords (March 1962), which put an end to French colonization, in effect ensured the protection of France's colonial advantages in return for massive economic aid.

In the post-Independence era, the Franco-Algerian relationship has never been simple to manage. It has been characterised by perpetual ups and downs, cyclical periods of cooling off and *rapprochement*. Under Ahmed Ben Bella (1962–65) and more so under Houari Boumediene (1965–78), the socialist and nationalist orientation of the new independent state led to complete state-control of the economy, thereby, adversely affecting French vested interests. In February 1971, the nationalization of 51% of the assets of the two French oil companies operating in Algeria was the last blow in France's progressive loss of control of Algeria's key economic sectors. It triggered what President Pompidou (1969–74) coined the 'banalization' of Franco-Algerian relations, that is a policy that was no longer to favour privileged ties with Algeria, particularly over Morocco and Tunisia. In effect, throughout the 1970s Franco-Algerian relations were lukewarm. Pompidou's somewhat conciliatory response to the oil producers' demands during the 1973 oil crisis did not forestall crises over such issues as immigration, gas prices, war archives, etc. Giscard d'Estaing's April 1975 trip to Algeria (which was the first visit of a French president to Algiers since Independence) did not succeed either in bringing France and Algeria closer. Under Giscard d'Estaing (1974–81), France's siding along with Rabat over the Western Sahara issue was a central cause of the deterioration of the *entente* with Algiers.

In the late 1970s, a series of factors led to an improvement in Franco-Algerian relations. Undoubtedly, one of the main factors in this improvement was Boumediene's demise and his replacement by Chadli Benjedid (1979–92). Less dogmatic than his predecessor, Chadli had also been an officer in the French Army before the insurrection of November 1954. His Administration became more French-oriented than that of Boumediene. When François Mitterrand was elected president in May 1981, the ground had thus been prepared for a *rapprochement*. In addition, the socialists endeavoured to give special attention to Algeria. One of Mitterrand's 110 electoral propositions was to establish privileged ties with Algeria[3] within the general framework of a foreign policy which would put emphasis on North/South co-operation and which, in the context of the Cold War, would back Third World states' non-alignment strategies. With the appointment of Claude Cheysson as foreign minister, it was not surprising that a special effort would be made in order to reinvigorate the relationship between the two states. Besides his third-worldist approach to international affairs, Cheysson has always been pro-Algeria, partly as a result of his official role as counsellor to the Algerian authorities in developing oil resources back in the 1960s. Also, Cheysson has always felt that France had to compensate for its large responsibility for the state of underdevelopment of Algeria. In the early 1980s, the 'impassioned' relationship which Cheysson had promised symbolically took shape with mutual presidential visits: Mitterrand went to Algiers in October–November 1981; Chadli Benjedid returned the visit in November 1983, his official trip being the first visit of an Algerian president to France since Independence. Concretely, the revival of Franco-Algerian relations came in the form of an over-market-price gas agreement (February 1982) and a comprehensive protocol of economic co-operation (June 1982) which were representative of the 'co-development' plan sponsored by Claude Cheysson and Jean-Pierre Cot (minister for co-operation and development).

Under the premiership of Fabius (1984–86) and under the first 'cohabitation' period (1986–88),[4] the euphoria of the early 1980s toned down principally because of an adverse economic environment both in France and Algeria. Crises subsequently erupted over such issues as gas, immigration, France's 'policy of equilibrium' in the Maghreb, the maintenance of French cemeteries in Algeria, the recovery of the *Pieds-noirs*' assets[5] and the custody of divorced mixed-couples' children. Without being icy, Franco-Algerian relations were thus somewhat chilly when Mitterrand was re-elected president in May 1988. As in 1981, the socialist Rocard government saw the settling of the gas conflict as a way of 'relaunching' the relationship on a healthier basis. The visit of the French minister for foreign affairs, Roland Dumas, to Algiers on September 3–4, 1988 was aimed at defusing the lurking crisis before Mitterrand's trip scheduled for October. Dumas succeeded in his mission by drawing up a firm schedule for the resumption of the gas dispute and by inscribing the prospect of the new gas accord within the larger framework of bilateral economic and financial co-operation.[6] The October riots then occurred and were to be the test of friendship.

During Mitterrand's first mandate, despite ups and downs in the bilateral relationship, France perceived the Chadli regime as much more open to co-operation and compromise than the Boumediene regime had been. France welcomed undergoing changes in Algeria. Chadli's steps towards economic liberalization were appreciated if only because economic reform was beneficial to French business.[7] Algeria's retreat from Third World activism[8] was also greeted because the French socialists' own Third World policy had lost much of its content as of 1984.[9] In the early 1970s, 'normalization' was a response to the French loss of direct control of Algeria's economic sectors. In contrast, in the latter part of the 1970s and in the 1980s, tension in bilateral relations stemmed from the wealth of the ties linking the two countries. At all times, however, crises were fuelled by the somewhat over-passionate climate that has surrounded Franco-Algerian relations since Independence. Colonization and the War of Liberation have, indeed, marked collective attitudes on both sides so that the context within which the Franco-Algerian relationship has been unfolding is highly emotional. Policy measures implemented by each of the two states, or events happening in each of the two countries have often been understood as discriminatory, as having the unpleasant taste of neocolonialism for the Algerians and of radical nationalism for the French. Slight disagreements over particular aspects of bilateral relations have sometimes degenerated into a (verbal) questioning of the whole relationship. Dramatisation has been reinforced by the civil societies' often passionate meddling with such issues as the maintenance of French cemeteries in Algeria, children abductions, racist attacks against Algerian immigrants in France, etc. Considering the emotions surrounding the relationship, no one will be surprised that it has often been described as one of simultaneous attraction and repulsion.

What policy and why?

The basic aim of this book is to look into France's Algeria policy particularly after the January 1992 coup d'état and to determine why the various French governments adopted a particular foreign policy course. The task before us is not easy because of the hidden face of foreign policy. Franco-Algerian relations are partly unfolding under the sway of informal networks which operate both at the economic and political levels. The impact of these informal networks on foreign policy-making is difficult to determine exactly, precisely because of their informal nature. The explanations brought forward in this book may, thus, not always provide a full picture of France's policy towards Algeria. But, to compensate for this inevitable shortcoming, the method of confronting words and deeds was systematically applied so as to unveil what the French governments exactly did as opposed to just what they said they were doing.

Confronting the official discourse to actual policy measures was conducted in relation to the socialist governments (1988–1993) in Part One and the right-wing governments under 'cohabitation' or not (1993–95) in Part Two. Both these sections are meant to provide answers to the question 'what policy?'. The essential conclusion to be drawn is that there was not one policy but several policies in relation to Algeria. Both the Left and the Right changed the initial course they had chosen for their Algerian policy at one stage or the other. In all cases, policy shifts revolved around the issue as to whether Paris should support a policy of conciliation with, or a policy of eradication of, the Islamist opposition. In turn, this implied a shifting positioning *vis-à-vis* the Algerian regime and its various strands. It must be made clear, however, that what mattered to French policy-makers was not the issue of conciliation / eradication in itself but the way in which each of these two options was perceived as affecting political stability in Algeria. The concern for political stability more than any commitment to democratization is, indeed, what led French policy-makers to make the choices they made.

Part One thus explains that, under the socialists, the official reaction to the January 1992 coup d'état was rather negative. Despite a formal concern about the inherent undemocratic character of the coup, French dissatisfaction with political developments in Algeria really stemmed from two factors. One was that the coup allowed the return to power of more nationalist figures than those of the Chadli era – a political development that was seen as adversely affecting French vested interests in Algeria. The other related to the Cresson government's view that political instability might grow out of the Algerian regime's attempts to force the Islamist movement out of the political landscape. Through behind-the-scenes diplomacy, the Cresson government actually advocated a compromise with the Islamist mainstream. It did not call for a formal integration of the FIS in the government but suggested that a political personality capable of engineering a synthesis between the Islamic and secular nationalist traditions of Algeria be propelled to the forefront of Algerian politics. The Quai d'Orsay (the French Ministry for Foreign Affairs) hoped that such a solution would be acceptable to everybody in Algeria, that it would preserve stability there and ensure the everlastingness of the way in which relations between France and Algeria have always operated. In the wake of its failure to convince the Algerian authorities to find an agreement with the Islamists, the Cresson government adopted a low-profile policy which was followed by Prime Minister Bérégovoy until January 1993. At that stage, a shift occurred to the effect that the French socialists saw political stability in Algeria as mere regime stability. The reasons for this shift towards a greater support to the Algerian authorities still remain unclear. It may, nevertheless, be speculated that in a context where it was believed that the Islamists might succeed in overthrowing the regime, France preferred to back the Algerian authorities than have to face a revolutionary Islamist regime.

Part Two reviews France's policy towards Algeria under the Right in the context of 'cohabitation' (the Balladur government, 1993–95) and in the early days of the new Chirac presidency (the Juppé government, 1995–97). The Balladur government's Algeria policy is analyzed in terms of the shift that occurred around September 1994. Prior to September 1994, the Balladur government also equated political stability with regime stability and, subsequently, buttressed the Algerian regime's 'eradicator' trend. In contrast, after September 1994, when it was realised that eradication had not succeeded to bring back political stability and that France was becoming isolated in supporting the eradicators, conciliation in Algeria was truly advocated. However, conciliation did not make unanimity within the government and, in practice, the Balladur government did not seek to dragoon the Algerian regime into conciliation. Under the presidency of Jacques Chirac (which is put under review only from May to November 1995, date of the Algerian presidential election), the advantages of conciliation over eradication were not forgotten. However, within the relatively conciliatory position adopted by the Juppé government, a shift towards greater support for conciliation occurred in October 1995 partly as a result of a controversy triggered by the French Socialist Party about a meeting scheduled between the French and Algerian presidents. As it was called upon to justify its policy in public, the Juppé government argued that if the return to democratic life was the key to political stability in Algeria, conciliation had to be part of the democratic equation. This meant that, in the wake of the Algerian presidential election, parliamentary elections in which the FIS would be allowed to compete would have to be organized. In practice, the Juppé government's firmer support to conciliation in October 1995 did not stem from its desire to promote democratization for its own sake. It derived from the view that allowing the FIS to compete in parliamentary elections (but not presidential ones) was the way to put some order back into Algerian affairs without taking too many risks. Juppé's government also seemed more resolute than Balladur's to push for conciliation when it warned that French economic aid might be tied to democratization in Algeria.

Part Three seeks to provide a rationale for the specific policy of opposing a FIS take-over by violence or by a negotiated settlement – a policy which, both under the Left and the Right, translated into French support to the Algerian regime at one stage or the other. Part Three brings forward and assesses two types of motives for French opposition to the FIS. One relates to the foreseen risks of the FIS coming into power. The other one deals with the ideological and 'psychological' dimensions of the French political elite's opposition to the FIS. Perceived risks entailed by the FIS coming into power are analyzed in terms of four issue-areas corresponding to the concerns expressed by the French political establishment with more or less emphasis: political instability in the Mediterranean by domino effect; immigration issues; national security issues and economic issues. Immigration issues raised by a FIS take-over or an inclusion of the FIS within the political process are identified as the central motive behind the French hostility to the FIS. The other factors are understood as having played a contributory role, especially insofar as opposing conciliation in Algeria was concerned. Opposition to the perspective of the FIS coming to power (by violence or not) is also explained by ideological and 'psychological' factors. It will be argued that, if French opposition to the FIS on ideological grounds was similar to most Western states' wincing at a new form of nationalism involving the ideological and cultural spheres, it was primarily motivated by the fact that this challenge to Western political culture came specifically from Algeria, that is from a country that has emotionally remained a part of France in the French collective imaginary. The FIS vote was lived in France as a 'psychological trauma' because it implied that part of the Algerian people did not recognize itself in France and its political paradigms. This was difficult to accept. This was also incomprehensible to the French political elite whose restricted contacts with the Algerian Gallicised elite have nourished a truncated vision of Algerian society.

Notes

1. In recent years a consensus has taken root in the academic literature dealing with the contemporary Islamic revival as to the terminology to use in order to describe religio-political movements which endeavour to reconstruct the social and political order of their societies within a framework inspired by Islamic Scriptures and which do so by aiming at state power. The generic term 'Islamism' generally applies to movements which advocate direct intervention in politics. 'Fundamentalism', on the

other hand, describes movements which restrict their religious activism to the moral sphere of private life without contesting the prevalent social and political order of their societies. On the issue of terminology, see F. Burgat (1988b).

2. To quell the rebellion, a state of siege was declared in Algiers, a curfew imposed and the tanks sent to the streets. 159 persons were officially recorded to have been shot by the Army throughout the country. Unofficial sources put the death toll over 500. Arrests were conducted *en masse* and disturbing cases of torture were reported. For details on the unfolding of the October 1988 riots, see among others K. Duran (1989).

3. F. Mitterrand (1981), p. 324.

4. 'Cohabitation' in French politics corresponds to a situation where the president of the Republic and the prime minister do not belong to the same political affiliations. Such a situation is made possible by the time lag between the presidential elections (held every seven years) and the parliamentary ones (every four years). In 1986, whereas Mitterrand's mandate was in its fifth year, the parliamentary election gave the majority to the Right. Accordingly, a right-wing prime minister had to be appointed. Jacques Chirac took the position and nominated his government. Mitterrand did not resign. A second cohabitation phase occurred during the period under review in this book. Whereas Mitterrand was re-elected in 1988, the 1993 parliamentary election brought the Right back to Matignon. Edouard Balladur became Mitterrand's prime minister until the 1995 presidential election in which right-winger Chirac won.

5. The French settlers in Algeria were called *Pieds-noirs*. When they fled Algeria at Independence, their properties and assets were expropriated.

6. For references on Franco-Algerian relations since Independence see: C. Wauthier (1995); J.F. Daguzan (1993/94); K. Basfao and J.R. Henry (1992); P. Naylor (1992); B. El Mellouki Riffi (1989); S. Mouhoubi (1989); P. Balta (1986); N. Grimaud (1986), (1984a&b); J. Damis (1984); I. Brandell (1981); D. Colard (1978); E. Kolodziej (1974); P. Balta and C. Rulleau (1973) and the international chronicle of Algeria yearly published in *Annuaire de l'Afrique du Nord*.

7. General literature on Algeria's liberalization policy can be found in K. Pfeifer (1992); A. Brahimi (1991) and M. Ecrement (1986). For a critical assessment of economic liberalization, see in particular M. Bennoune (1988). For a general account of Boumediene's strategy of development and its shortcomings, see R. Lawless (1984).

8. For details on Algeria's role in promoting the cause of the Third World in the 1970s, see A. Lassassi (1988); N. Grimaud (1984a) and R. Mortimer (1984). For details on Algeria's shift away from activism in Third World fora towards a focus on regional politics and international mediation under President Chadli, see N. Grimaud (1993); R. Mortimer (1992); B. Korany (1991); B. Allouche (1989) and J. Entelis (1986).

9. For references on French policy towards the Third World and its failures under Mitterrand, see e.g. F. Favier and M. Martin-Roland (1990); J. Adda and M.C. Smouts (1989); D. Levy (1987); J.F. Bayard (1984) and J.P. Cot (1984).

Table 1:   French and Algerian governments, 1988–95

FRANCE		ALGERIA	
President of the Republic	**Governments**	**Governments**	**President of the Republic**
Francois Mitterand	**Rocard (1)**	**Brahimi**	**Chadli Benjedid (e)**
(May 1981–May 95)	(May 1988–May 91)	(Jan. 1984–Nov. 88)	(Feb. 1979–Jan. 92)
	R Dumas (2) *P Bérégovoy (3)*	*A Taleb Ibrahimi* *B Benhamouda*	
		Merbah	
		(Nov. 1988–Sept. 89)	
		B Bessaih *Sid Ahmed Ghozali*	
		Hamrouche	
		(Sept. 1989–June 91)	
		Sid Ahmed Ghozali *G Hidouci*	
			President of High State Council
	Cresson	**Ghozali**	**Mohamed Boudiaf (a)**
	(May 1991–Apr. 92)	(June 1991–July 92)	(Jan. 1992–June 92)
	R Dumas *P Bérégovoy*	*L Brahimi* *H Benissad-* *Ghozali*	
	Bérégovoy	**Abdesselam**	**Ali Kafi (a)**
	(Apr 1992–May 95)	(July 1992–Aug. 93)	(July 1992–Jan. 94)

Table 1 (continued)

FRANCE		ALGERIA	
President of the Republic	**Governments**	**Governments**	**President of the High State Council**
	R Dumas	L Brahimi - R Malek	
	M Sapin	B Abdesselam	
			President of the Republic
Balladur		**Malek**	**Lamine Zeroual (a)**
(March 1993–May 95)	(Aug. 1993–April 94)	(Jan. 1994–Nov. 95)	
	A Juppé A Alphandéry - N Sarkozy	M S Dembri M Benachenhou	
Jacques Chirac	**Juppé**	**Sifi**	
(May 1995–)	(May 1995–1997)	(April 1994–Dec. 95)	
	H de Charette A Madelin - J Arthuis	M S Dembri M Benachenhou	
		Ouyahia	**Lamine Zeroual (e)**
		(From Dec. 1995)	(From Nov. 1995)
		A Attaf M Nenachenhou	

Notes: (e) = elected (within the limits of the Algerian political system); (a) = appointed; (1) = Prime Minister; (2) = Minister for Foreign Affairs; (3) = Minister for Economic Affairs.

Part One

The Socialists
(October 1988 – March 1993)

Introduction to Part One

Under the socialists, France's Algeria policy could best be understood in terms of three distinct periods corresponding to changed circumstances in Algeria. The first period opens with the October 1988 riots and ends with the January 1992 coup d'état in Algeria. The repressive turn of the October 1988 events caused embarrassment in the French political establishment which had supported the Chadli regime ever since the arrival of François Mitterrand to the presidency in May 1981. But, as the riots played the role of a catalyst in the progress towards democratization, the Rocard government did not condemn the repression. Instead, it brought its support to Chadli's democratization initiative as well as to his economic liberalization programme. Algeria's democratization process was concluded with the December 1991 free parliamentary election which was interrupted in January 1992 as a result of the victory of the Islamic Salvation Front (FIS) in the first round. The coup d'état generated a slight shift in French policy which, until January 1993, can be described as one of mixed support to the Algerian rulers. The interruption of the democratization process, indeed, generated a cool reaction in Paris both because of the dismissal of Chadli and the risks of greater authoritarianism involved. The discrepancy between the French president's discourse, emphasising France's strong reservations about the coup, and the foreign affairs minister's, stressing non-interference, should not be understood as a mere double-talk that allowed France to save face while effectively supporting the coup. It was a deliberate double-act meant to show France's dissatisfaction while at the same time maintaining the lines of communication open between Paris and Algiers. Indeed, France sought to influence the course of events in Algeria. It suggested that, in order to avoid the aggravation of the political crisis and of the security situation, a political personality, belonging to the National Liberation Front (FLN) but able to rally the Islamists' allegiance through his religious legitimacy, was needed. The proposal was judged as profoundly improper in Algiers. Relations between the two states became strained because of the socialists' unwillingness to effectively throw their weight behind Algeria's new rulers despite an official discourse of support and solidarity. In January 1993 – the starting-point of the third period – the Bérégovoy government initiated a *rapprochement* with the Algerian authorities. The minister for foreign affairs went to Algiers and invited the Algerian prime minister to Paris. Economic aid followed promptly. The underlying reasons for this firmer backing still remain mysterious for it occurred just when the socialists were about to be defeated in the March 1993 French parliamentary election whose results were rightly forecasted. It is possible that the change in French Ambassadors to Algiers played a role in the redefinition of French policy and that a reassessment of the power struggle between the Islamist armed groups and the authorities led Paris to alter its views.

In the following account, the French socialists' policy towards Algeria from October 1988 to March 1993 is thus analysed in terms of these three distinct periods: 1) support to Chadli's democratization and economic liberalization from October 1988 to January 1992; 2) mixed support throughout 1992; and 3) renewed support from January 1993 to March 1993. In each of these three sections, the marking events that occurred in Algeria are accounted for so as to understand the circumstances in which French foreign policy-making was made.

Chapter 1

French Support for Chadli Benjedid's Economic and Political Liberalization Policy (October 1988 – January 1992)

The October 1988 riots were to change the political face of Algeria. Indeed, they sparked off a fast-track democratization process that lasted for over three years before being brought to an end with the coup d'état of January 1992. During these three years, Algeria experienced an exceptional degree of political freedom in the Arab world. Civil society was freed. The one-party state system was brought down as political parties were allowed. Free local and regional elections took place in June 1990 and their results were accepted, thus bringing the FIS to power in the majority of local and regional councils. A setback occurred in June 1991 when martial law was enforced as a result of protests organized by the FIS against a new electoral law that gerrymandered the constituencies. The subsequent imprisonment of the FIS' leaders presaged what was to happen later on. However, to all appearances, the Algerian government seemed prepared to organize a 'clean and fair' parliamentary election. In parallel with democratization, Algeria accelerated its economic liberalization programme.

In face of the crushing of the 1988 riots, the Rocard government chose the 'telling silence' in the range of diplomatic formulae. It then proceeded to argue that Algiers needed help, not remonstrance, to overcome the socio-economic problems that led to popular discontent. Backing Chadli in the wake of Black October also came down to demonstrate support for the man himself at a time when he was challenged both from below and from within the political establishment. With democratization on track and economic liberalization accelerated, France brought its support to Chadli. Mitterrand went to Algiers in 1989. Significant economic aid was granted, although, to Hamrouche's despair, France refused to be accommodating with regard to Algeria's bilateral debt. The June 1991 setback led the French foreign minister to call for a rapid holding of the parliamentary election which was seen as the only means through which an Algerian government could get the legitimacy it had always been lacking. If the French government had foreseen the FIS' victory, it probably would have argued for 'the proper circumstances to be met' before holding the election.

The October 1988 uprising and the French response: non-interference and solidarity

Despite recurrent ups and downs in the Franco-Algerian relationship, the French authorities had supported the Chadli regime throughout the 1980s. When the brutal crushing of the popular rebellion occurred in October 1988, the Rocard government (May 1988 – May 1991) was faced with a dilemma. As explained by a high civil servant, 'supporting Chadli (...) mean[t] backing the repression, but supporting the Algerian people and freedom [came] down to disavow Chadli'.[1] While Algeria's youth was being shot at by the Army, the French foreign minister resorted to the traditional diplomatic phraseology by saying that the French government was very closely following a situation that 'appeared' worrying.[2] This foreshadowed the official position of non-interference in Algeria's domestic affairs spelt out both by the spokesman for the Elysée[3] and the Quai d'Orsay. On October 12, 1988, Foreign Minister Dumas argued at the National Assembly[4] that co-operation between Paris and Algiers should not be affected by these events. He explained that the French government had to express its solidarity towards Algeria because turning its back on the Algerian regime would not help solving the problems that were at the root of popular discontent. Dumas described the riots as an expression of the people's dissatisfaction with their socio-economic plight resulting from the deep developmental crisis affecting Algeria. He also mentioned the popular demand for greater political freedom, but, quite logically, hushed up the problem of the legitimacy crisis of the Chadli regime which had transpired during the riots through various slogans expressing only contempt for the president.[5] Dumas proposed to show France's solidarity by finding a solution to the dispute about gas contracts that had embittered bilateral relations – a proposal that he had already made in September 1988 during a visit to Algiers.

Apart from the fact that the Rocard government had perhaps already got wind of Chadli's political reform proposals made in his speech to the nation on the evening of October 10 (see below), the decision to support Chadli seems to have been taken primarily in light of his potential removal from power. In *Libération*, A. Valladao suggested that French support to Chadli was motivated by the fear that the Military establishment might return to the forefront of political affairs.[6] This was a prospect that the French government wanted to avoid, most certainly. For, even though the Military has always been the centre of power in Algeria, its direct management of political affairs would have had the effect of sapping the presentability stamp provided by the civilian government. But, in addition to this general issue, the maintenance in power of Chadli himself was at stake. Indeed, the nomination of the unique candidate for the next presidential election was on the agenda of the FLN's sixth congress scheduled for December 1988. Now, not only was Chadli openly challenged from below, but his policies had also alienated the conservative trend of the FLN party.[7]   Relations between the presidency and the Boumedienist trend of the FLN were particularly tense before the October riots broke out. The fact that part of the FLN party was pitted against Chadli boded ill for his nomination for the presidential election, even though, in the last resort, the decision lay with the Army.

In an interview with the author, Dumas confirmed that the French government wished Chadli to be maintained in power after the FLN congress.[8] Chadli was thought to be able to get his country out of crisis and his policies pleased the French government. In addition, the eventuality of his removal from power could only be apprehended with concern in Paris because of the uncertainty as to who would replace him and as to the future policies that would be implemented. French support to Chadli Benjedid did not imply that the French had a say in the nomination of Algeria's president. It did, however, signal that, with Chadli in power, the French authorities would be ready to help Algeria with its economic difficulties. The decision to back Chadli was thereafter reinforced by the Algerian president's democratization measures and his continued economic liberalization policy.

France stands behind Algeria's political and economic liberalization (October 1988 – June 1991)

Liberalization in Algeria

The bloody October 1988 events triggered a move towards political liberalization. In his speech to the nation on October 10, Chadli Benjedid promised, among other things, political reforms. On October 13, whereas the state of siege and the curfew had ended, the president announced a national referendum on a constitutional reform for November 3, 1988. He proposed to reorganize the executive power through the strengthening of the prime minister's function, henceforth empowered to conduct domestic affairs but also made responsible to the National Assembly. On October 25, the presidency proposed a reform of the FLN party. Chadli argued that the FLN had to 'definitively liberate itself from the temptation of hegemonic and direct exercise of responsibilities within the state apparatus, elected assemblies, the economy, and within the social and professional organisations'.[9] In effect, the presidency proposed the abolition of the one-party state system. After the dismissal of Mohamed Cherif Messaadia and his replacement by Abelhamid Mehri on October 30, 1988, the FLN endorsed the reform at its sixth congress (November 27–29, 1988). It also designated Chadli Benjedid as the unique candidate for the presidential election. Benjedid was re-elected for a third mandate on December 22, 1988. Two months later, on February 23, 1989, a new Constitution, opening the path to political openness, was put to referendum and accepted at 73.4% of the popular vote. The Constitution omitted reference to major ideological principles of the Republic, notably Socialism, Non-alignment, Third-Worldism and the promotion of a New International Economic Order. Mention of the FLN was done only in relation to its historical role in winning Independence from France. The Constitution fortified the separation of powers while reinforcing the presidential prerogatives. It secured the guarantee of civil liberties (freedom of expression, of association, right to strike, etc.) and introduced political pluralism by allowing for the creation of 'associations of a political character'. Moreover, article 24 no longer referred to the National Popular Army as the 'Guardian of the Revolution' and confined its activity to the sole defence of the territory.[10]

From February 1989 to June 1991, and particularly under the premiership of Mouloud Hamrouche (September 1989 – June 1991), political liberalization effectively took place.[11] During this period, the Army, without relinquishing its *de facto* predominance within the Algerian political system, withdrew from its positions in the direct management of political affairs: in March 1989, its officers left their functions in the FLN's Central Committee and, in July 1990, President Chadli Benjedid renounced his function as defence minister. In June 1991, he also relinquished his function as head of the FLN. The protection of civil liberties seemed secured with the April 1989 parliamentary approval of the UN convention against torture and the ratification of various international conventions on human rights, as well as the official recognition of the Algerian League for the Defence of Human Rights headed by Ali Yahia Abdennour in November of that year. The civil society was let to organize itself: a plethora of associations emerged, the press was freed, and political parties were allowed by statute 89-11 of July 5, 1989.[12] A year after the promulgation of this law twenty-one parties had officially been recognized. On the eve of the first round of the parliamentary election (December 1991), there were fifty.[13] The break with the past was symbolised by the return to Algeria of such opponents as Hocine Aït Ahmed, leader of the Front of Socialist Forces (FFS) in exile for twenty-three years and Ahmed Ben Bella, Algeria's first president who had spent fifteen years in prison before being released under Chadli Benjedid in 1980 and who thereafter went into exile in Europe. Anticipating the local and regional elections of June 12, 1990, the various political parties organized numerous demonstrations which were allowed. Democratization was also patent in the authorities' acceptance of the verdict of the June 1990 elections where the FIS triumphed over the FLN (see Table 2).

On the economic front, the appointment of Mouloud Hamrouche as prime minister gave a new impulse to the transition to a market economy. Hamrouche represented the FLN's reforming trend. Under the authority of the presidency, he had supervised a study workshop whose mission was to find solutions to the Algerian economic crisis. The fruit of this work was published in 1989 in *Les Cahiers de la réforme*.[14] It strongly inspired Hamrouche's own programme. The latter insisted on the necessity to associate all economic agents to the reform aimed at abolishing state-controlled economy. Under Hamrouche, the reform towards the managerial autonomy of state enterprises went ahead. State monopoly over foreign trade was further relaxed (August 1990) before being formally abolished (February 1991). Following the provisions of the March 1990 law of credit and money, the monetary and financial sectors were deregulated, the Central Bank was made independent from the Ministry of Finance and restrictions on foreign investments were removed. In accordance with an IMF programme accompanying a standby credit (April 1991), the Hamrouche government devalued the Algerian Dinar and introduced price deregulation and a new wage system meant to reflect productivity.[15] However, Hamrouche's endeavour to liberalize the economy was not achieved without difficulty as it questioned some well-established vested interests. In particular, foreign trade liberalization directly threatened the tidy commissions pocketed by the Army officers selecting foreign suppliers. The reform of public enterprises also prevented their infiltration by the Military Security. The June 1991 events offered the opportunity to remove Hamrouche from his function.

French support

In France, after the 'telling silence' on the crushing of the riots, the official stance was one of solidarity with the Algerian authorities. The appointment of Kasdi Merbah to the premiership had initially provoked some surprise. Merbah had headed the Military Security under Ben Bella and Boumediene and was not, therefore, the perfect incarnation of the democratization process announced by Chadli. Yet, it was also thought that as a man of authority, having good relations with the Military and having headed several ministries under Chadli, Merbah had the required experience and firmness to get the country out of crisis.[16] France's support was expressed through a diplomatic backing, illustrated by Mitterrand's visit to Algiers on March 9–10, 1989. There, he declared himself satisfied with Algeria's evolution towards pluralism and democracy.[17] As promised by Dumas, economic support was channelled through the settlement in January 1989 of the disagreement over the renewal of the 1982 gas accord[18] and the signature of a financial aid accord of FF7 billion (over \$1.1 billion) in February 1989. This financial package comprised a FF3 billion commercial credit line. It was also made up of a new financial device: a FF4 billion financial protocol constituted of long-term governmental credits (30 years) and of Coface guaranteed long-term private loans (10 years). The sum was to be paid out in two equal instalments in 1989 and 1990 and was meant to ease Algeria's balance-of-payments deficit and finance developmental projects.[19] This financial protocol indicated the French government's willingness to back the Algerian economy through state development aid, since, previously, French official development aid to Algeria had been very low.[20]

In the last months of his premiership, Merbah had been in open conflict with Chadli Benjedid over issues concerning the powers of the prime minister. Partly because of this quarrel, which was detrimental to governmental policy stability, the nomination of Mouloud Hamrouche was welcome in Paris. Hamrouche was a 'president's man'. He had been general secretary of the presidency since 1986. There were, thus, few risks of disagreements with the presidency. In addition, Hamrouche incarnated the FLN's reforming trend. His government comprised many young renovators. This gave credibility to his programme of reforms which he applied consistently and which was praised by the French political establishment.[21]

Prior to the visit of the French foreign affairs minister to Algiers on May 24–25, 1991, Hamrouche had stated in an interview with *Le Monde* that 'things were not going that well since 1988' between France and Algeria.[22] This was quite surprising since, as shown above, gestures of support had not been lacking even when Merbah was prime minister. When Hamrouche was himself in government, bilateral relations had been managed rather smoothly. Two marking events occurred when Hamrouche was leading the government: the Algerian elections (June 1990) and the Gulf crisis (August 1990 – April 1991). Neither had, however, a particular impact on Franco-Algerian relations. The June 1990 elections which brought the FIS to power in the majority of local and regional councils did not create a panic effect in France. As a consequence, they generated neither a stronger support to the Algerian regime than that existing nor an attitude of prudence toward the Islamist political force. The Islamist phenomenon was understood in Paris essentially as an expression of popular discontent deriving from Algeria's problems of economic development and its democratic deficit.[23] It was, thus, thought that the FIS vote of 1990 did not mean popular adherence to an ideology and that, subsequently, the popular protest which the FIS' success incarnated could be defused. This was the French Ambassador's message to the Elysée. It was also that of Algerian political figures, and notably of Hamrouche who went on a secret visit to Paris right after the elections.[24] There, he might also have explained that, however unexpected the extent of the FIS' success was, it would help undermining FLN hard-liners who protested against the Hamrouche government's liberalising economic measures. The French reaction to the result of the Algerian local elections – largely inspired by what was being said in Algiers – could not, therefore, be at the root of Hamrouche's harsh words.

As regards the effects of the Gulf War on Franco-Algerian relations, the issue is complex because of the different positions of the various actors involved. As in other parts of the Arab world, Algerian public opinion – in particular, the Youth and some intellectuals – was in favour of Saddam Hussein, partly in reaction to the disproportionate means engaged by the multinational coalition to destroy Iraq and the triumphal tone of the French news which are watched by about 12 million Algerians thanks to parabolic antennas. In their great majority, political parties also adopted a pro-Iraqi stance. The most active – Ben Bella's Algerian Democratic Movement (MDA) and the FIS – initiated a parallel diplomacy, travelling to various Middle Eastern capitals hoping to find a mediating solution. The FIS organized rallies, called on the government to dispatch volunteers to defend Iraq and announced its intention to set up military training camps.[25] This pro-Hussein activity must be partly understood in relation to the domestic context of Algeria and, notably, the run-up to the parliamentary election. Denouncing the multinational coalition was a means to differentiate one's policy from that of the government.

The Algerian government first reacted by condemning Saddam Hussein and calling for an unconditional withdrawal of Iraqi troops from Kuwait. However, while not making furious declarations against the coalition, the government did not lend its support to Saudi Arabia. At the Cairo Extraordinary Arab Summit on August 10, 1990, it abstained on a firm condemnation of Iraq and the sending of a pan-Arab force to Saudi Arabia. Its position was to argue for an Arab-monitored and peaceful settlement. Chadli Benjedid attempted a mediation and turned, among others, to France which had sought a compromise. At the UN in September 1990, Mitterrand had advocated a proposal to resolve the various conflicts besetting the region after the Iraq-Kuwait conflict would have been settled. In addition, although French forces were sent to the Gulf, they were not part of the multinational coalition until the offensive was launched. The French and Algerian positions, while not similar, were, thus, not far apart and Mitterrand agreed to meet Chadli in Paris on December 22, 1990. There, each party promised to do everything they could to avoid the war, even though they had doubts about their chances of success.[26]

There was in France, particularly in the press and among certain politicians such as Cheysson,[27] a certain fear that the Gulf War would provoke a fracture between France and Algeria. This perception was due to the trenchant discourse of the Algerian foreign minister. During his visits to France in January and February 1991, Sid Ahmed Ghozali had, indeed, been vehemently critical of France's participation in the Desert Storm operation which he denounced as submissiveness to the USA. However, Ghozali's position, although backed by a group within the FLN, was marginal within the Hamrouche government. This fact, underlined by the then French Ambassador to Algiers, also transpired in an interview with Georges Morin, responsible for the Maghreb at the International Secretariat of the Socialist Party. During the Gulf crisis, Morin went twice to the Maghrebi capitals as part of different initiatives to explain to the governments and the civil societies of the region that France's policy did not constitute a crusade against the Arabs. He affirmed that if, in general, France's intervention in the Gulf was criticised by the civil society, governments understood France's position and that, when Ghozali was virulent in his talks with Dumas, he was essentially trying to reflect the *doxa*.[28] It, thus, seems that the Gulf War did not have a strong detrimental effect on bilateral governmental relations, and that, in any case, Hamrouche's declaration that Franco-Algerian relations had not been at their best since 1988 was not motivated by a quarrel over the Gulf issue.

The only plausible explanation left refers to bilateral financial relations – an issue pointed out by Hamrouche in his interview with the daily; which proves that, in foreign affairs, what is perceived as the tip of the iceberg is sometimes the iceberg itself. In his interview, Hamrouche had reproached the lack of enthusiasm of French firms in investing in Algeria. More emphatically, he had criticised the French financial establishment for what he depicted as its negative attitude in relation to Algeria's proposal for a bilateral rescheduling of its debt towards France. A parenthesis is worth opening here about the issue of Algeria's foreign debt and its reluctance to sign a classical rescheduling operation sanctioned by an IMF accord.

Foreign debt has become a major troubling issue for the Algerian government since the later part of the 1980s as a result of several factors. First, the 1986 oil countershock drastically affected Algeria's export revenues which, for 95%, are drawn from the export of hydrocarbons. Thereafter, continuing falling oil prices and the dollar low value forced Algeria to borrow on the international market on a short-term basis to finance investment projects (besides, drastically reduced) and current imports. In the late 1980s and early 1990s, Algeria was, thus, faced with heavy debt reimbursements of both its short- and long-run foreign debt while its export revenues were at their lowest. This led to a rocketing debt service (principal and interests): between 1988 and 1992, it absorbed between 60% and 80% of Algeria's export revenues,[29] leaving but few resources left to finance imports and investments. Although the cost of debt servicing strangled the economy, the Hamrouche government and, later, the Ghozali and Abdesselam governments refused to implement a classical rescheduling of the debt service through the Paris Club (group of governmental creditors) because it required the signature of a stabilisation programme with the IMF and, thus, the engagement to economic restructuring. In official speeches, the refusal to sign such a programme as a counterpart to IMF financial help was justified by the ensuing loss of national sovereignty. However, the successive Algerian governments were less opposed to the nature of the economic policies to be implemented under a stabilisation programme than to the pace planned by the IMF. The recommended measures, such as devaluation, freeing prices, reducing wages and state expenditures, adversely affect purchasing power. Rapid restructuring was seen as containing the seeds of a social explosion which the regime wanted to avoid, considering the unstable political situation. The closure of international financial markets to rescheduling countries was also an element explaining that refusal. Instead of debt rescheduling, the different Algerian governments proposed bilateral debt 'reprofiling' operations with their major creditors. In terms of result, debt 'reprofiling' is a debt rescheduling since it aims at delaying the debt service payments. But it differs from a classical rescheduling operation because, by negotiating directly with the creditors and not with the Paris Club, the debtor avoids the requirement of dealing with the Bretton Wood institutions.

France, which holds about a quarter of Algeria's debt, always refused to satisfy Algeria's demand for 'reprofiling'. Financial orthodoxy partly explains France's refusal. The rule has always been that countries in payment difficulties go through a structural adjustment programme as a counterpart to a debt rescheduling. The successive French governments have never agreed to depart from it. As a compromise, they proposed, particularly after January 1992, to plead in favour of Algeria to obtain important funds from regional and international organisations and good lending conditions from the IMF. In addition, when Algeria first formulated its 'reprofiling' demand in 1989, there was an important contentious matter over the payment by Algeria of bills due to French firms. As part of a 1982 economic co-operation agreement, many French enterprises had participated to the construction of infrastructures in Algeria. Payments (FF 3 to 4 billion) had been blocked as a retaliation measure against the litigious gas negotiations of 1986–89. In times of financial difficulties, the Algerian government tried as much as possible to further delay them. The French Finance Ministry considered that, in these circumstances, the kind of help the Algerians were asking for should not be granted.[30]

Table 2:   Results of the Algerian local and regional elections, June 1990

Parties	Votes	Expressed Votes	Regis-tered Votes	APC		APW	
		%	%		%		%
FIS	4,331,472	*54.3*	*33.7*	853	*55.4*	32	*66.7*
FLN	2,245,798	*28.1*	*17.5*	487	*31.6*	14	*29.2*
Ind.	931,278	*11.7*	*7.3*	106	*6.9*	1	*2.1*
RCD	166,104	*2.1*	*1.3*	87	*5.6*	1	*2.1*
Others	310,136	*2.1*	*2.4*	8	*0.5*	-	-
Total	**7,984,788**	**98.3**	**62.2***	**1,541**	**100.0**	**48**	**100.1**

Registered Voters   12,841,769

Notes: APC: Assemblée Populaire Communale (local council); APW: Assemblée Populaire de Wilaya (regional council); Ind.: Independents.
*: indicates participation rate.
The numbers of votes correspond only to the local election. The results of the regional election (held simultaneously) were similar.
Source: Compiled from data in F. Rouziek (1992).

Hamrouche may not have been that bitter over France's rejection of bilateral 'reprofiling' if Italy had not agreed on May 3, 1991 to release a credit of $7.2 billion out of which $2.5 billion were meant to reschedule part of Algeria's short- and medium-term official debt towards that country.[31] For, on the whole, France's attitude towards Algeria had not been frosty. In July 1990, it had renewed its bilateral financial aid and had approved the principle of a rescheduling of part of Algeria's non-guaranteed debt by an international bank syndicate headed by the Crédit Lyonnais[32] – an operation that was not, however, concluded yet when Hamrouche formulated his grievances. In addition, France was active in promoting the European Community's 'Redirected Mediterranean Policy'.

Nevertheless, Cresson's minister for economic and financial affairs, Pierre Bérégovoy, was sent to Algiers on July 29, 1991 in order to respond to the Algerian authorities' complaints. Old commercial credits amounting to FF1.3 billion as well as a credit line of FF100 million for the creation of joint ventures were reopened. The revolving guaranteed credit of FF3 billion was increased to FF4 billion and a loan was granted for the import of cereals. Bérégovoy also promised to help in speeding up the Crédit Lyonnais's debt reprofiling operation and argued for 'a new impulse' in Franco-Algerian economic relations.[33] His visit, although dominated by economic issues, partly aimed at providing political support to the new Algerian government that had been appointed in June 1991.

The Quai d'Orsay urges elections (June – December 1991)

The June 1991 events in Algeria

The parliamentary election announced by Chadli Benjedid for June 1991 was eventually postponed to the end of the year in a highly volatile political context since, on June 5, 1991, martial law was enforced again and Hamrouche dismissed.[34] At the root of the street fighting that occurred between Islamist militants and police forces in early June was the controversy over a new electoral law which gerrymandered the constituencies. The secular parties denounced the bill, which also limited the number of candidates to two (as opposed to three as initially planned) at the second round, imposing the probable choice between the FLN or the FIS. The FIS' opposition to the law was reinforced by the adoption of decrees regulating the use of mosques and forbidding the Friday prayers to be turned into political rallies. It called for a general strike in Algiers on May 25, 1991 asking for the abrogation of the law and simultaneous parliamentary and presidential elections. The general strike was not followed but the FIS organized a sit-in at the main squares of Algiers for more than ten days. While on June 3 Abassi Madani had agreed with the Hamrouche government to end the demonstration, the *gendarmerie* was sent during the night to clear up the squares. The next day, demonstrations continued and, in the night of June 4, the Army intervened. Official sources recorded 17 dead and 219 wounded.[35]   Sporadic street fighting continued throughout the Summer[36] as the Army cracked down on FIS militants. Benhadj and Madani warned that armed resistance would be organized to meet the authorities' clampdown. They were subsequently arrested (June 30, 1991) on charges of conspiracy against the state. Several members of the FIS *majlis ash shura* (Consultative Council) were also arrested.

Table 3:   Results of the first round of the Algerian parliamentary election, December 1991

Parties	Votes	Expressed Votes %	Registered Votes %	Seats	% of Total Seats
FIS	3,260,222	47.3	24.5	188	43.7
FLN	1,612,947	23.4	12.1	15	3.5
FFS (b)	510,661	7.4	3.8	25	5.8
Hamas (ne)	368,697	5.3	2.8	-	-
Independents	309,264	4.4	2.3	3	-
RCD	200,267	2.9	1.5	-	-
MNI (ne)	150,093	2.2	1.1	-	-
MDA (b)	135,882	2.0	1.0	-	-
Others	349,386	5.1	2.6	-	-
Total	**6,897,419**	**100.0**	**51.7***	**231**	**53**

Registered Voters   13,314,771

Note: * represents participation rate; (b): boycotted the 1990 elections; (ne): non-existent at the time of the 1990 elections.
Source: Compiled from data in F. Rouziek (1993).

France urges elections

Following the enforcement of martial law in Algeria, the spokesman for the Quai d'Orsay deplored the violence whichever its origin.[37] The French minister for foreign affairs wished for calm to return and for a prompt resumption of the electoral process.[38] This was his constant message until December 1991 – his argument being that parliamentary elections were the key to political stability in Algeria:

> I think that Algeria will find a real balance only when the elections take place. These elections have to be held as soon as possible. (...) It is evident that [France] also has an interest in having an interlocutor whose governmental stability is confirmed.[39]

Surely, Dumas would not have been so insistent in calling for a rapid holding of the election if he had believed the FIS would win a parliamentary majority. He later confirmed that he assumed the FIS would not carry such a majority.[40] His statement is corroborated by Claude Silberzahn, head of the French secret services, who deplored that the French government had disregarded the DGSE's warnings about a likely FIS victory.[41]

At this juncture, reference must be made to the issue as to whether the Algerian authorities themselves expected the results of the first round of the December 1991 parliamentary election (see Table 3). Pierre Dévoluy and Mireille Duteil have argued that these results came as a complete surprise in Algiers.[42] Their argument is supported by the then French Ambassador to Algiers.[43] In contrast, Abed Charef and George Joffé have suggested that, not only did the Algerian Army anticipate the FIS' electoral victory, but that it had also favoured it in order to prove to foreign opinion that Chadli was incompetent, which justified the coup d'état that followed the first round of the parliamentary election.[44]

The contention that the results were unexpected in Algiers relies on internal information and is based upon the electoral forecasts of the Algerian Ministry for the Interior. The assessments of the Ministry conjectured that the votes would be divided in about three-thirds with a big third for the FIS, another for the FLN and the rest for the various contending political parties. This implied that an alliance between the FLN and the various parties in the future Assembly would put the FIS in the minority. The Algerian authorities' conviction that the FIS would not do badly, but not well enough to reach a majority, would have derived from three main factors. Firstly, there was a far greater choice in the parliamentary election than in the local and regional elections: fifty contesting parties as opposed to eleven in June 1990. Secondly, it was believed that the FIS had lost much of its popularity as a consequence of its management of the local and regional councils. The idea, conveyed in the Algerian and French press, that local Islamic governance had been catastrophic prove to be somewhat more partisan than objective. Economic results were perhaps not better than they had been. However, through various charitable activities, FIS-governed localities managed both to bring relief to the needy and to provide an activity for the young *hittistes*.[45] Equipping the slums with dustbins; regularly picking up the rubbish; offering free tutoring; setting up small shops managed by the unemployed; offering lower prices in the Islamic *souq*;[46] all this community work by local FIS leaders had made this brand of politicians much closer to the needs of their constituency than most of the FLN officials had ever been. With regard to the most publicised and contested measures allegedly implemented by the FIS, such as sexual segregation on the beaches, the ban on swimwear and shorts, or on alcohol sales, John Entelis has argued that he saw no evidence of such restrictions in the Tipasa municipality and that 'Islamic zealousness', although existent, had actually been much less important than the press had suggested.[47]

Thirdly, the Algerian authorities' belief in the FIS' partial defeat would have been grounded in the view that internal rifts crippled the FIS. Discord within the FIS appeared during the crisis of May–June 1991 and touched upon three main issues: the alliance of the FIS with other Islamist parties, which Abassi Madani had refused; the organization of the strike to protest against the controversial electoral law; and the participation to the parliamentary election. Dissidence even occurred as three members of the FIS Consultative Council criticised Abassi Madani's leadership on Algerian national television. After Madani and Benhadj were imprisoned, disunity was fuelled by the competition between the various currents making up the FIS for the party's leadership. Since its creation in 1989, the FIS has comprised two main currents: the *salafiyya* and the *djeza'ara*. The *salafiyya* has drawn upon the heritage of Ben Badis's Association of the Reformist Ulema which was created in 1931 as a reaction to colonial rule and which was inspired by similar Reformist movements in the Arab world. The *salafiyya*'s political ideal is the return to the Caliphate, which it sees applicable to the entire *umma* (the community of believers). The Algerian *salafiyya* is characterised by a generation split: its elders, who participated to the Association of the Reformist Ulema, who were involved in the War of Independence and who, during the process of state Islamisation, developed a religious opposition, see the reform of society as the prerequisite for the creation of an Islamic state. They, therefore, prefer a strategy based upon predication and social action, even though some *salafayyists* eventually joined Abassi Madani in creating a political party. The younger *salafayyist* generation, incarnated by Ali Benhadj, is often made up of 'radicalised militants' who never believed in the legal and political path chosen by the FIS to reach power. Essentially composed of veterans of Afghanistan (the 'Afghans') and of ex-Bouyalists,[48] this strand promoted the creation of armed groups in the wake of the 1992 coup d'état. The *salafiyya*'s pan-Islamic discourse contrasts with the Islamo-nationalist agenda of the *djeza'ara* which is mainly composed of educated technocrats who met with Islam at the university more than at the mosque. The *djeza'ara*, incarnated by Abassi Madani, Abdelkhader Hachani or Rabah Kebir, represents an elite which competes with the Westernised elite in power by using the vocabulary of Islam. The *djeza'ara* members' hope to obtain positions within the state apparatus explain their efforts to respect a legal framework in conducting political action.[49] In the wake of Madani's and Benhadj's imprisonment, the power struggle between the FIS' competing strands was eventually concluded by the take-over of the *djeza'ara* over the *salafiyya* during the Batna Congress of July 26, 1991. This Congress also allowed to marginalise proponents of the armed struggle. Despite the *djeza'ara*'s take-over of the FIS leadership, discord continued to hamper the party machine from running smoothly. Some FIS members argued for a boycott of the parliamentary election if the paramount FIS leaders were not discharged. This put Hachani, the president of the newly created FIS provisional executive bureau, in an uncomfortable situation. Running for the election without Madani and Benhadj could have been interpreted within his party as disloyalty to the 'historic' leaders. As a result, Hachani announced the FIS' participation in the parliamentary election just two weeks before the first round.[50] Analysts like Dévoluy and Duteil have argued that the Algerian authorities viewed the FIS' internal feuds as a factor undermining its electoral strength.[51] In contrast, Audibert, who agreed with the contention that the results were unexpected and the coup not premeditated, has affirmed that the Algerian authorities saw neither the quarrels between the members of the *majlis ash shura*, nor the hesitations of the new leadership in boycotting or not the election, as an electoral handicap since the FIS was leading campaign in the mosques.[52]

Charef's and Joffé's argument is that a clan, linked in some way to Major General Larbi Belkeir (the new Algerian Interior Minister appointed in the reshuffle of October 16, 1991 to supervise the forthcoming election) and to the FLN Boumedienist trend, was very well aware of the FIS' electoral import for the simple reason that it had bolstered it. These authors have underlined several troubling elements. One is the release of Hachani as well as the suspension of the ban on the FIS press one month prior to the election. Another is that the amendments to the new electoral law (passed on October 13) were of secondary importance. If gerrymandering to the benefit of the FLN was not questioned, nor was the majority vote principle whereas the latter favoured large parties and, as such, the FIS. Finally, Prime Minister Ghozali seemed to do everything he could to undermine the FLN party by sponsoring independent candidates in place of hard-liners, who by drawing upon the heritage of the Boumediene era, might have succeeded in prolonging the FLN's spell. The overall aim of this clan in preparing the FLN's bankruptcy would have been to demonstrate that Chadli, who had been the first to use the FIS as a means to undermine the Boumedienists, was 'incompetent at being able to control the genie it had itself unleashed'.[53] Deliberately bringing the country in front of a simple alternative – a FIS take-over or a coup d'état – this clan would, thus, have been seeking to make it obvious that a coup was the only reasonable path for Algeria.

Conspiracy or not in Algiers, Paris did not expect the FIS' *razzia* of the parliamentary seats. The idea that many FIS voters would withdraw their support as a consequence of the party's intolerant policies was relayed by the Algerian authorities in their contacts with the French political establishment.[54] Despite Dumas' claim that he was never won over by the Algerians on that point,[55] it seems that the argument was rather well accepted in Paris. Inasmuch as the extent of FIS support within the population was not properly gauged, there was no risk in calling for a rapid election. It was quite logically thought in Paris that, even though the FIS might be included in the government, the parliamentary election would bring the popular legitimacy that all Algerian regimes had hitherto been lacking and, thus, would provide the governmental authority required to bring back Algeria on the track of political stability and economic recovery.

Notes

1. Quoted in *Libération*, 11 October 1988.
2. Interview, 8 October 1988, quoted in *Le Monde*, 11 October 1988.
3. See the address of Mitterrand's spokesman in *ibid.*
4. MAE (September–October 1988), p. 86. See also his interview on France-Inter, 10 October 1988 in *ibid.*, pp. 71-2.
5. Despite this silence, Dumas's explanation of the 1988 riots is close to that found in the academic literature. In general, authors are split on two issues. Firstly, whether the uprising was primarily a 'semolina riot' (e.g. M. Akacem (1993), p.52) or whether it was essentially the product of a political crisis (e.g. H. Roberts (1993a), pp.434-6). Secondly, whether the rebellion was a spontaneous reaction to economic and political privations (e.g. J. Entelis and L. Arone (1992), pp.24-6; L. Rummel (1992); K. Duran (1989), pp.407-12), or whether the Youth had been manipulated either by the conservative trend of the FLN, as a means to destabilize the Chadli regime, or by the presidency itself, as a means to undermine the FLN party (see P.R. Baduel (1994), pp.8-12; A. Kapil (1992), pp. 515-21 and F. Rouziek (1990), pp.583-5). Whether or not the Youth was manipulated, it should not be forgotten that the 1988 riots were the peak of a movement of social discontent that had begun in the early 1980s.
6. *Libération*, 11 October 1988.
7. The FLN party absorbed the various nationalist movements at the time of the War of Liberation and thus became a coalition of different trends. It has never ruled Algeria despite its status of unique party. Its role has been limited to the control and

mobilization of the civil society – a function that it did not fulfil that well since Boumediene had to rely on communist activists to organize the Agrarian Revolution and since, in the early 1980s, an anti-establishment movement appeared both with the Berber and the Islamist mobilizations. Despite its weak position in the Algerian political system, the FLN had, nevertheless, a nuisance capability. This appeared clearly in 1985 during the debates around the 'enrichment' of the 1976 National Charter. The issue that crystallized opposition from the conservative or Boumedienist trend was Chadli's economic liberalization project. Some also argue that behind-the-scenes discussions on a reform of the FLN were at the root of the hard-liners' discontent. It is true that the official recognition of one of the three Algerian Human Rights Leagues and the easing of the conditions for the creation of associations in 1987 infuriated Mohamed Cherif Messaadia, head of the permanent secretariat of the Central Committee, precisely because it questioned the FLN's control over the mass and professional organisations, and, in the longer term, the FLN's status as unique party. On the relations between the presidency and the FLN hard-line conservatives, see A. Kapil (1992); F. Rouziek (1990) and (1989).

8. Interview with Roland Dumas, May 16, 1995.

9. Quoted in F. Rouziek (1990), p. 591. See also Rouziek's article for all events, dates and figures indicated for the year 1988. Algeria's democratization experience until the January 1992 coup d'état has been accounted for in many books and articles by now. Among them see e.g. J.J. Lavenue (1993); J. Entelis and L. Arone (1992); R. Mortimer (1991).

10. On the constitutional reform and for a reprint of the Constitution, see C. Rulleau (1989), pp.159-87.

11. The following marking events are drawn from the chronology provided in P. Eveno (1994); F. Rouziek (1992) and (1991).

12. The text of this law is reprinted in A. Djeghloul (1990), pp.200-5.

13. F. Rouziek (1993), pp.639-40.

14. The contents of *Les Cahiers de la réforme* can be found in G. Corm (1993), pp.12-16.

15. See G. Corm (1993); F. Rouziek (1993), (1992) and (1991).

16. Interview with Jean Audibert (France's Ambassador to Algiers from January 1989 to September 1992), June 7, 1995.

17. See his speech in MAE (March–April 1989), p.16.

18. The deadlock on the renegotiation of the 1982 gas contract opened in July 1986. It stemmed from disagreements between Sonatrach and *Gaz de France* (GDF) over the pricing formula and quantities. In addition to these problems, disagreements between the two companies appeared in late 1986 as Sonatrach continued to bill GDF's imports according to a temporary pricing agreement signed in March 1986 and designed to counterbalance the effects of depressed oil prices on the price of gas (pegged on the price of oil since 1982). The 1989 gas accord imposed a compromise between the positions of the companies and provided that GDF would pay the arrears (FF850 million) corresponding to the difference between the price paid by GDF and that billed by the Sonatrach. For details on the 1989 contract, see L. Blin and E. Gobe (1991), pp.

486-7. For details on the 1982 gas contract, see the debate between B. Abdesselam (1990) and A. Brahimi (1991); A. Sydnes (1989) and I. Zartman and A. Bassani (1987).

19. L. Blin and E. Gobe (1991), p. 486.

20. Throughout the 1980s French official development aid to Algeria amounted on average to FF300 million, accounting for 1 to 2% of French total official development aid (OECD, document obtained on request and ratios calculated from data in this document and the OECD's *Development and Co-operation* yearly reviews).

21. Interview with Jean Audibert, 7 June 1995. For an example of the French government's praise of Chadli and Hamrouche's reforms, see Dumas's press conference in Algiers on 25 May 1991 in MAE (May–June 1991), p. 41.

22. *Le Monde*, 28 May 1991.

23. This analysis was held by the French minister for foreign affairs and the co-operation minister as early as 1988. See respectively MAE (September–October1988), p. 72 and *Le Monde*, 13 October 1988.

24. Interview with Jean Audibert, 7 June 1995.

25. For details on Algeria's policy during the Gulf crisis as well as the parallel diplomacy of the MDA and the FIS, see R. Mortimer (1992), pp. 261-2 or N. Grimaud (1991), pp. 31-33.

26. Interview with Jean Audibert, 7 June 1995.

27. Cheysson, who is a close friend of Ghozali, criticised Mitterrand's decision to fight Iraq as a 'blind fidelity' to the Allies (interview with the author, 22 April 1994).

28. In August 1990, Morin accompanied Pierre Mauroy (ex-prime minister) who was sent by the Elysée in order to deliver France's message to Hassan II, Benjedid, Ben Ali and Arafat. In March 1991, Morin returned to the Maghreb, heading a socialist delegation of fifteen French people's representatives natives of the Maghreb. The delegation met members of government, opposition parties and human rights leagues (interview with Georges Morin, 29 June 1994).

29. IBRD (1994), p. 6. In terms of stock, Algeria's foreign debt rose at a high pace in the 1970s, passing from $940 million in 1970 to $19.4 billion ten years later. This resulted from the need to externally finance Boumediene's ambitious industrialisation programme. Whereas Algeria's debt decreased in the early part of 1980s, it grew again from 1986 to 1992, reaching by then $26.8 billion. In 1993, foreign debt stood at $25.8 billion. IBRD (1992), p. 2 and (1994), p. 6.

30. Interview with Jean Audibert, 7 June 1995.

31. M. Hernando de Larramendi (1993), p. 504.

32. *Le Monde*, 26 July 1990.

33. M. Hernando de Larramendi (1993), pp. 520-1 and 560.

34. The following account is drawn from A. Charef (1994), pp. 131-74 and F. Rouziek (1993), pp. 597-610.

35. A. Charef (1994), p. 167.

36. By 1 August 1991 official reports accounted for 55 dead, 326 wounded and 2,976 arrests and interpellations since 5 June 1991. *Ibid.*, p. 174.

37. *Libération*, 6 June 1991.

38. *Ibid.*
39. Interview, 27 June 1991 in MAE (May–June 1991), p. 137.
40. Interview with Roland Dumas, 16 May 1995.
41. C. Silberzahn (1995), p. 292.
42. P. Dévoluy and M. Duteil (1994), pp. 24-9.
43. Interview with Jean Audibert, June 7, 1995.
44. A. Charef (1994), pp. 222-31 and G.Joffé (1994a), p. 8.
45. The *hittistes* are the many young unemployed who spend their days outside, leaning back against the walls, waiting for time to pass.
46. See the interview of R. Bekkar on the FIS policy measures in Tlemcen in H. Davis (1992), pp.12-15.
47. J. Entelis (1992), pp.78-9. Francois Burgat (1994, pp.207-8) maintains for his part that, in connection with the FIS' management of local affairs, some of the facts the FIS was reproached with were pure fabrications on the part of an Algerian press whose objectivity and independence is still not really up to the mark. This argument partly undermines the view that the Algerian authorities would have done everything they could in order to boost the FIS' electoral success (see *infra*).
48. From 1982 to 1987 Bouyali headed the first Islamist armed group in Algeria.
49. On the various components of the FIS, see S. Labat (1995a), pp.75-102 and pp.129-75 and (1994), pp.41-67.
50. On the divisions within the FIS, see A. Charef (1994), pp.108-18 and 214-22 and JJ. Lavenue (1993), pp.122-7 and 162-6.
51. P. Dévoluy and M. Duteil (1994), p.26.
52. Interview with Jean Audibert, 7 June 1995.
53. G. Joffé (1994a), p.8.
54. See the article of Bernard Stasi (vice-president of the CDS and of the *Association France-Algérie*) in *Le Figaro*, 21 February 1991 and interview with Jean Audibert, 7 June 1995.
55. Interview with Roland Dumas, 16 May 1995.

Chapter 2

Political Upheavals in Algeria and Hesitating French Support (Winter 1992 – Winter 1993)

Algeria's first free election eventually occurred in late December 1991. The results of the first round indicated that the FIS would get a parliamentary majority. The Algerian Army subsequently intervened, staging a 'constitutional coup d'état' which removed President Chadli Benjedid from power. New ruling institutions were created and headed by a veteran of the Independence War, Mohamed Boudiaf, who accepted the Generals' proposition and returned to Algeria after a long exile. Although Boudiaf's coming to power generated hopes among the population, his rule was marked by tense relations with the Algerian political establishment as well as with the civil society. The regime's repressive drift, with its severe crackdowns on FIS militants and sympathisers, also initiated the repression-counter-violence spiral that has characterised Algeria's daily life in the 1990s. Boudiaf was murdered after six months of presidency, to all appearances, for having thought he could manage political affairs without the assent of the Army. The political reshuffle that followed Boudiaf's death in June 1992 brought back to power Boumedienists and, notably, Belaïd Abdesselam. As prime minister, he restrained economic liberalization and engaged into a political dialogue with political parties (excluding the outlawed FIS) which turned short mainly because political parties refused to back the regime's growing repression policy.

The French government reacted to all these events with great embarrassment. It did not clearly condemn the coup because it did not wish the FIS coming to power and because a condemnation would have been counter-productive in trying to influence the course of events in Algeria. The Cresson government did not, however, welcome the coup either because it involved the removal from power of Chadli and of his French-oriented Administration. Also, it was feared in Paris that the marginalisation of the Islamist current would generate political instability. Reservation, more than a wholesale condemnation, is the accurate term to describe the French official discourse in relation to the coup. Despite apparent governmental unity, the Socialist Party was split over the question of what France's attitude should be. But supporters of the 'preventive coup d'état' did not manage to influence foreign policy-making. Indeed, until January 1993, the French government's policy, despite talks of 'solidarity' and 'support', was rather one of minimal support to the new Algerian rulers. The relationship actually became strained. France's attempts at promoting a political compromise, by suggesting that a new political personality capable of rallying the Islamists' allegiance was needed, was a central factor in the deterioration of the *entente* between the two states until the French *volte-face* of January 1993.

Political upheavals in Algeria

The coup d'état

The results of the first ballot of the parliamentary election suggested that the FIS was heading for a clear majority in the second round scheduled for January 16, 1992. It had won 188 seats out of 231 and needed only an additional 28 seats to win an absolute majority. On the eve of the first ballot Chadli Benjedid had claimed that he was ready to 'cohabit' with the winning majority and that force would not be used. Rumours of a meeting with Hachani seemed to confirm that the president was ready to reach a compromise with the FIS. The FFS and the FLN called for the second round to be held as planned. Other parties, such as the Rally for Culture and Democracy (RCD),[1] the Algerian Movement for Justice and Development (MAJD)[2] and the Socialist Vanguard Party (PAGS),[3] as well as a number of non-political associations gathered around the workers' union (UGTA) in a National Committee for the Safeguarding of Algeria, demanded the interruption of the electoral process. The Army, which all along had warned that it would defend democracy and the institutions, intervened. Its plan was to make Chadli resign – which he did on January 11, 1992 – after making sure he had signed the decree dissolving the National Assembly and then to replace him by the president of the Constitutional Council instead of the president of the parliament, who was judged to be too close to the Islamist current. The flaw in this grand plan which, by resorting to the Constitution, aimed at protecting the legalistic image of the Army, was that the president of the Constitutional Council refused to assume presidential powers, pleading that the constitution was silent about the type of power vacuum generated by the resignation of the head of state. The ruling authorities were led to hold the reins of power: on January 12, the High Security Council, originally created to provide counselling on matters of security and defence to the president, took power. It annulled the results of the first round of the parliamentary election while cancelling the second round. Maintaining the Ghozali government, it then set up on January 14 a High State Council (HSC) to assume presidential powers until the end of 1993 with the assistance of a National Consultative Council. The HSC consisted of: Major General Khaled Nezzar (minister for defence); Ali Haroun (minister for human rights); Ali Kafi (secretary-general of the Organization of the Mujahidins); Tijani Haddam (rector of the Paris mosque); and, as president, Mohamed Boudiaf. Boudiaf had been one of the historic leaders of the War of Independence and was, therefore, representative of the generation of November. However, he had been in exile since 1964 and was, thus, untainted by the economic mismanagement and corruption associated with the FLN. Moreover, as he had criticised the authoritarian drift of the Ben Bella regime, he offered a certain guarantee of democratization.[4]

The Boudiaf leadership (January 1992 – June 1992)

Boudiaf was not to stay long in power. He was shot dead on June 29, 1992 by a second lieutenant, Lembarek Boumaarafi, who belonged to the security apparatus protecting the president during his speech at Annaba. The death sentence pronounced against Boumaarafi on June 3, 1995 has not dispelled the suspicions about the official version according to which a zealot would have acted on his own. Rather, it is widely believed that the killing was ordered by 'the politico-financial Mafia', afraid of losing its privileges in front of Boudiaf's determination to punish corrupted officials – a resoluteness illustrated by the arrest of General Mostefa Belloucif in May 1992.

During his stay in power, Boudiaf was isolated. Mistrusting the political system to which he now belonged, he had taken as advisors his close friends who, like him, had been out of Algeria for the past thirty years. Within the HSC, disagreements appeared with this 'Mister Clean' who projected to increase his popular legitimacy by purifying the system and creating his own support-base. Within the population, Boudiaf's past brought him some degree of legitimacy but his tragic end, more than anything else, now made him a national hero. As to the political parties, those who had initially supported the cancellation of the election and the establishment of the HSC were rapidly disenchanted.

Two aspects of Boudiaf's policy particularly worried the opposition. Firstly, as early as February 1992, Boudiaf had announced his intention to mobilize the people around a Patriotic National Rally (RNP) which would have played the role of a forum for discussion on a national programme for the establishment of a pluralistic democracy. As dialogue with the political parties was explicitly excluded (discussions were to take place within neighbourhoods and working premises), they denounced Boudiaf's initiative as a replica of the one-party system. The establishment, in April 1992, of the National Consultative Council which was to play the role of the dissolved parliament also generated opposition because its members had been nominated by the state and reflected the professional civil society (journalists, academics, unionists, etc...) rather than the political parties.

The second aspect of Boudiaf's policy which generated opposition concerned the growing repressive drift and its correlative dangers. Cracking down on the FIS, while coopting some dissidents,[5] was one of the first steps taken under Boudiaf. Most of the FIS leaders who were still free were arrested between January and February 1992 when the state of emergency was imposed (it is still in force at the time of writing); the control of the mosques was reinforced; the FIS press suspended. Ultimately, the FIS was outlawed on March 4, 1992.[6] In parallel with the crackdown on the FIS, gagging the media (through personnel reshuffles, financial pressures, temporary suspensions and judicial harassment of journalists criticising governmental policy) was reminiscent of the pre-1988 period. Equally worrisome was the dissolution of some local councils controlled by the FLN and the Independents. But, the issue that most generated concern was the emerging repression-violence circle. The banning of the FIS led those militants who had never believed that the political system could be reformed from within and who had always advocated armed rebellion as a means to take power to put their ideal into practice. Their influence over the FIS' sympathisers grew for two main reasons. First, the arrest of FIS leaders beheaded the party of its cadres who had until then checked the violent inclination of some FIS members. Second, because of the repressive drift, many militants and sympathisers joined the newly created armed groups in order to revenge their dead or merely in order to avoid being arrested. Rabah Kebir's calls for a peaceful solution to the political crisis were, thus, ignored by Abdezzerak Redjem, also a member of the FIS provisional executive bureau who went underground and published communiqués warning the authorities that, in the absence of a political dialogue and of a political party channelling Islamic aspirations, the political struggle would be led by other means. Redjem is reported to have sponsored the formation of the Islamic Armed Movement (MIA) around ex-Bouyalists such as Abdelkhader Chebouti.[7] In July 1992, Mansour Meliani, also a member of the former Bouyali Group, created the Islamic Armed Group (GIA)[8] which later became well-known for its attacks against the security forces, the intelligentsia, foreigners and laymen. In front of the emerging repression-violence spiral, the whole Algerian opposition – including the PAGS and the RCD which had approved the banning of the FIS[9] – called for the lifting of the state of emergency, the closing down of the seven detention camps opened in February, the respect of human rights and civil liberties, the establishment of a political dialogue and a schedule for the return to the electoral process.

Under Boudiaf, conflicts also characterised the economic scene. Ghozali had started his premiership by making the ostentatious announcement of the 'selling out of Hassi Messaoud', the largest oil field. The anticipated sale of gas and oil, as well as the new possibility for foreign firms to participate to the limit of 49% in the exploration and exploitation of new and existing oil and gas fields, was publicised as potentially generating a revenue of $7 billion, which would have allowed Algeria to face its financial difficulties. Because of the symbolic nature of oil as the source of Algeria's 'economic independence', opposition crystallised around the project at the National Assembly. The technocrats, such as Sadek Boussena, who, under Hamrouche, had prepared the bill on foreign participation in the exploration and production of hydrocarbons expressed reservations on the politicisation of this measure. They pointed out that it could not be used as an alternative to economic structural reforms because it would not accrue the kind of money Ghozali promised and that it would produce results only in the medium-term.[10] Ghozali's policies also alienated foreign and domestic economic agents. He promised the IMF and the IBRD privatization which never came. His refusal to impose price deregulation and currency devaluation at the recommended pace led to the blocking of an IMF credit in April. The Algerian employers' union protested against the insufficient funds and delays set by Ghozali for the financial stabilization of public enterprises. The UGTA denounced the low budget devoted to the social net meant to compensate for price increases. The scope of the economic and financial disaster was illustrated in June 1992 by Ghozali's breaking of the debt rescheduling taboo. He was, however, about to be dismissed.[11]

The Boumedienists' comeback[12]

Ali Kafi was elected by the High State Council on July 1, 1992 to replace Boudiaf as president of the HSC and Redha Malek was included within the presidential collegiate. Discharged, Ghozali was supplanted by Belaïd Abdesselam, who became prime minister as well as minister for the economy on July 8, 1992. Seven ministers of the Ghozali government were renewed in their functions, two of whom were Khaled Nezzar (defence) and Lakhdar Brahimi (foreign affairs). The image projected by the new ruling team was that of Algeria's nationalist past, reflecting the regime's attempt to recapture the legitimacy of the Boumediene regime. Kafi actively took part in the War of

Liberation and, after a diplomatic career, became the general secretary of the organization for the war veterans in 1990. Malek managed the governmental newspaper during the War, participated in the negotiations of the Evian Accords and in the drafting of Algeria's major doctrinal texts such as the Tripoli Charter and the 1976 National Charter. Malek had a diplomatic career, notably in Washington and London, before returning to domestic politics as the head of the National Consultative Council. As for Abdesselam, his return to politics marked a clear rupture with the Chadli era. As minister for industry and petroleum (1965–77), Abdesselam had, indeed, been a leading figure in the Boumediene era and had virulently criticised Chadli's policies.

It thus came as no surprise that Abdesselam's economic programme (September 1992), without wholly rejecting the principle of market economy, focussed on renewed state control and questioned some of the implemented reforms, such as the Central Bank's autonomy and trade liberalization. It also announced a 'war economy', centred upon drastically reduced imports, in order to repay the foreign debt. On the political front, the policy of the new team was characterised in the first months of power by two main orientations: an overture towards the opposition (FIS excluded) and an attempt to eradicate the Islamist armed groups which, with time, became identified with eradicating the FIS.

While Boudiaf had refused a dialogue with the political parties, Kafi announced in July 1992 his readiness to meet them in late September in bilateral talks provided they accepted his conditions: condemnation of terrorism and a clear commitment to establish a modern state and a pluralist democracy, and to uphold the unity of the nation and respect fundamental liberties. From the outset, the RCD and the PAGS were hostile to a dialogue which would include Islamist parties such as Hamas and MNI. The other political forces, on the other hand, favoured such discussions, seeing them as a way to organize the transition towards the resumption of the democratic process. As to the banned FIS, it declared itself ready to participate in the discussions on four conditions: the release of all prisoners; the end of arrests; the reinstatement of dissolved FIS local councils; and the organization of the second round of the parliamentary election. Whatever the FIS' conditions, the HSC was not willing to discuss political matters with it. The political dialogue eventually was cut short because the political parties refused to back the HSC's authoritarian policies.

The authorities' second aim was to put an end to the terrorist violence organized by the MIA and the GIA. A repressive security system was gradually put in place throughout the Summer to emerge fully in the Autumn with the adoption of a harsh anti-terrorist law (October 2), the systematic deployment of anti-terrorist squads and the enforcement of a curfew in seven *wilayas*

(December 2). If the terrorist violence organized by the armed groups had to be countered, the methods used by the Algerian authorities were soon to become as despicable as those of the terrorists.

France's mixed support (January 1992 – January 1993)

The French response to the coup d'état

As indicated above, the Cresson government urged a resumption of the electoral process when the parliamentary election was postponed in June 1991. It was, therefore, in the order of things that the spokesman for the Ministry for Foreign Affairs would welcome the event. A certain embarrassment as to the results of the first round was, however, discernible in his declaration as well as in Dumas': both refused to comment 'prematurely' on the results of the election. Nevertheless, the spokesman for the Quai d'Orsay adopted a well-disposed prudence towards the future parliamentary majority, arguing that:

> (...) whatever the choice of the Algerian people, the relations that unite them to the French people are so deep in all domains that they should maintain themselves. France, for its own part, will continue to promote their strengthening.[13]

As the intervention of the Algerian Army became evident, the minister for foreign affairs claimed that '(...) France does not intend at all to call on anybody to correct the [results of the] first round (...)',[14] which, without indicating whether France would condemn a coup, at least, denoted a willingness to keep at a distance from the coup in the making.

Weighing the pros and cons

The coup d'état put the French authorities in a very uncomfortable situation because, in practice, they could neither officially support nor condemn the event. They consequently chose a middle ground. It was clear that the French government could not *officially* back the coup. Even though the Algerian Army presented its intervention as a means 'to save democracy', it escaped nobody's notice that it had reacted chiefly to safeguard its own position within Algerian politics. The cancellation of the election represented a fundamental break in the democratization process initiated by Chadli. Since France had been standing for this democratization process, it could not suddenly retract and welcome the coup. In addition, this would have contradicted its official foreign policy orientation towards global democratization. No open support could, thus, be contemplated.

Without officially bringing its support for the coup d'état, the French government could, nevertheless, have seen the event with a willing eye. After all, the coup prevented the FIS from taking power. On the whole, the FIS was perceived as a reactionary and regressive political force. Its democratic credentials were questioned by Mitterrand. Commenting on the Algerian events in late January 1992, Mitterrand, indeed, argued that '(...) fundamentalism (...) does not appear to me as the surest way to reach democracy'.[15] Yet, whatever the French politicians' personal views about the FIS were, other considerations were at stake. First among all, the consequences of the coup had to be taken into account. Putting the issue of the FIS aside, some have argued that much of the French official anger about the coup stemmed from the fact that the dismissal of Chadli Benjedid allowed the Boumedienists to take over.[16] The Boumedienists' comeback was bad news for Paris because their nationalism has often translated into a preference for the USA over France precisely as a means to break free from neo-colonial influence. If, indeed, part of France's cool reaction to the coup can be explained in these terms, it would be reductive to stop at that. Concerns about political instability (more than about democracy) were also involved. Even though the scope of armed confrontation between the Islamist armed groups and the authorities was not anticipated, it was well suspected in Paris that the marginalisation of the Islamist current would not be done gently and that it would face some resistance. A new era of authoritarianism coupled with a greater state of instability (and, thus, uncertainty) was to be expected. The head of the secret services actually affirmed that he advised no support for the coup in order to preserve the future of Franco-Algerian relations in case the FIS later took power in less favourable conditions (i.e. through a coup d'état).[17] In order to form their opinion about the 1992 coup, French policy-makers also had to consider the issue as to how the FIS' inclusion within the government would affect Franco-Algerian relations. Within the administration of the Quai d'Orsay, the head of the Maghreb-Mashreq department, Pierre Lafrance, projected that a FIS government in Algiers would not dramatically affect France's economic and strategic interests. He also thought that, within the FIS, there were some moderates with whom the French authorities could find an understanding.[18] Part of this argument had found an echo at the Elysée. Indeed, the French president maintained that the Algerians were more dependent upon France than the reverse and that, consequently, the Islamists would have to tone down their anti-French positions, if in power.[19] Dumas, who had often insisted on the socioeconomic aspect of the FIS' success, argued in a press conference held in

Morocco in April 1991 that the FIS also represented 'the expression of Algerian identity, of the Muslim religious spirit and of its political tradition',[20] thereby conferring on it a certain political legitimacy. Since the FIS had won the votes of a quarter of the electorate, it was thought that it might have to be included in the political game. This judgement was reflected in an August 1992 statement when Dumas said in relation to Ali Kafi's proposal for a political dialogue excluding the FIS: 'Our hope remains to see a national dialogue taking place with the least exclusions possible'.[21] Explaining today what he meant by that, he answers he thought that it was a mistake on the part of the Algerian authorities to have cancelled the electoral process and then to have assumed that the Islamist political force could be defeated by combat. He also says he then thought that, if a dialogue there was to be, it had to be established not with self-appointed interlocutors but with those who were at the centre of the political rift.[22]

Three essential factors, thus, militated in favour of a condemnation of the coup d'état: (1) the consequence of the coup on the power structure of Algeria (return to politics of Boumedienists seen as inimical to French interests in Algeria); (2) the risks entailed by the coup (authoritarianism and political instability); and (3) the view that a political compromise taking the Islamic aspiration of part of the population into account was possible. Yet, in practice, the French authorities could not wholly condemn the coup. They would have had to take concrete measures, such as the non-recognition of the new authorities, a freeze of bilateral relations, etc... This was completely unimaginable because it would have implied that the French government wished the victory of the FIS, which was not the case. It simply wished the political situation to remain stable even if that meant that the Islamists be recognized as political partners, although under strict control. In addition, clearly condemning the coup would have had the consequence of blocking the channels of communication between the two rims of the Mediterranean. In that case, France could have lost a potential means of influence over the course of events in Algeria.

France blows hot and cold

In order to express reservations without a clear condemnation, the French authorities chose to talk with two voices. Whereas Mitterrand protested against the interruption of the election, Dumas cultivated a softer stance. The first statement of the French president (January 14, 1992) was undoubtedly critical of the Algerian authorities and the tone peremptory:

> (...) the engaged process towards elections in Algeria has been interrupted and that represents at the very least an abnormal act since it comes down to establish a state of exception. (...) the Algerian leaders have to knot again at the earliest the threads of a democratic life that had begun and which will have to (...) be carried through.[23]

Dumas' judgement on the Algerian High Security Council's decision was much less severe:

> It is not France's place to intervene in this affair. The Algerian leaders were faced to a difficult situation. They considered (...) that it was the least inadequate solution. We now have to trust them for things to be restored when the time comes.[24]

As to France's relations with Algeria, Dumas argued in the same declaration that France should maintain economic support to help stabilize the political realm:

> (...) France has to express its solidarity with the Algerian people. We have too many things in common not to take further interest in what happens in Algeria and to turn our back on this people and this country under the pretext that it is experiencing a difficult phase. (...) If we want to cure the causes [of the Algerian malaise], we have to (...) take measures to that effect, heal the disease, assist [economic] development so that this youth (...) finds a certain satisfaction in living at home rather than in finding refuge in extremist stances.

Whereas Dumas had argued towards the end of January that economic aid to Algeria was not to be closely tied to the restoration of the democratic process,[25] a week later, and in a context of emerging violence in Algeria, Mitterrand warned that:

> France is profoundly attached to the carrying-on and development of [Franco-Algerian] relations inasmuch as the principles that it judges as essential – and the progress towards democracy and the respect of human rights are part of them – will be respected.[26]

The deliberate discrepancy between the discourse of the president and that of his foreign minister aimed at showing that, even though the French government would not cease its relations with the new authorities in Algiers –

supposedly because of its solidarity with the people – it strongly encouraged them to move beyond the accomplished fact. If, this time, a 'telling silence' was not resorted to, it was because the French highest authorities were determined to put their message across. This, of course, generated strong reactions in Algiers. Ghozali denounced France's interference in Algeria's domestic affairs and – as invariably occurs in such cases – implicitly brought for consideration Mitterrand's ministerial functions in 1954 arguing that 'There are some people in France (...) who continue to live Algeria's problems as though they were theirs because they still have not accepted our independence (...)'.[27]

Divisions within the Socialist Party

On the whole, the Cresson and Bérégovoy governments showed great unity over France's policy towards Algeria. Nevertheless, there were divisions within the Socialist Party. They did not have any particular impact on the formulation and implementation of France's policy which was well under Dumas' control. Yet, they are worth mentioning. In general, the attitude adopted was one of wait-and-see in front of a dilemma that everybody would have preferred not to be confronted with. On each side of this general middle ground, two currents of opinion can be guessed from the public interventions made by party or government members. Some were in line with the substance of governmental policy but went slightly further than the official stance by pronouncing the very words that had been avoided by Mitterrand. Thus, Bernard Kouchner, minister for health and humanitarian action, declared in late April 1992 that 'the [Algerian] government was born out of a coup d'état' and that 'the progression of Islamism will not be stopped by force'.[28]

On the opposite side, and somewhat against governmental policy, some supported the 'preventive coup d'état'. It was the case, for instance, of Georges Morin or Claude Cheysson. On the basis of the analysis of the Algerian Army's officer corps,[29] they projected that the FIS' coming to power was bound to lead sooner or later to the Army's intervention because of the risks that such an eventuality entailed. The Algerian Army's analysis diagnosed three main risks. Firstly, Chadli might be too weak to resist an initiative of the FIS-dominated parliament to revise the Constitution. He would probably make some concessions to the FIS whose moderate wing would have to give in to the radicals so as to catch votes in the run for the presidential election. Presidential indulgence would generate opposition among the population, notably in Kabylia and in the Southern Sahara. There would, thus, be a risk of a secession war threatening the unity of the Army and, therefore, the cohesion of the

Algerian state. Secondly, by scaring off the world community, a FIS regime would isolate Algeria internationally whereas it needed foreign financial resources for its economy to recover. Thirdly, if the FIS attempted to 'export its revolution', it would seek to destabilize the neighbouring regimes and this threatened to suck the whole region in Algeria's political turmoil. Faced with risks of civil war, economic collapse and regional instability, the Algerian Army would intervene.

Within the French Socialist Party, those who supported the Algerian Army's line argued that, since the Army would intervene, it would be more efficient if it did so before the FIS controlled the wheels of government. They also had a four-point argument to rebuff those who, like Mitterrand or Kouchner, pointed their forefingers at the military-backed take-over. In the Socialist Party's newspaper and in *Le Monde*, Morin thus argued that: (1) emphasising the military nature of the coup was to ignore that for the past thirty years every Algerian governing institution had been military-backed; (2) democracy made no sense if it resulted in the access to power of a party that had vowed to destroy it; (3) with 3 million FIS-voters out of 13 million registered voters, the FIS hardly had a popular mandate to head for a revision of the Constitution towards the implementation of the *shari'a*; and (4) no one 'could take the liberty of telling the Algerians that they should have 'attempted the experience' at all costs'.[30] Morin was joined in his views by Cheysson (European MP, chairman of the European delegation for the Maghreb) who described as sheer nonsense Mitterrand's and Dumas' fixation on the interruption of the electoral process in a country where there is not yet a democratic tradition.[31] This current of opinion, critical of the chosen course for France's Algeria policy, did not, however, succeed in influencing governmental policy towards a greater support to the HSC. As examined below, until January 1993, France's backing of the Algerian regime was more a matter of words than of deeds.

A strained relationship

After the coup and until January 1993, when Dumas went to Algiers specifically to repair the troubled relations, France's policy towards Algeria was characterised by inconsistency between official discourse and actual deeds. The official discourse, after what had been perceived in Algiers as Mitterrand's diatribes, was one of support for, and solidarity with, the Algerian people and the regime. Dumas reiterated this policy stance all along. His address of February 5, 1992 to the Association of the Foreign Press sums up France's discourse:

On several occasions and since the arrival in power of a new team, France has renewed its willingness to continue to help Algeria. (...) I would like to say here to the Algerian authorities France's willingness to help Algeria and the Algerian people at this critical juncture which, I do not doubt, Algeria will be able to overcome if an effort is made – a significant effort to assist the economy of that country.'[32]

Yet, political relations did not illustrate France's discourse. Neither did economic co-operation.

After the coup, the relationship between the Cresson and the Ghozali governments opened with a crisis which resulted, on the one hand, from Mitterrand's harsh words and, on the other, from Dumas' manoeuvres. Immediately after the establishment of the HSC, Dumas sent Pierre Lafrance, director of the Quai d'Orsay's Maghreb-Mashreq department, to Algiers. Press reports described the visit as 'a mission of information and contacts with Algeria's political forces'.[33] For his part, the French Ambassador accounted for Lafrance's trip as a mission of contact with the HSC.[34] According to Audibert, the object of the visit was primarily to incite the Ghozali government to find a political remedy to the risks of instability stemming from the coup d'état by recognizing the force of political Islam. Lafrance had a ready-for-use solution: to find a political personality who, as head of state, could please every political currents and rally behind him the allegiance of the Islamists. This personality was Ahmed Taleb Ibrahimi, a politician with whom Dumas was on friendly terms. As a young lawyer, Dumas had defended FLN members during the War of Independence. Taleb Ibrahimi was one of them. Taleb Ibrahimi represents the religious current of the FLN which, ever since Independence, has played the role of a lobby within the state apparatus for Arabisation and Islamisation. With the rise of the FIS, he has come to be seen as a 'synthesis man' representing both historical and religious legitimacy, a 'link man' between the FLN and the FIS.[35] Lafrance's message made the Algerian foreign minister blanch all the more because Lafrance brought Iran into the picture. He argued that the *mullahs* could bring their help to a political solution by finding a way of cooling the FIS' ardour. Since the Rafsanjani regime was denounced in Algiers for meddling in Algeria's internal affairs – Iran had condemned the cancellation of the election and showed an open support for the FIS – the suggestion was not only wholly unacceptable for Algiers but also dismissed as improper.

The French Ambassador to Algiers, whose services had been short-circuited, had warned Dumas' emissary that the message would provoke 'reactions'. If the political strategy behind the proposal was not senseless (had not Ghozali brought Islamists into government?), he thought the approach ham-fisted. In addition to Lakhdar Brahimi's frank response to Lafrance, the Algerian government reacted by recalling its Ambassadors from Paris and Teheran. The Iranian Ambassador to Algiers was also expelled.[36]

Throughout the year, all sorts of signs, including the presence of FIS activists in France,[37] were underlined in the Algerian press as evidence of a Paris-Khartoum-Teheran axis conspiring against Algeria. *El Watan* spread rumours of contacts between the French secret services and the FIS (then referred to as 'France, Iran, Sudan') in Khartoum before the cancellation of the election.[38] *Le Matin* quoted the Spanish newspaper *El Pais* which leaked a French working document prepared for the account of the Elysée and in which the hypothesis of a FIS take-over was duly analysed.[39] Members of the ruling elite also resorted to this conspiracy theme, recurrent in Algeria's politics. In August 1992, the Algerian prime minister denounced the work of 'the foreign hand' – i.e. France in the Algerian political wording – in the bomb attack against the Algiers airport which killed nine people and wounded over a hundred.[40] At the end of the year, Ali Haroun, member of the HSC, condemned the French government for 'having two irons in the fire',[41] which meant it had a 'FIS joker' up its sleeve.

The Algerian press campaign and the authorities' unfounded accusations were a protest against the attitude of the Cresson and Bérégovoy governments. Quite apart from the crisis triggered by Lafrance's visit, the Algerian government soon discovered that, despite a discourse of support and solidarity, the French were, in fact, unwilling to throw their weight behind Boudiaf or Kafi. It was so because the Cresson government doubted Boudiaf's ability to pull Algeria out of crisis while the security, political and economic situation was worsening. Thereafter, his murder in June 1992 reinforced the view that resistance to a from-the-top reform of the Algerian political system was strong within the state apparatus itself. The return to office of Boumedienists and, particularly, of Belaïd Abdesselam was received with great reservation in Paris because of their nationalist and strongly anti-French, outlook.

In this general context, under Cresson and in the early months of Bérégovoy's premiership, the French government's policy was to maintain relations with Algiers, but to a strict minimum. Thus, the February 1992 financial accord amounting to FF5 billion (about $1 billion) was lower than before and was only made up of commercial credits. The French government did put pressure on American and Japanese banks to stay within the international bank syndicate headed by the Crédit Lyonnais and an accord was eventually reached on March 4, 1992, allowing the release of a $1.45 billion loan.[42] Although this helped Algeria in repaying part of its non-guaranteed debt, the French government's mediation concerned an operation in discussion since 1991. Throughout 1992, political relations were far from being at their best, as demonstrated by bilateral exchanges. Except for the visit of the Algerian minister for foreign affairs to Paris on March 4–5, 1992, there was no contact at high levels before July 1992, that is six months after the coup. Certainly, in June, the Bérégovoy government had sent the minister for agriculture and his counsellor (Georges Morin) to Algeria, as well as the deputy minister for trade, who headed the delegation of French enterprises at the commercial fair organized by Algiers.[43] Yet, the absence of an official high-state visit indicated the French government's unwillingness to bring too strong an approval to the policies of the Boudiaf regime. At Boudiaf's request, Mitterrand had accepted to meet him in Paris on July 16, 1992. The meeting did not occur since Boudiaf was killed before. But, significantly, the visit was to be secret.[44] Dumas eventually went to Algiers in order to attend Boudiaf's funeral and promised that 'France [would] not economise on its help to Algeria and that this [would] be visible in the days that follow[ed]'.[45] The Algerians were in fact to wait for another six months. In the meantime, it took an unusual four months for Sid Ahmed Ghozali, who had been replaced by Abdesselam and appointed in late July 1992 Ambassador to Paris, to be accredited (December 9, 1992) by the Elysée. The official justification for this delay – the French president's health problems and the protocol – may have been true, but it is evident that the difficult relations with Ghozali that occurred during the Gulf War and the role he played during the coup did not favour him in Paris. In any case, Ghozali's non-accreditation was perceived in Algiers as another mark of ostracism.

By the end of 1992, relations between France and Algeria were thus particularly strained. Neither political relations nor economic co-operation illustrated France's discourse of support to, and solidarity with, the Algerian regime. The coherence of France's policy was consequently seriously undermined. This was to change three months before the French parliamentary election.

Notes

1. The RCD, created by Saïd Sadi in 1989, was joined by militants of the FFS and the Berber Cultural Movement (MCB). The RCD is a Kabylia-based party, advocating secularism, social democracy and cultural pluralism. The FFS, born in 1963 but recognized only in 1989, shares the same objectives as the RCD. But the two parties differ on the issue as to how the FIS should be dealt with. The MCB, now legal, was

a clandestine association which sprang from the 1980 Berber Spring and whose prime objective is to defend the Berber cultural heritage.

2. The MAJD was created in 1991 by Kasdi Merbah (head of the Military Security from 1962 to 1979 and minister until 1989). Merbah supported the establishment of a pluralistic democracy, but put more emphasis on cleansing the Administration from corruption. Although the MAJD supported the cancellation of the parliamentary election, it later advocated conciliation with the FIS.

3. The PAGS was clandestinely set up in 1966 in opposition to Boumediene's regime. It was a resurgence of the Algerian Communist Party banned under Ben Bella. Made legal in 1989, the PAGS splintered in the early 1990s. One of the new parties, Ettahaddi, headed by Cherif el-Hachemi, advocates secularism, pluralism and socialism.

4. The account of the unfolding of the coup is drawn from A. Charef (1994), pp. 234-59; P. Dévoluy and M. Duteil (1994), pp. 34-100 and J.J. Lavenue (1993), pp. 173-81.

5. Saïd Guechi and Sassi Lamouri were included in Ghozali's third government (February 1992). Guechi, who had attempted to take over the FIS in July 1991, was appointed minister for employment. Lamouri, who belonged to an Islamist movement close to Hamas, was appointed minister for religious affairs.

6. Although it is incorrect to talk of the FIS, as opposed to the ex-FIS, when referring to the banned party, it has become usual to do so. I shall follow the norm.

7. *Le Point* (1124), 2 April 1994.

8. P. Dévoluy and M. Duteil (1994), p. 224.

9. For their parts, the FFS, the FLN, the MDA, the Algerian Renewal Party (PRA), Hamas and the Movement of the Islamic Renaissance (MNI) criticised the dissolution of the FIS as an unviable solution. The MDA was founded by former President Ben Bella in 1984 while he was in exile. The MDA was legalised in 1990. It advocates pluralistic democracy, reference to a tolerant Islam and soft economic liberalism. The PRA (headed by Noureddine Boukrouh and created in 1989), Hamas (Sheik Mahfoud Nahnah, 1990) and the MNI (Sheik Abdallah Djaballah, 1990) are three Islamist parties advocating the establishment of an Islamic state respecting democratic pluralism. They reject violence. Apart from the MNI, they fully support economic liberalism.

10. Interview with Sadek Boussena, April 19, 1994. S. Boussena was: minister for energy and petrochemical industries (1988–89); minister for mines and industry (1989–91); head of the Sonatrach (1988–90); and president of OPEC (1990–91).

11. The major events marking Boudiaf's leadership are drawn from J. Cesari (1994a), pp. 619-30 and A. Charef (1994), pp. 259-366.

12. The coming section concentrates on the policies of the HSC under Kafi only until Winter 1993, for it is then that French policy towards Algeria changed. For details on this period, see J. Cesari (1994a), pp. 630-51 and A. Charef (1994), pp. 366-441.

13. Declaration, December 30, 1991 in MAE (November–December 1991), p. 176.

14. Press conference in Abidjan, 8 January 1992 in MAE (January–February 1992), p. 24.

15. Press conference in Oman, 31 January 1992 in MAE (January–February 1992),

p. 92.

16. G. Joffé (1994a), p. 12.

17. C. Silberzahn (1995), p. 292.

18. Interview with Jean Audibert, 7 June 1995.

19. Ibid.

20. In MAE (March–April 1991), pp. 94-5.

21. Interview in *Réalités*, 13 August 1992.

22. Interview with Roland Dumas, 16 May 1995.

23. Press conference in Luxembourg, January 14, 1992 in MAE (January–February 1992), p. 55.

24. Interview on Radio Shalom, 21 January 1992, in MAE (January–February 1992), p.67.

25. Ibid.

26. Interview in *Al Hayat* on 27 January 1992 in MAE (January–February 1992), p.81.

27. Quoted in *Revue de Presse Maghreb, Proche et Moyen Orient*, January 1992, (361), p. 11. Between June 1954 and February 1955, Mitterrand headed the Ministry for the Interior. As such, he oversaw Algerian affairs since Algeria was assimilated to a French *département*. In his ministerial function, Mitterrand had to deal with the November 1954 national liberation uprising in Algeria. In these circumstances, he declared that with the Algerian 'rebels', 'There can be only one form of negotiation: war' (quoted in D. MacShane (1982), p. 61).

28. Quoted in *Le Monde*, 12 January 1993.

29. An account of the Algerian Army's analysis of the risks entailed by an eventual seizure of power by the FIS can be found in A. Charef (1994), pp. 253-4 or in H. Roberts (1993a), pp. 451-2.

30. *Le Monde*, 15 January 1992 and reprint given to the author by Morin of his interview with *Vendredi* in mid-January 1992.

31. Interview on 22 April 1994.

32. In MAE (January–February 1992), p.116.

33. *Le Monde*, 18 and 21 January 1992.

34. Interview with Jean Audibert, 7 June 1995.

35. Taleb Ibrahimi is the son of *Sheik* Bachir Brahimi who had been president of the Association of the Reformist Ulema after the death in 1940 of its founder, Abdelhamid Ben Badis. As a member of the wartime FLN, Ibrahimi was arrested by the French in 1957. Under Ben Bella, he was jailed (1963–65) for his criticisms of the regime and notably its socialist orientation. Under Boumediene, he benefited from the policy of co-optation of the *ulema* and was appointed minister for education (1965–70) and minister for information and culture (1970–77). Under Benjedid, he remained in government although he was attributed in 1982 a less sensitive portfolio – the Ministry for Foreign Affairs. He was dismissed after 'Black October'. Biographic information in J.J. Lavenue (1993), p. 228.

36. *Le Monde*, 21 January 1992 and *Middle East International* (417), 24 January 1992. Diplomatic relations with Iran were eventually broken off in March 1993.

37. FIS militants of a high profile such as Kameredine Kherbane, Rabah Kebir and Anwar Haddam stayed in France before being expelled. In addition, the Algerian Brotherhood in France (FAF), created in February 1991 to support the FIS electoral campaign, continued to function and evidence of fund-raising operations for the benefit of the FIS emerged with the dismantling of a counterfeiting trade operation in October 1992 (the *Lacoste* affair).

38. *Middle East International* (417), 24 January 1992.

39. *Le Matin*, 14 December 1992.

40. In *Le Monde*, 28 August 1992.

41. Haroun's interview in the French newspaper *La Croix*, quoted in *Le Matin*, 14 December 1992.

42. Y. Troquet (le) (1994), p. 500.

43. Y. Troquet (le) (1994), p. 500 and interview with G. Morin in *Le Soir d'Algérie*, 28 June 1992.

44. Interview with Jean Audibert, 7 June 1995.

45. Quoted in *Le Matin*, 14 December 1992.

Chapter 3

Friendship Otherwise Than Just with Words (January – March 1993)

Against all odds, Dumas made an official visit to Algiers only three months before the March 1993 French parliamentary election, initiating a *rapprochement* with Algiers just as the socialists were about to exit from the political game. Increased economic aid was immediately granted. Firm political backing was provided with the formal invitation to Paris of Abdesselam whose nomination as prime minister had generated strong reservations in Paris several months prior to the invitation. There are not yet any truly satisfactory answers to this paradoxical attitude. Two clues can, nevertheless, be identified. It seems that a reassessment of the Algerian crisis and of the power struggle occurred to the effect that the Bérégovoy government thought that it was too late to seek a compromise and that not supporting Algiers could indirectly help a FIS violent take-over. The change in French Ambassadors may also have played a role to the extent that the new Ambassador wished to start his mandate on a friendly footing with Algiers.

Dumas in Algiers – Abdesselam in Paris

The decision to organize a visit of the French minister for foreign affairs to Algiers was taken during the Autumn of 1992. The new Ambassador to Algiers, Bernard Kessedjian, had taken his position in late September 1992 with the aim of improving the troubled relations. In October, he announced that Dumas would soon come to Algeria to say that France wanted to maintain 'a sure, friendly and trustful relationship' with the Algerian Republic.[1] Because of the non-accreditation of Ghozali until December, Dumas' trip was, however, postponed until January 1993. After his visit on January 8–9, 1993, Dumas declared:

> I think my visit was useful. More than misunderstandings, a shadow existed on the relations between France and Algeria (...) During my trip to Algiers I had the opportunity to say (...) that during this difficult phase France would stand by the side of Algeria and of the

Algerians, and that this would translate into a political backing of
the leaders of today's Algeria, as well as economic [and] financial
support (...) As regards bilateral political relations as well as French
backing of Algeria on the international scene, things have become
normal again.[2]

In addition to Dumas' promises of a strong political and economic backing –
promises which were also made by Mitterrand in his message to the head of the
HSC[3] – the French authorities moved to reassure their counterparts on the issue
of Islamism. On January 7, the spokesman for the Quai d'Orsay expressed
France's concerns as to 'the rise of intolerance under the cover of democracy
in Algeria';[4] Dumas declared that 'France condemn[ed] terrorism and [had]
proved (...) that when it was aware of activities [on French soil] which, in one
way or the other, could lead to terrorist acts detrimental to Algeria, it took the
appropriate measures'.[5] To show that French reservations as to Abdesselam
were over, the Algerian prime minister was officially invited to France by
Bérégovoy.

In Algiers, Dumas had affirmed that it was 'normal that, in a period
such as this, friendship be expressed otherwise than just with words'.[6] Almost
immediately after his departure, the director of the French Treasury was
dispatched to Algiers to discuss a financial accord which was concluded on
February 13, 1993 by the French minister for economic and financial affairs,
Michel Sapin. The credit package totalled FF6.1 billion (about $1.1 billion) for
1993. It included: a FF5 billion commercial credit guaranteed by the Coface
(FF1 billion deferred credits for the purchase of vehicles and spare parts,
FF800 million still available from the FF4 billion revolving credit, FF2.2
billion fresh credits for miscellaneous purchases and FF1 billion for food
credits); a state loan of FF1 billion for balance-of-payments aid and the
financing of capital equipment purchases; a FF100 million loan financed by the
Caisse française de développement aimed at financing joint-venture operations.
The release of this loan, blocked since July 1991, was allowed by the signature
of a reciprocal accord on the protection of investments.[7]

In general, the Algerian press welcomed the new aid package.
However, *Algérie Actualité* pinpointed the fact that French financial help was
not more significant than in previous years and that the French authorities
continued to reject the principle of a bilateral rescheduling of Algeria's debt.[8]
As to the Algerian authorities, they seemed to make the best out of it since
Abdesselam accepted Bérégovoy's invitation and went to Paris on February
18–19, 1993. While Abdesselam's visit sanctioned the recovery of the dialogue
with the French socialists, its main object was to prepare Algeria's future. The
French parliamentary election was due in March and opinion polls predicted

the success of the Right. Avoiding tactlessness, Abdesselam's meetings with the opposition parties were not limited to the Right: he also met Georges Marchais whose Communist Party had called since January 1992 for strong French support to Algiers. Whether in front of the French highest authorities, the French political parties, the employers' union, or the emigrant community, Abdesselam defended his programme: a three to five-year transition period to let the economy recover before heading towards the resumption of the democratic process. Despite spectacular terrorist outrages such as the attempted killing of General Khaled Nezzar on the very day Sapin was in Algiers, the Algerian prime minister argued that the security situation was under control and that the Islamist armed groups were soon to be dismantled.[9]

Unclear motives

It is difficult to understand why the decision to bring a firmer support to Algiers was taken at that particular stage since the French parliamentary election was scheduled for March 1993 and the socialists defeated beforehand. In *Jeune Afrique*, Paul-Marie de la Gorce has argued that the idea that it was no longer possible simply to 'sulk' about the Algerian regime arose from two main considerations. First, in a context of growing political violence, it was unrealistic to believe in the possibility of a prompt return to democratic life. Second, France would have much to lose if the FIS, now radicalised by its armed struggle, came to power.[10]

Dumas explained his new policy in accordance with the first consideration. Indeed, on January 7, 1993, in his declaration to the personnel of his Ministry, he said:

> (...) the Algerians need our solidarity. The economic and social crisis that hits them directly has not allowed the pursuit of the democratic experience, let's regret it and go beyond our regrets. History commands us to keep up a dialogue in order to help them rediscover the way to development and democracy.[11]

When asked a couple of years later why the *rapprochement* with Algeria was decided, Dumas provides no additional clue. He repeats his January 1993 stance while emphasising that France dealt with the Abdesselam regime merely because it represented the legal government. France, he said, only aimed at supporting the Algerian people, not the regime.[12] All French governments have used this sophism in order to avoid criticisms highlighting compromising relations with a repressive and corrupted regime. Dumas' clarification, thus, does not help to understand the underlying reasons for the *rapprochement*. It merely indicates a willingness to minimise its impact.

In line with de la Gorce, it may be suggested that clearer support to Algiers as from January 1993 derived from a reassessment of the Algerian crisis and of the power struggle taking place in Algeria. The idea that the FIS was unable to overthrow the regime by force arose only in Summer 1993. Until then, the risk of a violent take-over and of the establishment of a radical Islamist regime was thought to be within the odds. Inasmuch as the Algerian authorities were unwilling to find a compromise with the FIS, not supporting them entailed the risk of indirectly helping a FIS take-over. The French government would have preferred a compromise with the Islamist substance in a framework where it could be controlled. In no way, however, did it wish to have to deal with a revolutionary Islamist regime in Algiers. Hence, it seems, the 1993 *rapprochement*.

The change in Ambassadors to Algiers may also have played a role in the redefinition of French policy. Kessedjian never hid his dislike for the FIS and was on relatively good terms with Abdesselam. In addition, Kessedjian had been Dumas' *cabinet*[13] director for several years and thus counted among Dumas' close acquaintances, which may explain why Kessedjian's initiative for a *rapprochement* was well relayed to the Quai d'Orsay.

To sum up, it is worth emphasising that, whereas the French media have tended to affirm that, in the wake of the January 1992 coup d'état, France's policy towards Algeria was one of unconditional support for the Algerian regime, the Cresson and Bérégovoy governments, in fact, led a very cautious policy which, as indicated by the minister for foreign affairs, consisted of 'manoeuvring on the razor's edge'.[14] The French socialists did not wish to see a FIS regime in Algiers. But they also feared that the exclusion of the Islamist mainstream from Algeria's politics would generate political instability. In maintaining relations with the HSC, the Cresson government hoped to be able to incite it to a compromise with the Islamists – a compromise whose outline was not well defined but which could have led, under the leadership of such a personality as Taleb Ibrahimi, to a political solution of controlled integration of the Islamists in the political game. The Socialist Party as a whole did not support this policy line but governmental unity was maintained. In addition, supporters of the 'preventive coup d'état' did not manage to influence Dumas' policy which, despite words of support and solidarity, was one of minimal contact with Algiers. In January 1993, after one year of tense relations with Algiers which accused France of having a FIS joker up its sleeve, the Bérégovoy government unexpectedly decided to more clearly back the Algerian regime. It seems that this change in policy was taken in the light of two considerations. First, that it was too late for conciliation to be reached in Algeria and, second, that the risk of a FIS violent take-over was possible. This policy of greater support to Algiers was also followed, at least until a certain point, by the new right-wing government appointed after the Right's triumph in the late March 1993 parliamentary election.

Notes

1. In *Le Monde*, 21 October 1992.
2. Interview on RTL, 10 January 1993 in MAE (January–February 1993), p. 27.
3. Reproduced in *El Moudjahid*, 10 January 1993.
4. Quoted in *El Moudjahid*, 8–9 16. G. Joffé (1994a), p. 12, January 1993.
5. Press conference on 9 January 1993, Algiers in MAE (January–February 1993), p.19. Dumas was referring to the expulsion of a few FIS militants.
6. Quoted in *Algérie Actualité* (1422), 13–19 January 1993.
7. *Le Monde*, 16 February 1993.
8. *Algérie Actualité* (1427), 17–23 February 1993.
9. El Moudjahid, 19–20 Fenruary 1993 and *Le Monde*, 21–22 February 1993.
10. *Jeune Afrique*, 4 February 1993.
11. In MAE (January–February 1993), p. 14.
12. Interview with Roland Dumas, 16 May 1995.
13. The French *cabinet* is the team of official and unofficial advisers grouped around each minister and thus bears no relation to the cabinet in the British sense.
14. Interview with Roland Dumas, 16 May 1995.

Part Two

The Right
(April 1993 – November 1995)

Introduction to Part Two

During the period under review, institutional instability in Algeria was particularly high. Three different governments were appointed. Two presidents (Kafi and Zeroual) headed different governing institutions. A presidential election also took place in November 1995, reconfirming Zeroual in his position (see Table 1). Despite these numerous and important changes, the Algerian leaders were all confronted with the same problem: getting their country out of a worsening economic and political crisis. They attempted to do so more or less in the same way. To deal with the foreign debt crisis, they finally agreed to reschedule the debt service (April 1994) and to implement the IMF's economic and financial guidelines. On the security front, they sought to eradicate the Islamist armed groups through methods that became more and more repressive for the population at large. On the political scene, they opened a dialogue with the opposition forces, including the FIS. It is by reference to these issues that the French Right had to define its policy towards Algeria. These issues will, thus, be explored before turning to an analysis of the Balladur and Juppé governments' discourse and policy.

In dealing with Algerian domestic politics, we shall mainly be concerned with the political dialogue process which was started by the Algerian authorities in order to bring the opposition to participate in the new political institutions they had created and in the 1995 presidential election. Particular attention is devoted to the Algerian government's dialogue with the FIS. Dialogue with the FIS is a key issue not only because the FIS was at the centre of the political rift in Algeria but also because dialogue with the FIS had, so to speak, institutionalised the 'eradicator / conciliator' split in Algerian politics and in the Algerian power structure. This split had important implications. First, its mere existence demonstrated that the Algerian struggle could not be read as a mere fight for 'democratic enlightenment' against 'totalitarian obscurantism'. Second, it implied that foreign governments could not support the Algerian authorities as a unit: they had to choose between supporting the conciliators or the eradicators in the government. Negotiations with the FIS were officially broken off in late October 1994 (even though they secretly continued thereafter). The failure of the dialogue with the FIS raises a few questions. Why did dialogue fail? Was it because the banned party adopted an uncompromising behaviour or, perhaps, because the Algerian authorities' dialogue initiative was designed to fail? What was the consequence of the failure of the dialogue on the organization of the opposition and what was the Algerian government's response to these organizational changes?

Once these questions are answered, the external context towards which French policy was made is set; it becomes possible to turn to the analysis of France's Algeria policy. The inquiry into France's policy *vis-à-vis* Algeria under the Right is conducted both in relation to the Balladur premiership (under Mitterrand's presidency) and the Juppé premiership (under Chirac's presidency). In both cases, the analysis deals with the shifting character of French policy which revolved around the conciliation / eradication paradigm. Under Balladur, a shift took place in September 1994. Prior to that date, the main feature of the French government's policy was its espousal of the Algerian eradicators' arguments for refusing to negotiate a political settlement with the FIS. By contrast, from September 1994 to the May 1995 presidential election which brought down the Balladur Administration, the French government showed more openness in favour of a conciliatory solution to the Algerian conflict. Regarding the earlier period, marked by French backing of the Algerian eradicators, the study focuses on the ambiguities and contradictions of the French official discourse with the aim to demonstrate that, despite a discourse emphasising the need for conciliation in Algeria, the Balladur government opposed a compromise with the FIS. In addition, the ways in which the French government brought its support to the eradicators in Algiers are examined. Other states' positions in relation to the Algerian crisis are briefly reviewed in the light of France's drumming up international support for Algiers. Insofar as the later period is concerned (i.e., after September 1994), the shift towards greater firmness *vis-à-vis* the eradicators is accounted for by showing the evolution of Balladur's Foreign Minister's discourse on the issue of political dialogue in Algeria. Particular attention is given to the issue of governmental disunity which characterised this period and which made France's policy look like a muddle. Finally, the reasons for Foreign Minister Juppé's change of heart are analysed as well as its limits: it was not accompanied by a change in policy measures, thus reflecting the Balladur government's unwillingness to force a conciliation with the FIS in Algeria.

Under Chirac's presidency (and Juppé's premiership), French policy was also characterised by a shift. Prior to October 1995, the Juppé government argued that the FIS should not be allowed back into the political game because it had not yet fulfilled the criteria of non-violence and democracy. Thereafter, although it still did not see the FIS fit to compete in the planned presidential election of November 1995, the Juppé government made no objection to the FIS' inclusion within the political dialogue and to its participation in future parliamentary elections. Very important as well was the government's view that French economic aid to Algeria may have to be tied to political conditions in order to push the Algerian regime into a political solution involving a wide political dialogue and democratization. This stance was new in comparison with what the Juppé government had itself maintained prior to October 1995. This stance was also what made the difference between the Balladur and Juppé governments since, as mentioned above, under Balladur there was no intention to force Algiers into conciliation. But, if as prime minister, Juppé went further than he did as foreign minister (under Balladur's premiership) in terms of his political discourse, what about his actions? Up to the time of writing, there was no evidence that the Chirac Administration had been politically effective in conditioning its economic aid to Algeria. Rather, Paris had been forced to work hard to smooth out the crisis that erupted in the wake of its policy shift.

Chapter 1

Domestic Politics in Algeria

From March 1993 to November 1995, several rounds of talks took place between the Algerian administration and the civil society (political parties, associations and various personalities). For the sake of clarity, it is best to differentiate the rounds of talks held between March 1993 and October 1994 from those held between November 1994 and November 1995. The talks of March 1993 – October 1994 aimed, first, at getting a national consensus around the Algerian authorities' proposal for the creation of new ruling institutions meant to replace the expiring High State Council. Thereafter, political dialogue aimed at winning the participation of opposition parties in these new institutions. By contrast, the talks held between November 1994 and November 1995 were organized in order to incite political parties to participate in the planned presidential election of November 1995. Another reason for distinguishing these two periods in the Algerian political dialogue process is that, after the official breaking off of the negotiations with the FIS in late October 1994, a change took place in the organization of the opposition: a 'conciliatory front' emerged, gathering the FIS, the FLN and the FFS.

This section first looks at the political dialogue initiative of March 1993 – October 1994. The various stages of the dialogue process and the Algerian government's goal in organizing such talks are briefly examined. The analysis then focuses on the authorities' negotiations with the FIS. In relation to this theme, two issues are reviewed in detail. First, we look at the political divide between 'conciliators' and 'eradicators' which has commanded much of Algeria's politics in the past few years. Second, we ask why the negotiations with the FIS failed and look at the issue of the genuineness of the authorities in talking to the FIS. Following the chronological order, section 1 then turns to the Rome initiative or the formation of an opposition front incorporating the FIS, before commenting on the results of the November 1995 Algerian presidential election.

Failed attempts at political dialogue (March 1993 – October 1994)

The aim of the dialogue: legitimacy

After the failure of September 1992, Kafi's attempt at starting talks with the opposition afresh was driven by the prospect of the expiring mandate of the High State Council (December 31, 1993). New ruling institutions needed to be created and Kafi hoped that, if a consensus could be reached through dialogue on such institutions, these would acquire the legitimacy which the HSC had lacked. For Kafi, dialogue was not a framework within which proposals for Algeria's future institutions could be advanced by the civil society. Rather, he saw it as a means to get a public approval of the HSC's own scheme which he had outlined on January 14, 1993 and which had been advocated by Abdesselam during his visit in Paris.

The backbone of the HSC's programme was the creation of a new governing body with a three-year mandate to oversee the transition to the return to the ballot box.[1] Most political parties were hostile to this proposal which they denounced as a means to maintain in power the HSC in another form. Yet, after discussions held with the civil society between March and June 1993, this was eventually the adopted solution in the 'Draft platform on the national consensus on the transitional period'.[2] Other rounds of talks were convened under the Malek government within the framework of a National Dialogue Commission.[3] They sought to bring as many parties into the consensus before a National Dialogue Conference was convened to sanction the blueprint on the transitional period. The blueprint provided for three ruling bodies: a state presidency, a government, and a National Transition Council supposed to replace the former Consultative National Council but not fundamentally different since its members were to be state-nominated.

The National Dialogue Conference took place on January 25–26, 1994.[4] Most political parties boycotted it; among them the FLN, the FFS, and the RCD. The RCD did so in opposition to the authorities' attempts at negotiating with the FIS (see below). The FFS, the FLN and other smaller parties said they were unwilling to participate in a 'great show' aimed at 'enthroning at the head of the state a candidate coming from the seraglio'.[5] Their boycott was also intended to protest against the government's neglect of their demands in favour of a return to civil peace: lifting the state of emergency, releasing political prisoners and ceasing executions. Hamas, the MNI, the PRA and others left the Conference because, on the eve of its opening, a provision on the selection process for the presidency of the Republic was reintroduced into the platform whereas they had previously obtained its abrogation.[6] The amendment of the platform implied that the military establishment would, as usual, nominate the president. Without surprise, it was exactly what happened. General Lamine Zeroual, who had been appointed defence minister in July 1993,[7] was designated president of the Algerian Republic on January 31, 1994. The Malek government was reconfirmed until April 1994. The National Transition Council was installed under Sifi's Premiership on May 18, 1994.

Since the most significant political parties had boycotted the Conference, the legitimacy which the authorities had hoped for was simply not achieved. Under (appointed) President Zeroual, the objective sought in continuing to propose a political dialogue was to obtain *a posteriori* such a legitimacy. Between March and September 1994, four rounds of talks were thus organized in order to bring the political parties that had boycotted the Conference to join the state-managed political game and to accept seats in the National Transition Council. During this period, the position of the political parties *vis-à-vis* the Algerian authorities was entirely dominated by the on-going debate on the place the FIS should be given in the political arena.

Dialogue with the FIS: the split between 'eradicators' and 'conciliators'

The issue as to whether FIS members should be invited to the negotiation table arose publicly during the round of talks convened between March and June 1993 under the Abdesselam government. It has never left Algeria's political debates ever since and has divided both the civil society and power circles into two categories: the 'eradicators' and the 'conciliators'.

Within the civil society, eradicators are represented by parties, such as the RCD and Ettahaddi; associations grouped around the UGTA in the National Committee for the Safeguarding of Algeria; most of the French-language press and part of the French-educated intellectual elite. Eradicators favour, as their name indicates, a strategy of eradication of the Islamist armed groups but also a strategy of complete exclusion of the Islamist movement from Algeria's political landscape. The Islamist political project, which they depict as archaic and totalitarian, is, in their view, wholly incompatible with their own, based upon the concept of a modern, secular and republican state. Organizing several protest demonstrations,[8] eradicators have denounced the Algerian authorities' contacts with the FIS. They have argued that no bargaining should be made with 'people who have deliberately and officially chosen murder and violence as a means to reach power'.[9] They have also maintained that no discussion should be held with any of the Islamist parties, whether or not they officially abide by the principle of democracy, for '(...) the

Islamist movement is one (...) [and] its incarnation in different parties is just an adaptation to the conditions of formal multi-party politics and a judicious distribution of roles and tasks'.[10] Proponents of the eradicator line have radicalised since Spring 1993 when they were taken into the whirl of violence: most politicians, journalists and intellectuals incarnating this trend have, indeed, been the target of the Islamist armed groups. Intolerance, which they denounce about the Islamists, has, however, progressively become one of their characteristics.

Conciliators are represented by parties with a greater electoral import than that of the eradicators. They notably include the FLN and the FFS, but also the MDA, the MAJD, the PRA, the PT (Trotskists) and legal Islamist parties such as Hamas, the MNI and the Contemporary Muslim Jazaïr. Organizations such as the Algerian League for the Defence of Human Rights headed by Ali Yahia Abdennour and personalities such as Ahmed Taleb Ibrahimi or Abdelhamid Brahimi[11] are also among the supporters of a compromising line. Conciliators, who do not necessarily share the Islamists' political project, have argued that the authorities must reintegrate the outlawed FIS within the political process for three main reasons. Firstly, in order to put an end to a civil strife which, by its very nature, hampers any return to democratization. Secondly, in order to bring the FIS to compromise and, thirdly, to satisfy those who have seen in this party an answer to their social demands.[12] It is worth mentioning that, even though politicians representing this trend have also been murdered, their respective parties have continued to support a compromising line.[13]

The split between eradicators and conciliators observed within the civil society also exists within power circles, whether at the civilian or military level. Within the military establishment, much has been said about potential disagreements between high- and low-rank officers, but the split also exists among senior officers. This became patent in April 1995: eight Generals called for reopening negotiations (officially suspended in late October 1994) with the FIS.[14] But, let there be no misunderstanding: if conciliator officers favour a negotiated solution to the state of violence, they do not intend to give up power. They are merely inclined to accept a civilian *façade* to their exercise of power. Concretely, this means that, as mentioned by Rémy Leveau, the Army's conciliator strand would be ready to accept the Islamisation of public behaviour and of urban society only if, as a counterpart, the autonomy of the military apparatus is maintained.[15] The readiness of conciliators and eradicators within the Algerian military establishment to drop one and the other must not be underestimated. Nevertheless, until now, preserving the unity of the Army has been held as a top priority by all its members, thus leading to compromises. In addition, it should not be overlooked that, for the Army's conciliator trend, eradication has never been seen as an option to be ruled out: the weaker the Islamist armed groups, the thinner the FIS' negotiating manoeuvre margin.

Fake or real negotiations with the FIS?

Overtures towards the FIS were initiated during Autumn 1993 as part of the Algerian government's offer for a political dialogue with the opposition. The opening move came with the High State Council's public statement on November 23, 1993 in which it affirmed its willingness to open 'a dialogue without exclusion'. As an outlawed party, the FIS could not participate in the dialogue. But it was specified that FIS members who respected the law and certain engagements could.[16] The option of a 'dialogue without exclusion' was upheld by President Zeroual in his speech of February 1994[17] and repeated by various political leaders until September 1994.[18] Contacts with the FIS leadership were established in Winter 1993/94 and multiplied towards the end of Summer 1994. The Algerian authorities accompanied their dialogue propositions with 'appeasement measures'. In January 1994, some of the Islamist prisoners held in the Saharan camps were released. House arrest sanctions against FIS militants who had sat in local and regional councils were lifted. In February 1994, two high representatives of the FIS, Ali Djeddi and Abdelkhader Boukhamkham, were released.[19] Finally, on September 13, 1994 – a week prior to the last round of talks scheduled for September 20, 1994 – the Algerian authorities transferred Abassi Madani and Ali Benhadj from prison to house arrest.[20] While this move suggested that the negotiations were unfolding in a satisfactory way, the last meeting was, in fact, concluded by the breaking off of the negotiations with the FIS. Indeed, Zeroual argued on September 21, 1994 that nothing concrete had come out of the discussions with the FIS. The official decision to cut the negotiations was announced by the Algerian president in a press communiqué on October 29, 1994 and repeated in his commemoration speech of November 1, 1954. The simultaneous promotion to a new ranking grade of Major General Lamari – the front rank man of the eradicators – was intended to show that eradication was the major item on the Administration's agenda.[21]

    Why did the negotiations fail? In tackling this question, I argue that the negotiation strategy adopted by the Algerian government could in no way lead to an agreement with the FIS. Dialogue with the FIS, thus, looked more like a sham than a real attempt on the part of the Algerian authorities to seek a political solution to Algeria's crisis by striking a compromise with the FIS. The reasoning then goes on to ask why the Algerian government endeavoured to talk to the FIS if the strategy underlying the negotiations had been designed to fail.

The Algerian government's negotiation strategy and its flaws

The authorities' bargaining strategy was the following. FIS representatives would be allowed into the political dialogue about the transitional period and its aftermath on two types of conditions: conditions applying to all political parties and conditions that were specific to the FIS. Conditions required of all parties varied from one round of talks with the Administration to the other. Those recurring were: respecting the republican character of the state; the principles of pluralism and of political alternation; observing private and civil liberties and rejecting violence. In addition to these general requirements, the FIS was asked to call for an end to violence.

In August 1994, Abassi Madani agreed to respect the 'constitutional fundamentals' required to participate in the dialogue.[22] He, however, refused to call for a cease-fire and presented counter-conditions: release of the FIS leaders; possibility for the *majlis ash shura* to meet; lifting of the ban on the party and of the state of emergency; general amnesty; return of the Army to its barracks; formation of a neutral government to oversee the transition before new elections or a referendum on the 'establishment of an Algerian republican state based upon Islamic principles'.[23] On September 6, 1994, in anticipation of the round of talks scheduled for September 20, the imprisoned FIS leaders also asked to include chieftains of the FIS' armed wing in the dialogue.[24] In response to the transfer of the paramount FIS leaders from prison to house arrest, Rabah Kebir, head of the FIS executive body abroad, suggested that Madani was ready to call a cease-fire before all his conditions were met.[25] The negotiations were then brought to an end.

The authorities' strategy had two flaws. They asked the FIS to call for an end to armed rebellion. This demand, if satisfied, would have led to an additional one: that the FIS guarantee the enforcement of a cease-fire. This was, indeed, an implicit condition for the FIS to be accepted in the dialogue. For, if the FIS called for civil peace without effectively enforcing a cease-fire, it would have been accused of taking back with one hand what it had given with the other. Was the FIS in a position to agree to call for an end to guerrilla action? No. It did not have control over the GIA and calling for a cease-fire threatened to further divide its armed wing within which dissension had appeared. The GIA has always claimed its independence from the FIS' political leaders in jail or in exile. It has also consistently denounced their negotiations with the Algerian authorities. The GIA is made up of several regional armed groups organized around a national structure. However, it is also an umbrella movement gathering a multitude of factions which often operate at the level of the neighbourhood independently of each other and independently of the GIA's national structure. The GIA's very loose structure makes it a body very difficult to control. This became a real problem for the FIS when its leaders accepted the principle of negotiations with the Algerian regime, on the one hand, and when the violence perpetrated by the GIA turned against the civilian population, on the other. In order to check the GIA's drawing power, notably on the youth, the FIS made an effort to channel violence for its own political goals through the MIA and, later, through the AIS (Islamic Salvation Army, July 1994) which federates several armed groups recognizing the authority of the FIS. However, the FIS' attempts at controlling violence led to important transfers from the FIS and the MIA to the GIA: Abdezzerak Redjem (head of the national commission of the FIS' provisional executive bureau and founder of the MIA) joined the GIA in May 1994, as well as Mohamed Saïd who had headed the provisional executive bureau after Hachani's arrest. Saïd Makhloufi, author of call-up instructions on civil disobedience and second in command of the MIA, seems to have joined the GIA by August 1994.[26] These defections suggested that calling for a cease-fire would generate additional shifts to the GIA, undermining further the FIS' control over the armed rebellion. By calling for a cease-fire, the FIS would have taken the risk to negotiate a truce which it would have been unable to enforce and which would, thus, have preempted it from being accepted within the dialogue.

The second flaw in the government's strategy was that it offered no guarantee to the FIS that if, indeed, it managed to restore order, it would be allowed to fully reintegrate into politics. The issue of the re-legalisation of the FIS, on the basis of the respect of the political conditions to which it agreed in August 1994, was addressed by the government as something that would need to be considered only once the authority of the state had been restored. Why would the FIS have run the risk of dissociating itself from the radicals if, in the end, it had no guarantee to be reinstated into legality?

Possible motives for a dead-end-dialogue with the FIS

It is possible to interpret the decision to hold 'negotiations without exclusion' as a genuine attempt by the conciliators within the power apparatus to eventually find a political solution to the crisis triggered by the January 1992 coup d'état. Under Kafi there had been signs of a willingness to move towards conciliation. Kafi had taxed political parties and associations urging 'a radical rupture with fundamentalism' with being 'pseudo-supporters of the rupture'.[27]

As defence minister, Zeroual had led a vigorous anti-terrorist policy. However, as the appointed president of the Algerian Republic, he seemed to be on the conciliatory side of the political divide. But, throughout 1994 and 1995, President Zeroual was unable (and, perhaps, also unwilling) to impose a fully conciliatory line on his colleagues in the eradicator camp. As a result, dialogue with the FIS could not succeed.

The May 1994 reshuffle of the military hierarchy is worth mentioning as evidence of Zeroual's limited manoeuvre margin. Zeroual then appointed his loyal men to the command of the ground, air, *gendarmerie* and police forces as well as that of the military regions. He also took two conciliators as ministerial counsellors.[28] Like the dismissal of Interior Minister Salim Saadi on the occasion of the appointment of the new Sifi government (April 1994), this military reshuffle was intended to reassure FIS leaders that eradicators were being marginalised. This, indeed, was the case. However, this reshuffle had been made possible only by maintaining Major General Lamari as chief of staff and by bolstering his authority: Lamari was given the right to sign decrees in Zeroual's name just before the reshuffle.[29] The important role given to Major General Lamari, the eradicator *par excellence*, could only foster doubts among the Islamists as to Zeroual's ability to force a compromise onto the eradicators. At a conference held in London, a FIS representative raised this very question:

> At present, the FIS is asked to give guarantees that it would be able
> to control the armed groups in order to be allowed in the dialogue.
> (...) In the Army there are people who believe in eliminating
> everyone else. What are the guarantees that Zeroual can provide to
> control these elements?[30]

Because of the eradicators' edge and because of the principle of preserving the unity of the Army, Zeroual was unable to impose the solution of a compromise with the FIS on his peers. He probably was also unwilling to take the risk, one may think, lest he would finish like Boudiaf or Merbah.[31]

If dialogue with the FIS was doomed to failure but nevertheless engaged, one can suspect that it accrued some advantages that pleased both the eradicators and the conciliators in government. Dialogue with the FIS, indeed, served at least two causes. One was that dialogue allowed the Algerian government to buy time from the international community which, as a whole, has not been as ready as France to buttress the Algerian regime in its eradication strategy.[32] Satisfying international opinion was particularly important to Algiers because it was then negotiating a stabilisation programme with the IMF. Another was that failed negotiations with the FIS contributed to discredit the option of conciliation with the FIS. On the surface, it looked as though the Algerian authorities were 'the good guys' since they had initiated a political dialogue and that the FIS leaders were 'the bad guys' since they had refused to compromise. For the eradicators, failed negotiations with the FIS simply showed that there was no need to talk to the FIS since the latter itself admitted that it did not wholly control the armed groups. For the conciliators or some of them, the failed dialogue could always help to justify a policy of political integration of the Islamist movement, but through less charismatic and more accommodating Islamist leaders than those of the FIS.

The conclusion that the dialogue initiative of November 1993 – October 1994 was, in effect, a sham more than a real attempt at finding a political settlement with the FIS is confirmed by the failure of other talks which initially took place secretly after the official breaking off in October 1994. These talks between the incarcerated FIS leaders[33] and the Algerian presidency were held in June and July 1995. They came within the framework of Zeroual's plan to hold a presidential election (see below) and were thus seen as 'the talks of the last chance' to find a compromise with the FIS. In these talks, the scenario was more or less the same as that adopted a year earlier. The dismissal on July 2, 1995 of Interior Minister Abderrahmane Meziane-Cherif, who had proved as much of an eradicator as Salim Saadi – his predecessor in the Malek government – was to be a token of goodwill. Yet, in their negotiations, the authorities did not waive their idea to link any concession to the FIS to an unequivocal call for a cease-fire and, implicitly, to an enforcement of a cease-fire.[34]

From the Rome conference to the presidential election (November 1994 – November 1995)

The road to the Rome conference

Eradicator opposition parties along with conciliator ones showed distrust in the regime's dialogue initiative with the FIS. This was not, in fact, very startling. Parties representing the eradicator line have always manifested their refusal of the very principle of negotiations with the FIS by boycotting all rounds and denouncing the risk of a 'Sudanisation' of the Algerian political system.[35] As to the conciliator parties, they were for dialogue with the FIS. But, they were unwilling to back the regime's initiative because they were fully aware of its limits. So, they coolly welcomed Zeroual when he asked them to help the authorities in bringing Madani and Benhadj to denounce terrorism. The FFS warned of a potential 'secret pact' between the Army and the Islamists that would exclude the democratic camp.[36] Whether Ait Ahmed truly believed in this possibility or not, the break in the negotiations with the FIS in October 1994 allowed the conciliator opposition to bring the FIS under its own wing with the view to preempting such an alliance or simply to face the authorities in a united front.

Under the sponsorship of the Catholic community of Sant'Egidio in Rome, conciliator opposition parties met FIS representatives twice: on November 21–22, 1994 and on January 8–13, 1995. The second meeting was closed with the adoption of a common 'Platform for a political and pacific solution to the Algerian crisis'. It was signed by the FIS, the FLN, the FFS, the MDA, the PT, the MNI, the Contemporary Muslim Jazaïr, and the Algerian League for the Defence of Human Rights. We review the content of the Rome platform below.

The 'peace offer'

It is worth emphasising that most of the provisions of the Rome platform could also be found in the platform put forward by the National Dialogue Commission. This underlines that a certain consensus as to the way in which Algeria could be disentangled from the crisis existed. There were similarities between the two platforms: in respect of the declaration of November 1, 1954 which established Islam as an integral part of the personality of the Algerian people; in respect of the 1989 Constitution; the rejection of violence as a means of gaining or holding power; respect for human rights and civil liberties; the establishment of political pluralism and of political alternation of office.

The Rome platform, however, contained other significant provisions. Some emphasised Berber heritage and religious freedom. Others were about guarantees of democracy: separation of powers; respect of popular legitimacy and rejection of dictatorship. In addition, the Rome platform put forward a series of concrete measures to be taken by the government and the FIS before negotiations between the regime and the opposition about future free elections could be started. Measures concerning the Algerian authorities included: lifting the ban on the FIS; releasing its leadership; closing the detention camps; lifting the state of emergency; ending censorship, torture and reprisals on the population. The FIS' obligations were to condemn violence and call for an end to the killing of civilians and foreigners and to the destruction of public goods.[37] The advantage for the FIS of this opposition platform was that, provided it condemned the murder of civilians and took the necessary steps to enforce the cessation of the violence perpetrated by the AIS, it did not need to restore complete order to be accepted within the political game.

A word on the FIS' position about violence is necessary at this stage because of the confusion that surrounds the question. It is important to recall, first of all, that when the FIS was created in 1989 it subsumed various currents and included proponents of armed struggle who had been, for most, activists within Bouyali's Armed Islamic Movement (1982–87) or veterans of Afghanistan. Until the cancellation of the results of the December 1991 election and the outlawing of the FIS, partisans of the armed path had been marginalised within the party by those advocating a legalist way to reach power. When the FIS was banned and repression against Islamist militants organized, armed groups were formed and joined, not only by those who had always advocated armed rebellion, but also by militants threatened by repression.

At first, the political wing of the FIS, without claiming the terrorist attacks perpetrated by the armed groups, did not condemn them either, arguing that the first violence came from the state. Playing upon comparisons between the policies of the colonial state and of the current Algerian regime, it presented armed rebellion as a legitimate resistance against state oppression.[38] In March 1993, the armed groups' strategy shifted from merely attacking security forces to eliminating civil servants, intellectuals and journalists. FIS representatives argued that the killings were justified as a response to active or passive collaboration with the authorities:

> Who are these so-called intellectuals? Among them there are members of the National Consultative Council which has usurped the place of the people's elected representatives, persons who wrote murderous editorials, and those who, as psychiatrists, advised torturers on how to obtain confessions. The Algerian people has chosen as targets only those individuals upon whom the military-security system in Algeria relies.[39]

FIS representatives also underlined that none of these intellectuals 'had lifted a finger' to denounce state repression against the Islamists and that they had, therefore, chosen sides.[40]

As regards the killings of foreigners, which started in September 1993[41] and which have been claimed in their great majority by the GIA, the evolution of the position of the FIS is difficult to assess accurately because press reports did not systematically account for the declarations of FIS representatives. What can be said with a measure of certainty is that while maintaining that 'It [was] not the policy of the FIS to kill foreigners (...)',[42] FIS representatives did not clearly condemn the killings until February 1994, arguing that foreign regimes supporting the Algerian authorities had to expect a reaction.

It is, it seems, the GIA's intimidation campaign against the civilian population, clearly engaged since 1994 in order to establish Islamically ruled pockets,[43] that brought the FIS – then, in negotiations with the Algerian authorities – to condemn 'the attacks against all individuals – Algerians and foreigners, civilians and soldiers – who do not participate in the operations of the security forces conducted with the use of force'.[44] Since February 1994, this has been the official line of FIS representatives who make a distinction between 'terrorism' and the 'armed struggle'. The armed struggle is defined as targeting the security forces. Terrorism is understood as aimed at the persons not involved in the security forces' violent operations. During the Rome conference Anwar Haddam was clear on this point. He also declared that the FIS condemned terrorism but supported the armed struggle with the specification that: 'the armed struggle is not an end in itself, it is a means. If its goal can be reached through peaceful and civilian ways, we are for [them]'.[45] Kebir also made an important move in January 1995 when he condemned 'any act which aims at innocents whatever their tendencies or their religion and whoever the authors of such acts are'.[46] The formulation 'whoever the authors of such acts are' was significant since it implied that were the AIS to commit terrorist attacks, in the sense defined by the FIS, the latter would no longer justify such acts.

In concrete terms, despite the February 1994 declaration, the exiled FIS leadership has continued to adopt an ambiguous stance with regard to . In general, it has been readier to strongly condemn terrorist attacks against foreigners or against foreign countries[47] than attacks against Algerians in Algeria. For instance, although both Haddam and Kebir condemned the bomb attack in the Mostaganem cemetery which killed four children on November 1, 1994, they also accused the regime for the attack.[48] The car bomb attack against the police station of Algiers which killed 38 persons and wounded over 250 (January 30, 1995) was unequivocally condemned by Kebir. For his part, Haddam condemned the attack but recalled that the police station had been turned into 'a centre for torture'.[49] The continued equivocal attitude of the FIS' political wing towards violence largely stemmed from its attempt to remain credible in the eyes of its radicals.[50] The reason that brought the FIS so desperately to look for this credibility was that, without it, the FIS could not hope to be recognized as a necessary party to any negotiations with the Algerian authorities.

Reactions to the Rome conference

In general, the West reacted positively to the January 1995 Rome conference. We deal later with France's reaction to the Rome initiative in greater detail.[51] Suffice to say here that, globally, the 'peace offer' proposed by the Rome parties was apprehended abroad as a possible breakthrough in the Algerian deadlock. Therefore, many states brought their support to the Rome initiative.

By contrast, in Algeria, the Rome conference was denounced by the eradicators as well as by the Islamist armed groups. Fearing to be left out from a possible agreement, the GIA initially announced that it was ready to 'cease the war' under certain conditions (recognition by the authorities of the Rome platform; release of its chief Abdelhak Layada; dissolution of the communist parties and application of 'the law of God' against the Generals). However, as the AIS itself rejected the Rome platform, the GIA then withdrew its support and called for the establishment of the caliphate through armed combat. The attitude of the AIS, which denounced the Rome agreement on the ground that its signatories had showed 'unjust towards the mujahidins' by condemning violence as a means to reach power, could be understood as a dropping of the FIS. However, in retrospective, the AIS' continued allegiance to the FIS tends to suggest that its condemnation of the Rome platform was, first and foremost, a means to put pressure on the political wing of the FIS so as to prevent it from 'selling out'.[52]

As for the Algerian government, it simply condemned the Rome initiative and accused the Catholic community of Sant'Egidio of interference in Algeria's domestic affairs.[53] Although it recognized later that the Rome platform contained some good points, the government never recognized the 'Rome front', thus, aborting the entire project put forward by the Rome parties. Instead, the Algerian authorities went along with their project to hold an anticipated presidential election.

The Algerian presidential election (November 1995)

President Zeroual disclosed his plan for a free presidential election to be held before the end of 1995 on the very day he officially announced the failure of the negotiations with the FIS, that is, October 31, 1994. Through this anticipated presidential election, the Algerian authorities hoped to gain the legitimacy that neither the HSC nor the institutions having replaced it ever enjoyed. In order to ensure the success of the election, the Algerian authorities endeavoured to include the opposition in the preparation process. To that effect, they organized three rounds of talks with opposition parties on a bilateral basis from January to August 1995.

**Table 4:   Results of the Algerian presidential election,
                November 1995**

Candidates	Votes	Expressed Votes %	Registered Votes %
Lamine Zeroual	7,088,618	61.01	46.18
Mahfoud Nahnah	2,971,974	25.58	19.36
Saïd Sadi	1,115,796	9.60	7.29
Noureddine Boukrouh	443,144	3.81	2.89
Total	**11,619,532**	**100.0**	**75.72***

Registered Voters	15,351,475	

Note: * represents participation rate.
Source: Le Monde, 26–27 November 1995.

        Initially, the political parties which had signed the Rome platform in January 1995 rejected Zeroual's call for consultation. The Algerian government had condemned their initiative and had remained deaf to their proposals for a return to civil peace. As a result, the Rome parties argued that no discussion should be held with the authorities as long as the latter did not change their behaviour. As a front, the Rome parties also rejected the bilateral character of the talks proposed by the government. Instead, they proposed the organization of a national conference for the preparation of the election.[54] In April 1995, the FLN, the FFS and the MDA did, however, meet with President Zeroual on a bilateral basis. But this did not lead to any form of agreement. Zeroual maintained that the presidential election would go ahead without the FIS as long as the armed groups would not cease from strife. The signatories of the Rome platform stood by their opposition to the exclusion of the FIS from the political process.[55] They, subsequently, boycotted the last round of talks of August 12, 1995 where the date and the mode of organization of the presidential election were fixed.[56] Finally, affirming that the dice were loaded in favour of the regime, the Rome parties boycotted the presidential election and called on their sympathisers to abstain from voting.[57]
        In other political quarters, the prospect of the presidential election did produce some excitement: no less than 40 candidates – conciliators and eradicators – were ready to take their chances for the presidency.[58] Only four

managed to fulfil the electoral requirements. They were: outgoing President Lamine Zeroual; Mahfoud Nahnah (Hamas); Saïd Sadi (RCD) and Noureddine Boukrouh (PRA). The official results of the first round of the presidential election, as published by the Algerian Constitutional Council, gave an absolute majority (61%, see Table 4) to Zeroual. He was, therefore, elected (on the very first ballot) president of the Algerian Republic for five years.

Commentators in the international press generally underlined two marked features of the election. Firstly, the high participation rate (75.7%). Whereas doubts have been cast on the accuracy of the stated performances of the Algerian candidates, the participation rates were generally held to be close to the real figures.[59] Massive popular participation, in a context where the Islamist armed groups threatened those who would go to the polls with death, was interpreted as a clear popular demand for civil peace. Secondly, commentators argued that perhaps precisely because the results of the election were probably fake, they provided us with an indication of the Algerian administration's plans for the future. In that respect, Saïd Sadi's low score (7.3% of the registered votes) combined with the persistence of the electoral weight of Islamism, as represented by Hamas' score (19.4% of the registered votes) was interpreted as a victory for the conciliator camp in the political system. This generated hope the Zeroual would be able quickly to promote a conciliatory solution to Algeria's political crisis.[60] The assassination of one of Zeroual's allies, General Mohamed Boutighane, on the very day the new Algerian president was sworn in,[61] however, also suggested that the eradicators would not give Zeroual a free hand. And, indeed, during his term, Zeroual failed to go beyond the boundaries that the governmental eradicators set to his national reconciliation programme.

Notes

1. *MEI* (442), 22 January 1993.
2. *The Financial Times*, 23 June 1993 and *Algérie Actualité* (1447), 6–12 July 1993.
3. The National Dialogue Commission was created on 13 October 13, 1993. It was headed by five civilians and three Army Generals. *Le Monde*, 17–18 October 1993.
4. The convening of the Conference having been postponed to January 1994, the HSC's mandate was prolonged for a month. On the Conference, see *Le Monde*, 30–31 January 1994 and 1 February 1994.
5. H. Ait Ahmed in *Le Monde*, 27 January 1994.
6. A reproduction of the amended platform can be found in *Liberté*, 24 January 1993. Initial versions and amendments are outlined in *El Watan*, 24 January 1993. For details on the National Dialogue Conference, see *Liberté*, 24 January 1993; *Le Monde*, 25

and 27 January 1994.

7. Zeroual replaced Major General Khaled Nezzar who kept his function within the HSC (*MEI* (455), 23 July 1993). Zeroual was reconfirmed in his function as defence minister in the Malek government and he kept this portfolio after having been appointed president. The High Security Council, the same body that dismissed Chadli, chose Zeroual as president. It was then composed of Khaled Nezzar, Major General Mohamed Lamari (chief of staff), Salim Saadi (interior minister), Redha Malek and Mourad Benachenhou (economy minister). *MEED*, 38 (6), 11 February 1994.

8. E.g. the demonstration of 22 March 1994 where marchers – bolstered by Sadi's call for 'resistance' against the Islamist armed groups' attacks – threatened to organize themselves into self-defence groups (*Financial Times*, 25 March 1994), or the march of 29 June 1994 for 'a republican rupture', aimed at 'defeating fundamentalism and the regime that produced it' (see the Movement for the Republic's call published in *El Watan*, 27 June 1994. This Movement was created in December 1993 and is headed by Saïd Sadi). Counter-demonstrations were also organized by the 'conciliators' such as that of 8 May 1994 where demonstrators called for a 'national reconciliation' through a dialogue with the banned party (*Le Monde*, 10 May 1994).

9. Saïd Sadi (RCD) interviewed in *Le Monde*, 27 September 1994.

10. Hachemi Cherif (Ettahaddi) in *El Watan*, 15 June 1994.

11. Taleb Ibrahimi and Abdelhamid Brahimi (prime minister, 1984 to 1988) created in September 1991 a National Committee for the Support of Political Prisoners. They subsequently campaigned for the re-legalisation of the FIS and its full reintegration in Algeria's political realm. See, for instance, Brahimi's attempt at relaunching the Rome initiative in London (meeting of the signatories of the Rome platform without, however, the FLN and the FFS at the Royal Institute for International Affairs on 22 March 1995 (*The Guardian*, 23 March 1995)). See also A. Brahimi (1994).

12. See the FLN's declaration in *Algérie Actualité* (1422), 13–19 January 1992; the interviews or declarations of Hocine Ait Ahmed (FFS), in *Algérie Actualité* (1422), 13–19 January 1992; *Le Monde* 27 January 1994 and 23 February 1995; Mahfoud Nahnah (Hamas) in *Algérie Actualité* (1434), 6–12 April 1993 and in *El Watan*, 21 April 1994; Nourredine Boukrouh (PRA) in *Algérie Actualité* (1408), 8–14 October 1992.

13. It was reported that, from January 1992 to December 1994, 200 political militants were killed, out of whom 50 were affiliated to the FLN (*Le Monde*, 24 December 1994). Islamist moderates of Hamas and the Guidance and Reform Association have also been the target of murderous attacks (*Le Monde*, 20 September 1994 and 14 October 1994). Whether they were all killed by the GIAs remains in question.

14. *Le Monde*, 8 April 1995.

15. R. Leveau (1995), p. 114.

16. *Algérie Actualité* (1468), 30 November–6 December 1993 and *Le Monde*, 11 December 1993.

17. *Le Monde*, 9 February 1994.

18. Notably by Prime Minister Sifi, see *Le Monde*, 23 July 1994.

19. *Le Monde*, 21 January 1994 and 24 February 1994.

20. *Le Monde*, 15 September 1994. Madani and Benhadj had been sentenced to twelve years of jail on July 15, 1992 following their arrest in June 1992.

21. *Le Monde*, 24 September 1994 and 1 and 2 November 1994.

22. Confirmed by the Algerian foreign minister in *Le Monde*, 1 October 1994.

23. Content of the letters of 25 August and 27 August to Zeroual in *Le Monde*, 8 September 1994. It can be noted that between December 1993 and August 1994, one of the FIS' conditions for participation in the dialogue was dropped: the abrogation of the laws passed since January 1992 which implied among others the abrogation of the annulment of the results of the parliamentary election. For details on the conditions put forward by the FIS, see Kebir's statement in *Le Monde*, 19–20 December 1993 and the content of Ali Benhadj's letter to Zeroual in *Le Monde*, 23 August 1994.

24. *Le Monde*, 11–12 September 1994.

25. *Le Monde*, 18–19 September 1994.

26. For details on the Islamist armed groups, see S. Labat (1995a), pp. 227-43 and L. Martinez (1995), pp. 39-70.

27. Quoted in *Algérie Actualité* (1428), 23 February–1 March 1993 and (1431), 16–22 March 1993.

28. *Le Monde*, 7 May 1994 and 19 May 1994 and *MEED* (38)(20), 20 May 1994.

29. *Le Monde*, 23 March 1994. As head of the ground forces, General Lamari was involved in the June 1991 crisis which was perceived by the FIS as a betrayal on the part of the regime. After having been dismissed from this function under Boudiaf (although kept as counsellor to the defence minister), Lamari was appointed commander of the anti-terrorist squads in September 1992. He was, thereafter, promoted to the rank of Major General and appointed chief of staff in July 1993.

30. Paper read in Rabah Kebir's place at the conference on 'The Future of the Maghrib' organized by the Geopolitics and International Boundaries Research Centre, 6–7 October 1994, Royal Institute of International Affairs, London.

31. Kasdi Merbah was assassinated on the very day Malek was appointed head of the government. Merbah had proposed to Zeroual, then defence minister, to play the role of a mediator between the FIS and the authorities before they enter into direct contact with the banned party. The murder has been blamed on (and claimed by) the GIAs but, as in the case of Boudiaf, the accusing fingers are all pointing at the eradicator army officers. See P. Dévoluy and M. Duteil (1994), pp. 304-10.

32. See section 'Multilateral support' below.

33. Between February and June 1995, the whereabouts of the two paramount FIS leaders were unknown. In early June 1995, the Algerian minister for the interior confirmed that Madani and Benhadj had been re-imprisoned (*Le Monde*, 4–5 June 1995).

34. On the secret talks, see *Le Monde*, 4 and 13 July 1995.

35. Saïd Sadi in *Liberté*, 19 April 1994.

36. *Le Monde*, 24 and 25 August 1994.

37. The Rome platform is reproduced in *Le Monde Diplomatique*, March 1995.

38. See M. Al-Ahnaf et. al. (1991), pp. 129-41. The parallel with the debate in France during the War of Independence over the issue of the legitimacy of the FLN's terrorist

acts is obvious. At the time, some French intellectuals such as Jean-Paul Sartre or Francis Jeanson argued that the 'the violence of popular resistance' could not be equated with the 'violence of aggression' and that counter-violence to the initial violence produced by the colonial political system was legitimate.

39. Anwar Haddam (October 1993) quoted in A. Zerouali (1994), p. 164.

40. Abdelbaki Sahraoui on *Transit*, 'Algérie: comment sortir de l'impasse?', Arte, November 1993.

41. From September 1993 to (early) September 1995, 93 foreigners (out of whom 32 were French) were killed in Algeria (*Le Monde*, 5 September 1995).

42. Rabah Kebir (October 1993) quoted in A. Zerouali (1994), p. 164.

43. Intimidation measures include the killing of unveiled school girls (the first having occurred on 28 February 1994), threats to public transport owners to incite them to impose sexual segregation, or to traders to bring them to reduce their prices (*Le Monde*, 22 February 1994). In August 1994, the GIA also threatened schools and universities of forced closure on the ground that current education programmes deviate the youth from the path of God (*Le Monde*, 7–8 August 1994). By October 1994, over 600 schools had been partially destroyed and some 50 academics murdered (*Le Monde*, 8 October 1994).

44. A. Haddam in *Le Matin*, 3 February 1994. See also R. Kebir in *Le Monde*, 23 November 1994.

45. A. Haddam in *Le Monde*, 12 January 1995.

46. In *Le Monde*, 7 January 1995.

47. See, e.g., the FIS' condemnations of the killing of a French monk and a French nun (8 May 1994; *Le Monde*, 17 May 1994); of the hijack of a French Airbus (24 December 1994; *Le Monde*, 5 January 1995); of the killing of four White Fathers (27 December 1994; *Le Monde*, 7 January 1995) and of the wave of terrorist attacks in France during Summer and Autumn 1995 (*Le Monde*, 15 September 1995).

48. In *Le Monde*, 4 November 1994.

49. In *Le Monde*, 4 February 1995.

50. See on this point, S. Labat (1995b), pp. 87-110.

51. See Part 2, Chapter 2 for discussion of this matter.

52. On the positions of the Islamist armed groups, see *Le Monde*, 17 and 24 January 1995.

53. *Le Monde*, 20 January 1995.

54. *Le Monde*, 26–27 March 1995.

55. *Le Monde*, 11 and 19 April 1995.

56. *Le Monde*, 18 August 1995.

57. *Le Monde*, 30 August 1995, 3 and 20 October 1995. Note that the Contemporary Muslim Jazaïr did present a candidate to the election. This was understood by the Rome parties as a unilateral withdrawal of this party from the Rome agreement (*Le Monde*, 26 September 1995).

58. *Le Monde*, 3 October 1995.

59. By contrast, Algerian opposition parties and, in particular, the Rome parties have either contested the validity of the participation rate or denounced pressure by the

Algerian authorities to force people to go to the polls (see, for example, *Le Monde*, 19–20 November 1995).

60. See *Le Monde*, 19–20 November 1995.
61. *Le Monde*, 30 November 1995.

Chapter 2

The Meanders of French Policy Under the Right: 'Cohabitation' (April 1993 – May 1995)

France's Algeria policy under the premiership of Balladur is quite difficult to decipher. Two main factors made France's policy look like a muddle. First, France's words did not always match the deeds. Quite cleverly, this gave France's Algeria policy an air of constancy that it did not have in reality. Foreign Minister Juppé always argued that the status quo was no longer tenable in Algeria. As a consequence, it seemed that ever since its coming to Matignon the Balladur government had supported conciliation in Algeria. In fact, the Balladur government did so only after September 1994. But, as of then, there was no governmental unity as to whether the Algerian government should open negotiations with the FIS and as to whether the French government should encourage such negotiations. This brings us to the second point. During the last nine months of the Balladur government's term, France voiced different opinions about what its Algeria policy should be. Quarrels between the Elysée and Matignon and, most importantly, between the Quai d'Orsay and Place Beauvau (the Interior Ministry) gave a dim picture of France's approach to the Algerian conflict.

To make sense of France's Algeria policy under Balladur, the following analysis focuses on the two periods characterising his shifting policy: buttressing governmental eradicators in Algeria until September 1994 and showing greater firmness against them afterwards. Eradicators were first praised as reasonable politicians seeking a political solution and then accused of blocking a political solution in Algeria.

Buttressing the eradicators (April 1993 – September 1994)

It is no longer a matter open to debate whether the Balladur government supported the Algerian regime or not. Its economic and military assistance to Algiers as well as its intelligence and police co-operation and its role as Algeria's defender on the international scene made it obvious that France was siding with the Algerian authorities, at least until Autumn 1994. The question, therefore, is whether by buttressing the Algerian regime the French government was supporting its conciliator or eradicator strands. It is the contention of the following account that, despite a conciliatory discourse, the Balladur government supported the eradicators. In order to underline the ambiguities and contradictions that point to this conclusion, the official discourse must be expounded first. After showing that France backed the eradicators, I shall focus on the policy measures which were implemented.

The official discourse

The Right in the opposition

Prior to their victory in the French parliamentary election at the end of March 1993, some politicians in the opposition had clearly indicated that a right-wing government would support an anti-Islamist policy. After the first round of the Algerian 1991 parliamentary election, some public statements reinforced the Algerian Army's viewpoint that, were the FIS left to relish the fruits of its victory, Algeria might be ostracised at one stage or the other. Such signals came from Charles Pasqua (chairman of the RPR at the Senate) and François Léotard (MP, UDF). Both claimed that a right-wing government would revise its co-operation policy with Algeria if the FIS came to power. Léotard specified that a FIS regime would not be backed if it did not respect the principles of democracy, pluralism and equality between the sexes. What the FIS would have done seemed, however, clear to him since he compared it to Hitler's National Socialist party.[1] Reference to Nazism has been the principal credo of the Algerian government and of the eradicators to legitimise the coup. By reformulating their claim, Léotard was, thus, indicating that he agreed with the thesis justifying the coup. For his part, Alain Juppé (general secretary of the RPR) had followed a cautious line, avoiding saying anything that could have been interpreted as some form of 'aiding and abetting'. His hope that the FIS' electoral success would provoke a 'salutary shock' to Algeria's 'democratic opposition'[2] was, nevertheless, indicative of his concerns regarding a FIS take-over. Generally, in right-wing circles, the cancellation of the election was thus welcomed with relief. Valéry Giscard d'Estaing (UDF) was the only centre-right personality who openly criticised the popularised view that the coup served 'to save democracy'.[3]

After the coup in Algeria, until it came to office in April 1993, the Right criticised the socialists for being unsupportive of the Algerian regime.

During his visit to Algiers in early December 1992, Juppé deplored the socialists' low profile on the Algerian file. He then promised that inasmuch as 'France, has an interest in Algeria being a stable and modern state', the Right, if elected, would intensify relations with Algeria.[4]

Balladur in Matignon

'Cohabitation' between the socialist president and the right-wing government did not cause many problems throughout Balladur's premiership, at least in so far as Algeria was concerned. President Mitterrand made very few statements on France's policy towards Algeria, perhaps because of his sickness or simply because he preferred to remain cautious. With the exception of his proposal of February 1995,[5] he took no initiative. Mitterrand reasserted that 'one cannot be a democrat here, and contest to a people over there the right to decide for itself of its destiny'.[6] But he was in line with Matignon when arguing that France must support those forces promoting the establishment of a 'modern, tolerant and hospitable state',[7] for France could not wish '(...) the victory of whoever would make the mores [and] the institutions regress back to medieval conceptions'.[8] In general, his declarations expressed a certain disillusionment and detachment:

> We wish (...) the Algerian people to put its business in order by itself in the best way, the best known [and] the most evident manner, and become able to pronounce itself through the ballot box: naturally, we are far from it.[9]

In the absence of presidential initiative, France's Algeria policy was primarily designed by the government. Because Prime Minister Balladur did not have a specific policy line to impose on his ministers,[10] French policy was chiefly conceived by the Quai d'Orsay and Place Beauvau. This did not generate a dual discourse before Autumn 1994. Until Autumn 1994, the Balladur government was led to determine the orientation of its Algeria policy by the basic idea that, while a FIS take-over would be 'a catastrophe', it was not 'ineluctable'. Upon this consideration, it was decided, in the words of the foreign minister, Juppé, that everything had to be done in order to avoid the risk of a FIS take-over.[11] With this objective in mind, the Balladur government threw its weight behind the Algerian regime and, in particular, behind the eradicator strand. While backing the Algerian regime, the Balladur government suggested in August 1993 a crisis-overcoming scenario based upon Juppé's argument that 'the status quo is not tenable'. As Foreign Minister Juppé invariably explained, moving beyond the status quo meant the implementation of two courses of action by the Algerian government: (1) rescheduling Algeria's foreign debt and completing the transition to a market economy; and (2) with a view to returning to the electoral process, opening a political dialogue with opposition forces provided they respected the principle of democracy and disavowed violence.[12] Although the French government advocated this change to the status quo as a means to solve Algeria's crisis, it always maintained that it would not intervene in Algeria's domestic affairs and that, consequently, it would not seek to impose this solution on the Algerian authorities.

The policy line of transcending the status quo was defined in a particular context. It was spelt out ten days before the dismissal of the Algerian prime minister. Throughout Abdesselam's premiership, the rumour had always been that he might depart soon, so unpopular at home and abroad was his economic policy and his political statements so at odds with the HSC's decision to open a political dialogue.[13] Whether or not the French government knew exactly when Abdesselam would be dismissed and by whom he would be replaced, the definition of its policy line at that particular moment can be understood as a signal of what it wished the new Algerian government to do. It was an encouragement to find an agreement with the IMF and to continue discussions with the opposition (then excluding the FIS) within the framework of the National Dialogue Commission scheduled for Autumn 1993. The appointment of Redha Malek as prime minister was welcomed in Paris precisely because he satisfied these expectations.[14]

Even though France's policy was defined in this specific context, it remained its constant message throughout Balladur's mandate. France's discourse was so static because things evolved slowly in Algeria. As seen previously, the political dialogue process unfolded over two years before reaching a virtual deadlock. In the economic realm, the Algerian government was driven into a corner by a debt service forecast to exceed export revenues in 1994 and by creditors' warnings that new funds would be channelled only once an agreement with the IMF was reached. As a result, the Malek government agreed to the principle of a debt rescheduling in December 1993.[15] However, between the time Malek was appointed prime minister and the time he actually sent a letter of intent to the IMF (April 1994), about a year elapsed.[16] Another reason for such an unchanging discourse was that it was so general and steeped in ambiguities that it applied to both the pre- and post-September 1994 periods. Constancy did not necessarily mean consistency.

Putting the discourse to the test: ambiguities and contradictions

The Balladur government's discourse on its Algeria policy was characterised by several ambiguities and contradictions, of which two are underlined below. They concern the issue of the integration of the FIS within the political process in Algeria and that of economic aid.

On the inclusion of the FIS in the political process

Despite its apparent simplicity, Juppé's discourse on the political dialogue contained a major ambiguity: it was never crystal clear on the issue of the inclusion of the FIS within the dialogue. In the following analysis, I attempt to demonstrate that the Quai d'Orsay – as much as Place Beauvau – did not support the inclusion of the FIS within the political process at least until September 1994, that is until the negotiations between the Algerian authorities and the FIS were about to break down.

It is noticeable that Foreign Minister Juppé apparently always refused to answer reporters' questions whether he included the FIS in his vision of the dialogue that had to be opened by the Algerian government. His response was to repeat the necessity of a confabulation and to say that if 'Islamic forces' were ready to play by the democratic game, they should be included in the process. He then hastened to add that it was not up to him to designate which such forces were, for this would have come down to interfering with Algeria's domestic affairs.[17] This argument allowed the French government to avoid falling out with the eradicators and conciliators of the Algerian regime. Perhaps more importantly, it also left open the possibility for the Balladur government to change its course of policy without having to change its discourse.

There are, however, several elements that allow us to affirm that Juppé, along with Pasqua, did not wish the integration of the FIS in the political dialogue and, more generally, in Algeria's political landscape. These are to be found in their speeches which emphasised the French government's opposition to a FIS takeover as well as in their claim that there was no such thing as an 'Islamist moderate'. The Balladur government's soft attitude *vis-à-vis* the Algerian authorities' negotiation strategy with the banned party also gives added weight to the argument that, while calling for a conciliation, the French government opposed a compromise with the FIS. Finally, the way in which crackdown operations against FIS militants and sympathisers were conducted in France suggests that the French government made no difference between the Islamist militants who advocate violence and those who do not. This undermined its public claim that a dialogue could be opened with Islamic forces rejecting violence. These four elements shedding light on the Balladur government's actual position concerning the inclusion of the FIS in the political process are reviewed in turn.

The Balladur government constantly made it plain from June 1993 to September 1994 that it was opposed to a FIS take-over. On several occasions,[18] Foreign Minister Juppé argued that the coming to power of the FIS would be a 'catastrophe'. But he never specified whether he was thinking of a take-over through violent means (with the revolutionary radicalism that it would have involved) or of a coming to power through a negotiated settlement. Logic would want that, since Juppé had consistently appealed for a political dialogue, he had in mind a take-over through violence. But, in explaining why France would side with Algeria in its struggle against 'fundamentalism', Juppé underlined France's opposition to the *political project* of Islamism:

> (...) we will not be lenient with political movements whose values, objectives, [and] aims are exactly in contradiction with everything we believe in. (...) I believe that we have nothing to gain in showing indulgence vis-à-vis *political Islamism* (...).[19]

By April 1994, Juppé no longer referred so bluntly to the 'clash of civilisation'. In substance his argument remained, nevertheless, the same. From then on, he stated that, if the FIS came to power in Algiers, the confidence of similar Islamist movements throughout the Muslim world would be boosted and anti-Western regimes might thus mushroom.[20] Inasmuch as the French government was opposed to the political project of the FIS and highlighted its anti-Western outlook, whether the FIS seized power by force or came to office through a negotiated settlement, did not make much difference: in either case it would have had consequences which the French government wanted to avoid (these are spelt out in chapter three). This implied, in turn, that the French government saw no prospect in a middle-of-the-road solution involving the FIS in the government. Consequently, there was no point in trying to associate it to the political dialogue on the transitional period.

The French authorities also gave an informal support to the Algerian eradicators when arguing that there were no moderates within the Islamist movement as a whole. Although the interior minister is remembered as the one who said that '(...) the idea that a moderate Islamist regime might emerge is nothing but rubbish',[21] he was never alone in saying so. In a May 1994 press conference in Washington, the foreign minister argued that:

> (...) there may be here and there this or that representative of the FIS with whom one can talk, but globally and in its very essence, it is an

extremist, terrorist, anti-European [and] anti-Western movement (...).[22]

Moreover, it was argued in the Quai d'Orsay that the legal Islamist parties such as Hamas or the MNI were mere 'screens' of the FIS.[23] This contention implicitly meant that their formal allegiance to the principle of democracy was not to be taken seriously.

The third way in which the Balladur government showed its hostility to an inclusion of the FIS within the political process appeared through its attitude *vis-à-vis* the strategy of the Algerian authorities in their negotiations with the FIS. As pinpointed earlier, this strategy could not lead to the success of a political perspective because the FIS was not given sufficient guarantees that it would be allowed back into politics. In front of this vitiated negotiation strategy, the French government congratulated the Algerian authorities for their political openness while blaming the deadlock on the FIS and other political parties. Thus, Juppé declared in June 1994:

> The willingness to talk exists on the side of the political establishment. The whole problem is to know with whom [hold negotiations]. It is evidently very difficult to negotiate with someone who puts a kalachnikov on the table pointing the barrel directly to your chest! But I note that, while maintaining a security policy that is often rough, the government proves more and more open to discussion.[24]

And he concluded in October 1994:

> (...) unfortunately, [the dialogue] has not progressed since the political parties such as the FFS or the RCD as well as the FIS still refuse to get involved in the dialogue.[25]

Juppé feigned to ignore the fact that, in the same way as the Algerian authorities had imposed conditions for participation in the dialogue, opposition parties had their own prerequisites. By putting forward their own terms, opposition parties showed that they were not against the principle of a dialogue but that they were willing to participate in negotiations only if they were meaningful to them. As regards the FIS, it had signalled in December 1993 that it was not shut to the idea of a dialogue since it had submitted its conditions which were, moreover, open to bargaining. When Abassi Madani wrote in his letters of August 1994 that he accepted the Algerian government's conditions to participate in the dialogue, his flexibility was greeted with skepticism by the Quai d'Orsay: it was argued that 'we shall wait and see how things evolve' and that Madani's renouncing violence had to be 'verified and confirmed'.[26] Surely, Juppé was right in expressing some skepticism towards the FIS' new position. However, his contrasting attitude with regard to the Algerian regime's dialogue initiative revealed an over-enthusiasm that would not have existed if the French government believed that a political perspective in Algeria required the reintegration of the FIS within the political game.

The last indicator of the Balladur government's reluctance to see a compromise being reached with the FIS is revealed by the way in which some of the round-up operations against FIS militants and sympathisers were conducted in France. Under the Balladur government four large-scale crackdown operations took place.[27] Only one point need be made now about the French government's contradictory stance. The French authorities themselves recognised that the first two crack-downs – that of November 1993 on the Algerian Brotherhood in France (FAF) and that of August 1994 which led to the expulsion of twenty suspected FIS militants and sympathisers to Burkina Faso – did not concern persons involved in terrorist activities or in the armed struggle in Algeria. Indeed, the house arrest sanctions against some of the defendants rounded-up in November 1993 were lifted because 'the reproached militancy [did] not relate in any way to what is usually called terrorism'.[28] Regarding the second crack-down, the board for civil liberties and legal affairs attached to the Interior Ministry openly declared that the majority of persons who had been expelled were expelled for grievances of an ideological nature while only a small minority was suspected of giving logistical support to the FIS networks in France.[29] The official recognition that most persons had been indicted or expelled because of their opinions and political militancy wholly discredited the Balladur government's public stance on political dialogue in Algeria. For, indeed, whether or not the Islamists left 'the kalachnikov in the cloakroom', they had to be fought because, for the French government, what was really at stake was not violence but ideology.[30]

By emphasising its opposition to the FIS on ideological grounds, by arguing that there were no FIS moderates, and by backing the Algerian authorities' negotiation strategy, the Balladur government showed, simply through its discourse, that debating with the FIS was not considered as an option of the political solution it was, otherwise, calling for. For all that, did France's discourse contribute to obstructing the chances of a conciliation, as suggested by Hugh Roberts?[31] The argument, however logical at first sight, requires careful examination. The causal relationship between France's discourse and the unfolding of the events in Algeria is, indeed, difficult to establish with certainty. By upholding compromise rather than eradication, the socialists probably managed to boost the conciliators' confidence. However, this did not translate into a breakthrough in favour conciliation. There is, thus, no *a priori* reason for the French Right to have succeeded where its predecessors had failed. It is doubtful that the Balladur government actually hampered a conciliatory solution through its mere discourse. What may be most important is perhaps less what France says than what it does. In supporting the Algerian regime the Balladur government essentially acted in three ways. It refused to tie its economic aid to political conditions as demanded by some Algerian conciliator parties and segments of the French public opinion. It impeded the progress in France of Islamist networks. And it encouraged the international community to follow in its wake. In doing so, more than through its declarations, the Balladur government contributed to the obstruction of a conciliatory solution, since it allowed the Algerian eradicators to buy time. Yet, it is unclear whether the conciliators in government would have appreciated any other policy on the part of France. For, in attempting to compel the Algerian regime to negotiate a true conciliation, France would have forced it to negotiate in a position of weakness and this was (and remains) the governmental conciliators' worst scenario.

On economic assistance and non-intervention

Under the Balladur government, as under the socialists, bilateral economic assistance to Algeria was justified as a support to the people as opposed to the regime.[32] Less than a contradiction, this justification came close to a lie. Financial support did certainly benefit (some of) the people, at least by ensuring a level of imports. But it, first and foremost, helped the regime in three main ways. Firstly, as a general rule, financial aid symbolises no ostracism and, as such, provides political backing. Secondly, this financial aid allowed the Algerian government to allot funds – otherwise devoted to finance current imports, investments, or debt repayments – to repression expenditures: buying anti-guerrilla hardware, regularly and well paying the security forces in a context of collapsing living-standards, etc. Finally, considering the corruption system surrounding import contracts,[33] France's tied commercial loans indirectly allowed the military establishment to distribute this income and buy its clientele. The irony in the whole issue about conditioning economic aid lay in the fact that when it came to bring Algiers to sign an economic agreement with the IMF, the Balladur government no longer saw economic aid as a help to the Algerian people but very much as a pressure tool that could be used against the Algerian regime. Because the Balladur government lied in the first place about the end use of economic aid to Algeria, it was caught in its own trap. In effect, it ended up saying that a worse economic plight in the short-term was worth its price for the sake of economic liberalism but not for the sake of human rights and democratic records.

It is also noteworthy that, by warning that France's 1994 financial aid would be made dependent upon Algeria rescheduling its debt and implementing economic structural reforms, the Balladur government contradicted its initial claim not to force, but merely incite, a departure from the status quo. French willingness to directly intervene in the Algerian economic sphere partly ensued from the belief that acting on the economic lever meant serving Algeria's long-run political stability.

Bilateral and multilateral support: the means

If the Balladur government's official discourse did not bluntly refer to its backing of Algeria's eradicators, the concrete support that it lent to Algiers left few doubts as to what kind of solution it contemplated for Algeria's political crisis. Under Balladur, France's support to the Algerian regime took two forms: bilateral and multilateral. On the international scene, France advocated the adoption of policies similar to its own, notably, economic support and constraining the activities of exiled Islamist militants. But France did much more than that bilaterally.

Bilateral support

The Balladur government expressed its bilateral support to the Algerian authorities through traditional diplomatic means such as speeches and visits, through economic and military aid as well as by clamping down on exiled Islamists.

Until Autumn 1994, bilateral visits were relatively numerous and of a relatively high standing. In addition to regular meetings, they included the visits to Paris of Foreign Minister Malek in June 1993[34] and of Prime Minister Sifi in June 1994.[35] Foreign Minister Juppé and Defence Minister Léotard went to Algiers in early August 1994 in order to pay homage to the three *gendarmes* and the two agents of the French Ministries for Foreign and Economic Affairs killed in Algeria.[36] If this visit had an impromptu character, it had been preceded in July by the trip of a senatorial delegation headed by the president of the foreign affairs and defence commission of the French Senate, Xavier de Villepin, who also happened to be the director of Juppé's *cabinet*.[37] On the whole, during these visits, the Algerian emissaries explained the merits of their government's policy in the political realm. At first, they also attempted to convince the Balladur government to 'reprofile' Algeria's bilateral debt. As Paris refused, they pleaded for its support in international institutions. Most Algerian visits to France preceded an international forum pending which Algeria's financial problems or its political situation were to be discussed (e.g. Paris Club meeting, EU summit in Corfu, G7 summit in Naples). The French authorities assured their Algerian counterparts of their support and understanding: President Mitterrand transmitted messages of support to President Zeroual and the Balladur government positively responded to Algeria's lobbying.

Regarding financial flows, after disbursing the amount of the Sapin financial accord without economic conditionality, the Balladur government threatened to cut off the tap if Algeria did not reach an agreement with the IMF. It also warned that its efforts at mobilising international finance would be dependent on Algeria's signature.[38] Once Algeria signed its letter of intent in April 1994, Paris kept its promises. In May 1994, a three-year financial protocol (FF200 million) for the purchase of pharmaceuticals was signed.[39] It was followed in July by a new credit package worth FF6 billion ($1.1 billion). The first portion of the package was a FF1 025 million protocol of mixed loans from the Treasury and from the export credit agency which were allotted for balance-of-payments relief and project financing. The second component concerned a FF2 billion guaranteed trade credit available for three years and meant for the purchase of medicines, vehicles, and consumer goods. The third component was a FF1 billion credit to finance the purchase of French cereals. The remaining sum of about FF2 billion comprised private project financing guaranteed by the Coface.[40]

If this financial package was quite traditional in relation to both its amount and structure, Balladur's support to the Algerian regime was best illustrated by military assistance, police and intelligence co-operation. Both are reviewed in turn. French military co-operation with Algiers has never been very intense. Just as with many of France's ex-colonies, military assistance has mainly concerned the supply of equipment to, and the training of, forces responsible to the Algerian Interior Ministry: the *gendarmerie*, the police, the Republican and Presidential Guards.[41] In November 1994, it was revealed that France was supplying Algeria with helicopters and night-vision material used in anti-guerrilla warfare.[42] Although not particularly important quantitatively, these military supplies were highly symbolic of France's agreement to assist the eradication strategy. In December 1994, in order to avoid criticisms, the Balladur government announced that France had cancelled its anti-guerrilla material supplies. Helicopters were still being sold but, it was argued, in a 'civil version'.[43] Their final use, however, raises few doubts.

A tight police and intelligence co-operation was also established with Algiers (as well as with Rabat and Tunis) with a view to restraining the activities of exiled Islamists in France. As the various operations of the French police have shown, the Islamist networks implanted in France have not merely been concerned with political militancy. Some have also brought a concrete support to the armed struggle in Algeria by raising funds for the purchase of arms, explosives and military equipment, by operating arms traffics, by providing Algerian guerrillas with forged papers and by organizing the infiltration / exfiltration of *'mujahidins'*. It makes no doubt that these activities must be repressed not only because they imply outlawed practices but also because they are at the basis of violent action. This being said, it must be emphasised that the Balladur government's crack-downs on exiled Islamist militants and sympathisers served other objectives than just curbing down their support to the armed groups in Algeria. One of these objectives was internally motivated: round-ups, expulsions and the banning of Islamist literature[44] was one way for the French government to hamper the influence of Islamist networks within the Muslim community in France. I shall return to this domestic issue in chapter three. Another objective of the clamp-downs fits within the category of punishment and dissuasion: the first two large-scale round-ups of FIS militants and sympathisers were a response not to what such militants and sympathisers did in France but to what the armed groups did in Algeria: namely, the kidnapping in October 1993 of three consulate agents (who were eventually freed with a message warning the foreign community in Algeria to leave the country within a delay a month) and the killing, claimed by the GIA, of five French nationals (three *gendarmes* and two civil servants) on August 3, 1994.[45] Lastly, cracking down on exiled Islamists was one of the means by which the Balladur government backed Algiers politically. As I indicated earlier, crackdowns not only targeted people involved in concretely supporting the Algerian armed groups but also persons involved in lawful political militancy. Measures taken against these persons amounted to the muzzling of a political opposition movement. In this regard, it is noticeable that prior to the first large-scale round-ups, Juppé, who had pledged to 'help Algeria in struggling against extremism and fundamentalism' during Malek's visit,[46] justified such assistance less on anti-terrorist grounds than on ideological ones. Juppé certainly invoked the possibility of 'violent activities undertaken from our soil against this friendly country'.[47] But the main argument lay in the following claim:

> Since the month of April [1993], the new government has made it
> clear that it would not be lenient with religious extremism, simply

because this extremism is a vehicle for values and ideas that are not ours and are against us (...).[48]

It was only after the first round up of November 1993 that Juppé argued that France refused to become 'a rear-haven for terrorism' and that it should not 'show leniency towards those who have made terrorism and violence the essential feature of their programme'.[49] Pasqua, however, underlined that, despite a preoccupation for terrorism, the principal concern was subversion:

> (...) the Republic cannot accept that, under the cover of cultural associations, operations of a subversive type be put in place with the view to destabilizing a neighbouring country or even to conduct later subversive or terrorist actions in France.[50]

Multilateral support

The Balladur government played the role of Algeria's defender on the international scene, undertaking an active advertising campaign in favour of the regime and selling its product to major international actors. There are two main reasons explaining the 'diplomatic campaign' launched by the Balladur government. First of all, considering Algeria as France's backyard, the international community waited for Paris to show the way – even though, in practice, it has not systematically followed France's recommendations. As to the French government, it felt directly concerned by the Algerian crisis not only because of the multiple ties that link France to Algeria but also because of the foreseen consequences of this crisis for France itself. But it did not want 'to go it alone', as underlined by the French minister for foreign affairs, primarily because the international community's financial help was necessary. In addition, the Algerian crisis raised fundamental issues about political change in the Arab Muslim world. Beyond its specificities, the Algerian crisis was thus for France a co-operation test between the North towards an increasingly turbulent South.

In its endeavour to drum up international support for the Algerian regime, the Balladur government sought financial support from international and regional organizations as well as from individual states. It also advocated the adoption of its own restrictive behaviour towards exiled FIS militants. If, in the process, it managed to get clear political statements backing the Algerian regime, this was of course welcomed. The Balladur government reached its aim concerning financial support but found it harder to obtain a consensus about the merits of its own policy with regard to exiled Islamists and the exclusion of the FIS from dialogue. These three issues are reviewed below by focussing on the European Union, individual European countries and the USA.

On the whole, the EU's political statements on the Algerian political crisis were very close to those of France. At the fourth meeting of the EU–Algeria Co-operation Council (February 7, 1994), for instance, the Union appealed for a 'frank and open national political dialogue with those who renounce terrorism and support the return to democracy and the reconciliation of all Algerians'.[51] During its visit to Algeria on May 30, 1994, the European troika also showed satisfaction with the Algerian authorities' conduct of the dialogue. The Greek foreign minister noted 'the sincerity of the Algerian government in its will to face political and economic challenges' and the Belgian foreign minister, Willy Claes, declared:

> We will return to Brussels with the conviction that the Algerian government is determined to boost national political dialogue with all the nation's active forces.[52]

The EU formally showed a greater interest than the Balladur government in voicing concern about human rights violations in Algeria.[53] However, no sanctions were taken to protest against Algeria's poor human rights record. The second instalment of an ECU 400 million loan was suspended in March 1992.[54] But this freeze was not prompted by the European foreign ministers' willingness to tie economic aid to Algeria's 'respect of human rights, tolerance and political pluralism', as they had suggested after the 1992 coup.[55] It was linked to Algeria's refusal to go through IMF structural reforms.

Despite this apparent consensus between France and the EU, it would be wrong to conclude that all member states were in complete agreement with Paris. As time went by and as the option of supporting the Algerian regime did not produce greater stability, some expressed skepticism as to the eradication strategy. Schematically, states closer to the scenes of violence gradually became more independent from France's own position. Thus, the other three Southern European states – Italy, Portugal and Spain – became more inclined to publicly support the view that the Algerian regime was 'illegitimate' and that a distinction had to be made between Islamist moderates rejecting violence – with whom dialogue had to be established – and Islamist radicals supporting terrorism.[56] By contrast, Northern European countries such as Britain or Germany, in general, supported the Balladur government's approach. This was less because of their total agreement with it than because of their concern to avoid a public quarrel with France over an issue which remains, after all, peripheral to their interests. But, if Britain and Germany did not attempt to block France's initiatives, neither did they issue political statements supporting the Algerian regime.[57] Their case must, therefore, be differentiated from

Belgium whose foreign minister argued in June 1994 that it was 'naive' to advocate a dialogue with Islamist moderates who, if they existed at all, were to be found 'on the benches of the national conference' (i.e. the legal Islamist parties) and not elsewhere.[58]

Within the Clinton Administration the debate between supporters and detractors of a political recognition of Islamism has been settled to the advantage of the former. Since the Algerian government's initiative to open 'a dialogue without exclusion', the USA has constantly advocated the solution of a power sharing between the regime and what Clinton has called 'dissident groups not involved in terrorism',[59] a category within which the FIS is included. The position of the American Administration on Algeria derives both from a general viewpoint on political Islam and an assessment of the Algerian situation itself. Contending that 'Today, Islamic political groups vary in their attitudes and ideas about how to address the needs of their societies',[60] the Near Eastern affairs department has firmly argued that existing extremist and anti-Western groups do not represent the Islamist movement as a whole and are not an inherent expression of the Islamists' political agenda. The department has concluded that political accommodation should be sought with Islamist movements which agree to work within existing political structures to effect change. Regarding the Algerian situation, the American Administration (which did not at first condemn the coup) made the simple assessment that: 'Events of the past two years demonstrate that Algeria's leaders cannot ease the crisis through over reliance on repressive policies'. Washington subsequently urged Algeria to broaden political participation and encompass 'all political forces in the country, including Islamist leaders who reject terrorism'.[61]

Apparently, the solution advocated by the Clinton Administration was similar to that of Balladur's since the latter never explicitly argued that the FIS should be excluded from talks. But the difference between the two Administrations concerned this very issue. It showed in a difference in discourse over two main points. Firstly, whereas the French purposely blurred the frontier between the GIA and the FIS, the Americans maintained that the FIS was not responsible for the acts committed by the GIA[62] which has been on their terrorist movements list since May 1995. Secondly, the Americans adopted a harsher discourse towards the Algerian regime than France did. The acting assistant secretary for Near Eastern affairs, Mark Parris, emphasised that the violation of human rights in Algeria was not unilateral.[63] Likewise, whereas the Balladur government congratulated Algiers despite its vitiated political dialogue strategy, Parris expressed doubts about the Algerian government's sincerity in attempting to open a political dialogue. On March 22, 1994, he declared before the House Foreign Affairs subcommittee on Africa:

I regret to say (...) that despite the stated intention of all Algerian governments in the past two years to undertake genuine political and economic reforms, we have seen little progress toward these goals. The failure of the government-sponsored 'national conference' in January, which all major opposition parties boycotted, demonstrated that the regime has yet to convince opposition elements of its willingness to permit them a meaningful role in governing during a transition period.[64]

The Balladur government's position on the political dialogue, from which it wished to exclude the FIS, and on the political support that had to be provided to the Algerian regime's eradication policy was, thus, progressively contested by some European countries and the USA. France's efforts at bringing the international community to constrain the activities of exiled Islamists did not meet with particular success either, at least until the beginning of 1995.

In early August 1994, the USA, Britain and Germany which had hosted official FIS members (as well as high figures of other Islamist movements) were asked to restrict the political activities of FIS representatives by limiting their freedom of movement and by imposing on them the 'duty of reserve'. Indeed, the deputy spokeswoman for the French Foreign Ministry then indicated that contacts with a number of states had been taken so that they would do everything to prevent exiled FIS representatives from 'engaging in political activities and renewing declarations that were inadmissible.'[65]

In response, the USA, Britain and Germany defended a policy of abstaining from crackdowns on Islamists as long as there was no evidence of a shift from political activism to terrorist or illegal activities. The White House indicated that no special measures against Islamists could be undertaken as long as expatriates were on American soil lawfully and as long as there was no proof of their financial support to listed terrorist groups.[66] Germany, where Rabah Kebir and the sons of Madani obtained asylum status, declared that Kebir's role was essentially political and that, in these circumstances, he could not be subjected to special surveillance. He was fined in August 1994 for disregarding his obligation not to express publicly his views on the Algerian political crisis, but the German authorities did not expel him.[67] Britain maintained that, as a matter of principle, political refugees benefit from freedom of expression. In supporting their viewpoints, the three states concerned were in line with the EU. In October 1993, a communiqué of the European Parliament had urged member states not to allow FIS representatives living in their borders to condone acts of violence.[68] But the Council had specified that 'political action must not be confused with terrorism'.[69]

Nevertheless, the failure of these states to meet France's demand led Interior Minister Pasqua to depict as an 'unfriendly act' the fact that they sheltered 'persons who not only did not disavow attacks but underwrote them'.[70] Much of the anger in Paris stemmed from the use of the freedom-of-expression argument in relation to Algerian Islamists when such freedom may be restricted for opposition movements to regimes with which these states enjoy good relations. If Paris could in theory understand why Britain, for instance, was harsher with Saudi political opponents or Germany with Kurd opponents than with FIS militants, in practice, it viewed their behaviour as an unwillingness to collaborate with France. Britain, in particular, was the target of French criticisms because the fax through which the GIA claimed the assassination of the first two French citizens killed in Algeria in September 1993 was sent from London. Criticisms towards Britain did not only emanate from the French political establishment but also from the media which, throughout Summer and Autumn 1994, denounced Britain as being too 'soft on Islamists'. French reporters pointed at several 'elements of proof' of Britain's 'laxity': the Home Office's unwillingness to ban the Wembley and Sheffield meetings respectively organized by *Hizb el Tahrir* and the Islamic Mission of the United Kingdom on August 7 and August 28, 1994; the granting of asylum rights to Rashid Ghannoushi (leader of the Tunisian *al-Nahda*) and to FIS militants such as Mohamed Dnidi (ex-director of the FIS' newspaper); and the Royal Institute for International Affairs' hosting of meetings where FIS representatives were present in June, September and October 1994. In practice, however, Britain did co-operate with France: the French police was allowed to interrogate Dnidi in England[71] and the Home Office refused to grant a visa to Anwar Haddam who was invited to a conference at the Royal Institute for International Affairs in September 1994.[72]

By early 1995, a series of factors led the European countries to become more responsive to the Balladur government's requests for greater collaboration. One of the main reasons that drew European countries closer to France was the development in their borders of Islamist networks connected to Algeria. By the end of 1994, several reports, for instance, in Switzerland and Germany indicated that supplies of arms and of various materials to the Algerian armed groups were organized from their territory.[73] Throughout Spring 1995, various police operations in Belgium (the Zaoui trial),[74] Germany,[75] Italy[76] and Switzerland[77] led to the dismantlement of arms trafficking networks. Pressure from Arab regimes confronted to Islamist opposition movements is also one of the factors that led European countries to increase surveillance over the political activities of exiled Islamists. As an example of Algeria's pressure on European countries, one can note General

Lamari's visit to Switzerland on November 8, 1994 where he asked for the extradition of about ten political opponents suspected of belonging to the Islamist movement.[78] Lastly, the terrorist attacks undertaken by Algerian armed groups against France (hijack of an *Air France* plane in December 1994 and wave of bomb attacks in France during Summer and Autumn 1995, see below) did generate some solidarity throughout Europe. Immediately after the hijack of the Airbus, the British interior minister promised his support to Pasqua in combating 'Islamic terrorism'.[79] Although the German secret services continued to maintain that Kebir's role was limited to political militancy, they now began to monitor his movements and phone conversations as well as those of Madani's sons.[80]

To conclude on this point, it may be argued that France's efforts to bring the international community to curb the activities of exiled FIS militants had mixed results. On the one hand, it is true that, with time, other European states came closer to France's position on the necessity of restricting the political militancy of exiled FIS representatives. On the other hand, these states reached that conclusion less through a full community of viewpoint with France than under the pressure of the growth within their borders of Islamist networks involved in the support of terrorism. The only area where France's multilateral diplomacy in favour of the Algerian regime produced immediate and tangible results was the financial one.

While refusing 'bilateral debt reprofiling', France declared itself ready to lobby in favour of Algeria in order to obtain flexible and advantageous conditions from the IMF and the Paris Club as well as fresh financial loans from regional institutions and individual states once Algeria had rescheduled. Parallelling Algeria's financial diplomacy,[81] France first exhorted Japan and Italy to accept the principle of a rescheduling of Algeria's debt and then attempted to gather international support for fresh credits to be channelled to Algeria. In Spring 1994, Juppé multiplied his foreign visits, calling for economic support notably in Tokyo (April 1), Luxembourg (April 18) and Washington (May 12).[82] Emphasising the risks of destabilization throughout the Mediterranean, Juppé criticised the view that the West should prepare itself for, instead of opposing, a FIS take-over and argued that the economic card was one way of ensuring stability in Algeria.

All the governments contacted by Algeria and France agreed to support Algeria's case within international organizations on condition that Algeria signed a stabilization programme with the IMF and filed its rescheduling dossier with the Paris Club. However, with the exception of France and Belgium,[83] none immediately granted new bilateral financing. This may be because they preferred to wait for their bilateral rescheduling agreement to be finalised after the signature of the framework agreement with the Paris Club. This may also be because, while recognising the necessity for rescheduling and international financial support, they were unwilling to give too much moral and material support to the Algerian regime. Such was the USA's stand.[84]

After its rescheduling operation, Algeria, thus, received new financing mostly from international institutions. In addition to the IMF standby loan, Algeria benefited from a series of loans from the IBRD. In July 1994, the blocked $175 million second tranche of the World Bank's structural adjustment loan was released, triggering the disbursement of the remaining $150 million instalment of a programme approved in 1991 and co-financed by the Import-Export Bank of Japan. The IBRD also planned the granting of new loans for the development of the agrarian and housing sectors.[85] In May 1994, the EU agreed to release the frozen second tranche (ECU150 million, $180 million) of the 1991 balance-of-payments loan.[86] In Summer 1994, it also paid into a locked account of the Algerian Central Bank an ECU70 million ($84million) structural adjustment grant to finance work in the housing sector.[87] Lastly, in December 1994, the EU signed with Algeria a new credit of ECU 200 million ($240 million) for balance-of-payments relief. Its first instalment of ECU100 million was granted in May 1995.[88]

Greater firmness towards the eradicators (September 1994 – May 1995)

During the last nine months of the Balladur government, France's Algeria policy was most confusing. A dual discourse appeared within the government. Whereas Foreign Minister Juppé (as well as Defence Minister Léotard) made an overture towards the conciliators, Interior Minister Pasqua maintained the previous policy line of support for the eradicators. Yet, Pasqua also engaged in a secretive diplomacy, initiating contacts with the FIS. This contradicted both France's official policy and Pasqua's apparent alignment with the eradicators. A rift also occurred between the Elysée and Matignon over the issue of organizing an EU conference on Algeria in order to unlock the crisis. It was, nevertheless, short-lived. Juppé soon recognised that Mitterrand's February 1995 proposal was not completely unsound. These quarrels and contradictory attitudes stemmed in part from the French electoral context. However, it would be a mistake to believe that the prospect of the French presidential election of April – May 1995 had a significant impact on policy-making. The main consequence of the battle for the presidency was to allow governmental disunity to appear to the public eye. The Juppé / Pasqua split and its consequences regarding the coherence of French policy are expounded below. Then, the causes and the limits of Juppé's shifting vision will be analysed.

The Juppé / Pasqua split

It has been argued that the Juppé / Pasqua split was discernible as early as August 1994 and that it came out in open light after the hijack of the *Air France* Airbus by a GIA commando in December 1994.[89] Because Juppé did not change his views from one day to the other, choosing a date is necessarily somewhat arbitrary. Nevertheless, September 1994 may represent the best compromise. Juppé had, indeed, fully developed his new stance before the hijack occurred. Hence, the hijack cannot have played the role of a 'catalyst' in the adjusting of his policy. The crisis of confidence that crystallised during this event between the Quai d'Orsay and the Algerian authorities merely reinforced Juppé in his newly formed views. Regarding the other side of the time-scale, the starting-point of Juppé's personal doubts as to the merits of supporting the eradicators may well have arisen in August 1994. However, he did not share them publicly before his speech to the Senate on September 15, 1994. There he warned that political dialogue between the Algerian government and the Islamists may not succeed because on both sides some wished to torpedo it.[90] Intra-governmental disagreements occurred notably between Place Beauvau and the Quai d'Orsay in August 1994. This explains why many observers chose this date as the starting-point of Juppé's changed perceptions. It is not, however, absolutely certain because Juppé did not publicly indicate a policy change prior to mid-September 1994. Consequently, there is a risk of interpreting the quarrel between Juppé and Pasqua as stemming from disagreements of substance over France's Algeria policy whereas it might have derived from mere disagreements of form. The tension might also have been the sole result of intra-governmental competition. For instance, Pasqua's tough call on 'allied countries' to clamp down on exiled Islamists irritated the diplomatic corps. But, as was mentioned earlier, the Quai d'Orsay issued a communiqué confirming that steps to that effect had been taken. Disagreement was, thus, less driven by a fundamental difference in viewpoints than by Pasqua's large interpretation of the powers allocated to him through his interior portfolio and by his undiplomatic manners. Similarly, the war logic into which Pasqua entered after the AIS and the GIA had issued threats to protest against the internment of twenty-six Islamists in Folembray might have been perceived by the Quai d'Orsay as over-dramatic[91] and dangerous for the security of French nationals in Algeria. But Juppé had also always maintained that France would not let Islamist networks operate in France. In the midst of this confusion ensuing from bureaucratic politics, it is thus safer to choose the date of the official text clearly instituting the difference in viewpoint as the starting-point of the Juppé / Pasqua split.

Overtures towards the conciliators: the Juppé line

Between September and December 1994, Juppé changed his views by feeling his way along as events unfolded in Algeria. Because of this gradual process of change, his speeches on Algeria and on France's policy incorporated both old and new elements. On the one hand, Juppé reiterated that France would not be lenient with terrorism on its own soil; that it would struggle against ideologies that combat what France represents; that it would continue to promote political dialogue in Algeria and that it would pursue its policy of financial help as long as the Algerian authorities maintained their economic liberalization policy.[92] On the other hand, Juppé adopted a more conciliatory attitude towards the FIS and a harsher one towards the eradicators, thereby moving towards a more balanced policy stance.

Juppé's perceptions on the FIS partially evolved. By early September 1994, he recognised that the Islamist movement was divided[93] – a point that the French authorities had hitherto been unwilling to publicly uphold. Juppé still expressed a certain scepticism regarding Madani's written acceptance of the authorities' conditions to participate in the discussion table. He also refused to pronounce the expression 'Islamist moderate'.[94] Yet, he tried to play down Pasqua's declaration (and his own) according to which there is not such a thing as an Islamist moderate. He argued that the interior minister's statement aimed solely at the terrorist movements with which no dialogue was to be considered.[95] Claiming that the solution to Algeria's crisis was to be found in 'the reconciliation of the different trends of the Algerian society',[96] Juppé seemed convinced as from early September 1994 that the most representative Islamist party would have to be integrated within the political process. If he did not exclude the principle of a coalition government,[97] he nevertheless consistently maintained that the arms would have to be laid down first and that strong guarantees from the FIS that it would respect the principle of democracy, and notably political alternation, were needed.[98] This was essential to prevent any dominance or 'hijack' of the government by the FIS once it was accepted within its fold.

If Juppé's perceptions of the FIS partially evolved, a change also occurred *vis-à-vis* the Algerian government. Between September and December 1994, Juppé became more critical of the eradicators. In his speech

to the Senate, five days before the last round of talks (September 20) between
the Algerian regime and opposition parties, Juppé depicted as kith and kin die-
hards in the Algerian government and the Islamist armed groups, and notably
the GIA. He suspected both of doing their best to block a political perspective
in Algeria. On the very day the first Rome conference was held (November 21,
1994), he further declared that 'our party in Algeria is the party of
democracy'[99] and specified in early December that this was addressed to all
'hawks' whether on the side of the Algerian authorities or of the 'extremist
opposition'.[100] This new firmness towards the eradicator trend was also
reflected in the defence minister's discourse. In September, Léotard claimed
that 'the best solution for Algeria would have been to accept the poll of
December 1991'.[101] This U-turn provoked the summoning of Kessedjian, the
Ambassador to Algiers, by the Sifi government. More skilful in the art of
diplomacy, Juppé made a clever declaration which, while apparently intended
for the Islamists, also concerned the Algerian authorities:

> (...) when one wants to participate in a democratic process, the rules
> of democracy must be respected. The basic rule of democracy is
> alternation, that is, when one wins elections, it is fine; but when one
> loses, one goes. (...) A certain constitutional framework, the respect
> of the fundamental rights of the human person (...) must be
> accepted. If there are some Islamic forces ready to play by the game
> (...) they must be allowed into this [political] process.[102]

Rather than criticising past decisions, which would have amounted to
questioning the soundness of France's policy, Juppé focussed on the near
future. In particular, he issued warnings about the planned Algerian
presidential election. While arguing that the FIS had to recognise democracy
to participate in it, he was addressing the Algerian government when he stated
that the election should represent a '*true* democratic consultation' and that it
could not occur in 'such a climate that its legitimacy could be contested'.[103]

The hijack of the *Air France* Airbus by a GIA commando did not
generate a return to a one-way tough stand on the 'religious fanatics of the
FIS'. Rather, it drove Juppé to be even more explicit in his criticism of the
eradicators. He now designated them as those who 'satisfy themselves with
repression and an all-security line'.[104] While consistent with his new more
balanced position, this qualification expressed his degree of irritation towards
the Algerian authorities. Their attitude during the tragic event and, notably,
their misinformation as to their intentions on how to manage the crisis had
antagonised Juppé who feared both the execution of hostages by the hijackers
and an intervention by the Algerian special forces which could have turned into

a blood bath. He felt that the Algerian government was unjustly playing with the hostages' lives by refusing to accept the commando's demand to let the plane take off. The Algerian attitude seemed only intended to demonstrate the government held the situation under control – a fact that Juppé obviously doubted.[105]

The fact that, from September 1994, Juppé was no longer opposed, as a matter of principle, to an integration of the FIS within the political process is reflected in the French government's attitude towards the second Rome conference. The Quai d'Orsay brought its support to the Rome initiative only through hints: on January 16, 1995, the spokesman for the Ministry for Foreign Affairs called on all the political forces in Algeria to engage in a dialogue.[106] But Léotard was clearer in saying that the Rome initiative was 'rich in hope to get Algeria out of the bloody face-to-face that tears it' and that the Rome platform represented 'a groundwork from which Algeria ha[d] to initiate the process towards the return to a democratic order'.[107] There was, indeed, nothing more explicit than this statement to indicate to the Algerian authorities that France now tilted towards conciliation. Let us note that the change in France's discourse was reflected in the EU's statements. On September 23, 1994, the EU asserted that all parties had to be included in the political process in order to reach political conciliation and the return to stability.[108] In January 1995, the European Commissioner for relations with the Mediterranean countries openly said that the moderate wing of the FIS should be allowed to share power.[109] For its part, the European Parliament recognised the Rome platform as a working basis.[110]

After the second Rome conference and the problems surrounding the organization of the presidential election in Algeria, the Balladur government issued few statements on its policy. Juppé maintained that France supported dialogue between the conflicting parties and that 'all initiatives allowing dialogue dynamics to engage ha[d] to be taken into consideration'.[111] But his statements became noticeably less harsh when aimed towards eradicators.

Maintaining support for the eradicators: the Pasqua line

Whereas the Ministries for Foreign Affairs and Defence partly revised their positions on France's policy towards Algeria, the Ministry for the Interior maintained the previous course, grounded in the view that even though the Algerian regime was not 'a model of democratic government', 'the choice [was] between the capacity of the (...) regime to control the situation or the coming to power of the fundamentalists'.[112] The Pasqua / Juppé split became patent over two main issues: the recognition of the existence of Islamist moderates and the Rome initiative. While Juppé had realised that the Islamist movement was divided and had played down the 'no Islamist moderate' line, Pasqua reiterated in October 1994 that:

> (...) there are some moderate Muslims, but, in this case, they are not Islamists (...). Is anyone capable of telling me, in relation to the Islamist movement, where the FIS stops, where the AIS and the GIA begin, knowing that, anyway, in Islamist circles, double language is considered an integral part of politics, that the right hand should not be knowing what the left hand does?[113]

In contrast with Juppé and Léotard, Pasqua did not regard the Rome conference as a positive step in the resolution process of Algeria's crisis. He stood, in fact, with the Algerian eradicators, questioning the popular representativeness of the opposition parties having subscribed to the platform, questioning 'angelism' – the attitude consisting in believing that 'FIS people would become democrats' and arguing that:

> To believe for two minutes that these people will abandon the idea of an Islamic Republic appears to me unreal. What is at stake is the return to the application of the shari'a (...) that is [to] the Muslim society of the seventh century'.[114]

Although in his official statements Pasqua made it clear that, to him, Islamists were all backward fanatics prone to terrorism, he initiated behind-the-scenes contacts with the FIS through his special mission man, Jean-Claude Marchiani. Press reports indicated a meeting with Kebir in April 1994 where a French mediation between the FIS and the Algerian government would have been proposed as well as talks with the two paramount FIS leaders and a meeting with AIS representatives in October 1994.[115] There were also rumours of contacts initiated by the French government with Khartoum to incite the Sudanese regime to work towards a *rapprochement* between the FIS and the Algerian regime. Whereas the occurrence of contacts with Hassan al-Turabi were officially denied,[116] Marchiani's manoeuvres were not.

The rationale behind Pasqua's secretive diplomacy is difficult to establish. Meetings with the FIS contradicted France's official policy of not being in touch with the banned party. They were initiated by the person in government who was apparently the least inclined to arrangements with the FIS. In trying to find an explanation, it may be suggested that these contacts came within the framework of Pasqua's security policy. In November 1993, following the kidnapping of three consulate agents in Algeria, Pasqua had already approached a founding-member of the FIS (the expatriated imam of the *Khaled-ibn-Walid* mosque, Abdelbaki Sahraoui) in order to get his help for the release of the French hostages.[117] Meetings with the FIS can also be seen as part of an attempted mediation to bring the outlawed party to a give-and-take policy. Asserting that negotiations are out of the question and conducting secret talks on the side is standard practice in conflict settlements. The discrepancy between Pasqua's discourse and his acts is consequently not that baffling. What is most troubling is that, if these contacts are to be seen as a mediation attempt, this raises questions about Pasqua's apparent alignment with the eradicators. Unfortunately, as long as it remains unknown whether we are dealing with mere confabulations or with hard bargaining – in which case the very terms of Marchiani's negotiations are important – it will be impossible to ascertain whether these contacts invalidate the thesis according to which Pasqua sided with the eradicators all the way.

A muddle

To add to the confusion created by intra-governmental disunity and Pasqua's parallel diplomacy, a dispute occurred between the Elysée and Matignon. It arose on February 3, 1995 when Mitterrand launched the idea of organizing a conference on Algeria within the framework of the EU with the aim of enhancing the chances of a national reconciliation on the basis of the Rome platform.[118] The government which had not been informed of Mitterrand's idea protested. Juppé reacted by saying that there was no plan to take any new initiative on the Algerian issue.[119] The Quai d'Orsay deplored Mitterrand's lack of subtlety. Calling so bluntly for the organization of a dialogue upon the basis of a platform that the Algerian government had rejected could only be met by a refusal in Algiers. All the more since the conference would be organized by a foreign forum. In the eyes of the Ministry for Foreign Affairs, the proposal was not only useless but could also prove counter-productive because of the nationalist sensitivity of the Algerians.[120] Actually, the Algerian regime reacted strongly to the proposal. It denounced it as an intervention in Algeria's internal affairs and recalled the Algerian Ambassador from Paris. The newly appointed French Ambassador, Michel Lévêque, was also summoned to receive the Algerian government's protestations.[121]

Despite the Quai d'Orsay's initial disapproval, by the end of February, Juppé was apparently no longer opposed to the principle of an EU mediation. Indeed, he argued that if France had no right to tell the Algerian authorities what they should do and with whom they should talk, other powers could, precisely because they were not France and had not the same past with Algeria.[122]

Parallel diplomacy, reversals of discourse and dissension within the state apparatus generated perplexity among observers. Discord between the Elysée and Matignon was to be expected in those days of 'cohabitation'. Intragovernmental disunity and, even more so, its being allowed on the public space, produced puzzlement. As minister for the interior, Pasqua was in charge of immigration, security and religious affairs. He was at the crossroads of problems raised by the Algerian crisis and, thus, naturally led to make statements relating to Algeria. However, he meddled with Juppé's business when making statements that did not relate to the domestic consequences of the Algerian conflict. It was all the more shocking as Pasqua, whose statements did not comply with official policy, was never called to order by the prime minister. This phenomenon stemmed, in part, from the electoral context in France which burst the principle of governmental unity. The great peculiarity of France's presidential election of April – May 1995 was that two candidates belonging to the same party ran for the presidency: Prime Minister Edouard Balladur and MP Jacques Chirac. This double RPR candidacy had the effect of splintering loyalties within the government: whereas some, as Pasqua or Léotard, supported Balladur, others, as Juppé, backed Chirac. Instead of maintaining governmental unity, Balladur gave his two lieutenants a free run to express their views. Whereas Léotard's statements stayed in line with the position of the Quai d'Orsay, Pasqua's did not.

Causes and limits of Juppé's shift towards conciliation

Causes

Juppé's and Léotard's shift towards accepting the principle of a political dialogue encompassing the FIS primarily flowed from their analyses of the Algerian situation and from France's growing international isolation. As demonstrated below, electoral calculations did not play a significant role (if any) in the shift.towards conciliation. For, very few criticisms had been voiced in the civil society against the government's support to the Algerian regime. Three main factors explain why Juppé and Léotard gradually came to favour conciliation. First, their progressive awareness that eradication had failed in its objectives and that it did not constitute a viable long-run strategy. Second, their view that the FIS was bound to negotiate with the regime since it could not overthrow it.[123] Third, their sense that in opposing conciliation France was increasingly alone and that this may later prove a hindrance in its relations with

Algeria. These explanatory factors are reviewed below before turning to the issue of electoral calculations.

The Foreign and Defence Ministries' shift in favour of conciliation in Algeria thus started with the assessment that eradication had not produced the expected results. Despite the Algerian authorities' constant assurances that terrorist groups would be neutralised soon, the guerrilla war has continued unabated. As from 1994, the duel between the Army and the armed groups also changed in nature. As indicated by a confidential report, dated March 23, 1995 and drafted by the French Defence Ministry, both state and terrorist violence now aimed at the civilians:

> Throughout 1994, one has progressively passed, from one side or the other, from a war logic (...) to a terror logic aimed at isolating the adversary from the population, at weakening it and at causing it to splinter. Ever since then, on both sides, the target of the acts of violence is the population and the method, terror: massive repression on villagers by official troops, or collective assassination of bus passengers by the Islamists, what difference does it make? The counter-guerrilla strategy used by the armed forces is quite a simple technique of terrorisation of the population (...). In the same way, the violence dynamics created by the GIA prevails more and more over selective violence.[124]

The equally despicable behaviour of the Army and the armed groups probably contributed to Juppé's and Léotard's tougher stance on the eradicators. But this new stand derived principally from the view that state repression had added fuel rather than water to the flames. If this was to continue, there was a risk of turning a fratricidal war into an all-out civil war or, as the Defence Ministry's report indicated, a risk of 'Somalisation'. While the security advantages of eradication were thus undermined, it was also realised that, even if the armed groups were eliminated, there would be a political and social survival of the Islamist current. Some Islamist parties were still allowed to function in the Algerian political system. FIS cadres were still alive, even though imprisoned. There also was a functioning Islamist associational fabric. Accordingly, it was illusory to believe that, by neutralising the armed groups, the problem of the political force of Islamism would be solved.

The view that the FIS would have to negotiate its share of power, since it was not in a position to overthrow the regime, was also important. It implied that the FIS would have to work from within the political system to effect change and that a *modus vivendi* would have to be struck with the authorities.

Revolutionary fury would thus be avoided. Coupled with Juppé's more sceptical view on eradication and with the risk of the Algerian crisis bogging down, this argued in favour of a compromise.

Lastly, as the USA and some European countries voiced their support for a negotiated solution to the Algerian conflict, France felt more and more isolated. At the same time, since it was recognised that a lasting solution to Algeria's protracted conflict might require a compromise with the FIS, stubbornly backing the eradicators could only prove detrimental to France's future relations with Algeria; it could eventually cause a new government in Algiers to broaden its horizons somewhat away from the ex-colonial power towards those states that had shown more understanding during the crisis. As dealt with in Part Three, the Algerian government – whatever its ideological outlook – could not wholly question the relationship with France. It could, however, question some of its aspects to the benefit of other countries, undermining, thereby, France's multi-dimensional influence in Algeria.

The change in Juppé's discourse derived from these considerations rather than from electoral calculations. In general, the view expressed, notably in the press, that the French presidential election had played a role in the formulation of France's Algeria policy related not to the shift in Juppé's stance but to the policy of support to Algiers. It was suggested that the French government had backed the Algerian regime in order to avoid political change in Algeria prior to the French election. The risk of an immigration flood which threatened to boost the constituency of the extreme right would have been the prime motive behind France's categorical refusal to see the FIS associated to a political perspective. This argument became difficult to uphold with the September 1994 change in discourse which preceded the French election by eight months. The French government probably preferred the status quo to be maintained until the presidential election in order to avoid a panic effect in France. Yet, the prospect of the election did not hamper a change in policy stance and, in that respect, did not have an inhibiting role in policy-making.

If the prospect of the French presidential election did not play an inhibiting role in policy-making, did it, by contrast, trigger Juppé's change? In other words, is Juppé's shift towards conciliation in Algeria to be explained, at least in part, by pressure coming from French civil society? The answer is quite certainly negative. Neither political parties, public opinion, the media nor the intellectuals voiced strong criticisms about France's support to Algiers before August 1994. It was the reprisal threats issued by the AIS and the GIA in August and the Airbus hijack in December that provoked a general recognition that, by backing the Algerian regime so strongly, France had created enemies among people who might become its interlocutors in the future. Because this recognition was almost concomitant with the change in Juppe's discourse, it is unlikely that the criticisms to which it gave rise were at the root of his policy change.

French political parties in the opposition were surprisingly silent over the Balladur government's policy. Parliamentary questions to ministers were essentially about the domestic dimension of the Algerian conflict: security of French citizens in Algeria and the FIS' influence on the Muslim community in France. Reservations were expressed only when the Algerian conflict clearly crossed the Mediterranean as in August and December 1994. Such reservations came from the centre-right but only from specific persons who were either particularly interested in international affairs or directly concerned by Algeria. Jean-François Deniau called for a 'double distance' from the Algerian government and the FIS.[125] Bernard Stasi, head of the *Association France-Algérie*, claimed that France 'should not give the feeling it unconditionally supports the Algerian government, an incompetent, corrupted and illegitimate government.' In his view, the Algerian government was to be helped only 'provided that it clearly manifest[ed] its will to establish a dialogue with those among the Islamists who condemn[ed] violence'.[126] The Socialist Party also expressed some criticisms against France's support to the Algerian regime. In August, Dumas opposed his 'balanced policy' to Juppé's.[127] In December, Henri Emmanuelli, the Socialist Party's general secretary, urged the Balladur government to reconsider its policy, arguing that French support to the Algerian regime's repressive policy had shown its limits.[128] However, the socialists remained split over the Algerian issue. This transpired in Cheysson's reaction to the criticisms against Pasqua's August 1994 crackdown on Algerian Islamists. Cheysson then declared that:

> The fundamentalists are declaring war on us; we must fight them. Even though I am a socialist, I consider that the current government is showing more enlightened on this issue than the previous one (...). It is out of the question to pursue a policy of dialogue under these conditions.[129]

The same internal disagreements seem to have occurred within the Communist Party. Whereas its leader, Robert Hue, argued in August that the French government should stop giving a blind support to the Algerian authorities,[130] Paul Euziére questioned the political reality of moderate Islamism in the Communist Party's periodical of September 1994.[131] In general, the PCF preferred to criticise the Balladur government for having driven Algiers to accept 'the diktat of the IMF' and for refusing to cancel Algeria's debt[132] rather than for its support to the Algerian regime. This may be explained by the

Communist Party's embarrassment towards Algerian communists who, in general, sided along with the eradicators.

Those political parties or politicians who criticised France's unconditional backing of the Algerian regime did so during the very period Juppé changed his own discourse. That these criticisms may have played a role in the change in the official discourse cannot be wholly excluded. But, their timing may essentially reflect a general acknowledgement that supporting a regime opposed to a political perspective was no longer tenable. For, in their electoral run, political parties did not attempt to entice voters with their proposals on Algeria. Out of the nine competing candidates only three (Independent Jacques Cheminade, Communist Robert Hue and Socialist Lionel Jospin) mentioned their future policy regarding Algeria in the electoral brochures mailed to voters. Only Cheminade, who, as a black horse, had nothing to lose, wrote in black and white that he supported the Rome platform.[133]

Even less than political parties can public opinion be seen at the source of Juppé's change. The average French person has formed her/his understanding of the Algerian conflict through the images projected by the media. On the whole, the French media have consistently given a simplistic vision of this conflict as a war between enlightenment and obscurantism, where the good secular democrats were being beheaded one by one by the bad and unscrupulous zealots. Television news, by far the most popular means of quick information, have been the privileged channel for this message. Television programmes on Algeria have reproduced this flaw as they were invariably about the struggle of the French-speaking Algerian 'democrats'.[134] In the press, until August 1994, few journalists argued that the FIS should be included in the political process. Few criticised France's support for eradication. If they did,[135] the impact of their statements was annihilated by the numerous articles focussing merely on the barbarity of the conflict and particularly on 'Islamic barbarity'. Although *Le Monde*, for instance, began talking of state violence in October 1993,[136] it rarely emphasised this aspect of the conflict until December 1994. The French media's bias in favour of Algerian French-speaking 'democrats' upholding no dialogue with the religious 'regressive forces' was reflected in the almost total monopoly of expression they benefited from on French television and in the newspapers. The numerous interviews conducted with Algerian supporters of eradication rather than with representatives of secular or Islamist conciliator parties have resulted in the generalisation of a truncated vision of Algerian society, which is perceived by the French layman as wholly opposed to the Islamist political project.

In general, the French intellectual community has also failed in providing a balanced criticism of governmental policy towards Algeria. While some openly supported the 1992 coup d'état, arguing that 'between two ills, the lesser must be chosen, that is secular authoritarianism that saves us from fundamentalist totalitarianism',[137] many intellectuals were torn by their antipathy for the Islamists and their recognition that 'the lesser evil' still proved to be one. As a consequence of their embarrassment, French intellectuals chose not to meddle with Algerian politics, claiming it was not their business to recommend or condemn a specific solution to the Algerian crisis.[138] They preferred to devote their energies in existing or new associations to provide moral comfort and material support to Algerian intellectuals, academics and artists threatened by the Islamists.[139] Accordingly, their criticism of France's policy towards Algeria was confined to its immigration aspect only. Intellectuals joined associations for the defence of human rights or for foreigners' rights and participated in demonstrations against the government's restrictive attitude in granting tourist visas and asylum status to their Algerian peers seeking refuge in France. They put forward 'the duty to host' and the crime of 'non-assistance to endangered persons'.[140] It was not before Winter 1994/95 that the French intellectuals suggested what they thought France's policy towards the Algerian conflict should be. They then signed the *Algérie urgence* communiqué accompanying the demonstration of December 3, 1994 in which French trade unions, associations and political parties as well Algerian parties participated. They then all argued for a 'double distance' from 'murderous fundamentalism' and the 'authoritarian, violent, corrupted and discredited regime'.[141] By then, Juppé had already made his harsher declarations on the eradicators and advocated a conciliation which had, nevertheless, some limits as underlined below.

Limits

Despite the adoption of a new policy stance over the way to resolve Algeria's political crisis, no concrete measures were implemented under Balladur to illustrate an eventual determination to actively promote conciliation in Algeria. There was no policy output under Balladur for at least three reasons which, more than appearing from the government's discourse, can be inferred. First, the decision to support conciliation was taken somewhat reluctantly. As a result, the policy line to follow was not clear in the minds of the policy-makers themselves. I asked a high civil servant of the Quai d'Orsay who exactly was comprised in the 'party of democracy' that Juppé had singled out as having France's backing. While declining to answer, this high civil servant pointed out

– honestly, I believe – that the French list of the Algerian parties encompassed in the 'party of democracy' changed every two months or so. This is testimony to the difficulty encountered by the Balladur government in deciding exactly what position to adopt towards the FIS even after the shift of September 1994. But, even if the government had been completely convinced of the validity of supporting a political compromise with the FIS, there are two other reasons which explain France's lack of action: first Juppé never envisaged intervening, otherwise than through diplomatic means, in order to break the Algerian political deadlock and, second, direct interference entailed risks of retaliation from the eradicators.

In January 1995, Juppé clearly indicated that foreign interposition was out of the question:

> It is up to it [Algeria] to create for itself a real society project which will not be imposed by anyone, neither from the interior nor the exterior, for it can only be the fruit of a dialogue between the different political and social components of the Algerian people.[142]

Juppé seemed convinced that foreign intervention in order to dragoon the Algerian regime into conciliation was not the best strategy for Algeria's long-term stability. In thinking so, he was probably right. It is, indeed, difficult to imagine how an externally forced compromise with the FIS could be sustained in the long-term. Without a consensus between governmental eradicators and conciliators over the issue of striking a deal with the outlawed party, there are few chances of a return to calm. If governmental conciliators were to find a give-and-take deal with the FIS under duress, they would have to oust eradicators from the spheres of decision-making. Conspiracies to overthrow the new rulers could not be excluded. If a coup d'état orchestrated by dismissed eradicators were successful, nothing would be solved while a new problem would arise: how to restore the authority of the previous government? By sending troops? A scenario *à la* Haiti is hardly applicable to Algeria, if only because of the psychological impact that sending French troops to Algiers would have in both countries. By cutting aid? It is very unlikely that France, which has a commercial interest in granting loans to Algeria, would decide to wholly close the tap. Reactions from Algiers would also need to be considered. Would not France be in danger of becoming a target for state-sponsored terrorism?

This question, apparently so far-fetched, brings us to the second point explaining Juppé's reluctance to bring pressure to bear upon the Algerian regime. Direct intervention entailed risks of reprisals. The change in the Balladur government's discourse generated protests on the part of the Algerian authorities. They showed their irritation by resorting to codified diplomatic behaviour (recalling their Ambassador, convoking the French one) and by denouncing *via* interposed media the existence of a pro-Islamist lobby within the French establishment. The Algerian regime, or some of its elements, also used less classical methods. It is quite seriously suspected that some foreigners killed in Algeria were assassinated under the indirect orders of the Algerian Military Security which had infiltrated the GIA. Suspicion surrounded the murder of a French nun and a French monk in May 1994 and of four White Fathers (of whom three were French) immediately after the December 1994 Airbus hijack.[143] In addition, a survivor's account of a May 1995 attack in which five foreign technicians were killed by an Islamist commando underlines the sense that the Algerian Army was not always there to protect foreigners against reprisal operations triggered by its habit of displaying the bodies of killed Islamists in the street for half a day.[144] Knowing that the Algerian Army prided itself on acting as it would when playing pool,[145] one wonders whether, in this particular case, the Army aimed at a specific ball (the killing of Islamists) merely to move another one (the killing of foreigners). The Military Security's underlying motive for killing foreigners, *via* the GIA, would be both to generate further antipathy against the Islamists and to dissuade foreign governments from actively supporting conciliation. The French government was aware of the risks entailed by its turnabout since, several months before Juppé's September 1994 change of heart, I was informed by someone close to the government that the latter feared terrorist attacks as much from the GIA as from the Algerian regime:

> For a long time, we thought that there would not be any attack against French nationals in Algeria because we thought that radical forces – whether on the side of the Islamists or on the side of the Military Security – would not dare stepping over this threshold since this was to risk vigorous reactions on the part of counter-powers. It was done and, as a consequence, one does not see what would hold them from doing the same thing one day (...), elsewhere, in Southern Europe.

One may also suggest that the French government knew the risks to which it was exposed inasmuch as it had had a compromising hand in the shady business of Algerian Military Security in relation to the Mécili affair (1987)[146] and perhaps also in the kidnapping of the three French consulate agents (September 1993). There have been many unanswered questions about the circumstances and unfolding of this kidnapping and some have argued that it was a fake abduction.[147] True or not, it is worth mentioning that this kidnapping absolved the Algerian regime for its repressive excesses. It also justified the crackdown on the FIS' relays in France – a crackdown that had more in common with a frame-up than with a terrorist-hunt, as the Kraouche affair was to demonstrate.[148] Being tempted by the devil does not shield one from becoming its victim, however. This probably explains quite well why the Balladur government did nothing to promote conciliation and why Juppé, after having lost his temper with the eradicators, stripped from his discourse his severe remarks.

Notes

1. Pasqua's statement is quoted in *Le Monde*, 7 January 1992 and Léotard's in *Le Point*, 11 January 1992.
2. Quoted in *Le Monde*, 29–30 December 1991.
3. Interview on France-Inter on 17 January 1992, BIPA.
4. See *El Moudjahid*, 2 December 1992.
5. See section on the Juppé/Pasqua split ('A muddle') below.
6. Interview on French television, 10 May 1994 in MAE (May–June 1994), p. 68.
7. Best wishes address to the diplomatic corps in January 1994 reported by *El Watan*, 9 January 1994.
8. Quoted in *Le Monde*, 2 September 1994.
9. Speech to the French Ambassadors, 31 August 1994, quoted in *ibid.*
10. Balladur made few statements on the Algerian crisis. He intervened mostly at times of crisis to reiterate the principles of non-intervention in Algeria's internal affairs and of refusing that France become a terrorist haven. See his radio interview reproduced in *Le Monde*, 16 August 1994.
11. These considerations appear in various interviews and statements. A. Juppé's interview in the Tunisian newspaper *Réalités* on 30 June 1994 (in MAE (May–June 1994), p. 360) mentions them all.
12. A. Juppé interviewed on Europe 1, August 11, 1993 in MAE (July–August 1994), pp. 103-4.
13. Although Kafi had been critical of the eradicator parties, Abdesselam went further, taxing them with being 'secular-assimilationists', which, by referring to the colonial question of Independence / assimilation, implied that they belonged to the 'party of France'. In addition, whereas the HSC had opened negotiations with political parties (September 1992 and March–June 1993), Abdesselam had maintained that 'the parties represent only themselves and are, consequently, of no use'. See *Algérie Actualité* (1431), 16–22 March 1993 and (1459), 28 September–4 October 1993.
14. See Juppé's statement (24 August 1993) on the nomination of Malek in MAE (July–August 1993), p. 115.
15. *Le Monde*, 16 December 1993.
16. Algeria's letter of intent secured a standby loan worth $1.04 billion as a

counterpart to a one-year stabilization programme as well as the release of several credits from the World Bank and the EU. By 1 June 1994 a framework agreement with the Paris Club was reached to reschedule $5.3 billion of official debt over 15 years with a four-year grace period. As the standby agreement expired in May 1995, Algeria signed a three-year IMF extended fund facility of $1.8 billion accompanying a structural adjustment programme (1995–98) which provides, among others, for the privatization of the public sector, currency convertibility, and complete trade liberalization. A second agreement with the Paris Club concerning the rescheduling of another $7.5 billion in official debt was reached in late July 1995. In parallel, after seven months of negotiations with the London Club (group of bank creditors), Algeria signed in May 1995 an accord to reschedule $3.2 billion of private debt over 5 to 10 years. See *Le Monde*, 3 June 1994; 14–15 May 1995; 24 May 1995 and 23–24 July 1995.

17. See e.g. his interviews on 9 February 1994 and 17 December 1994, respectively in MAE (January–February 1994) and (November–December 1994), pp. 173 and 367.

18. See, for instance, his speech to the French parliament on 21 April 1994 (in MAE (March–April 1994, p. 210), his press conference in Washington on 12 May 1994 and his interview in the Tunisian newspaper *Réalité* on 30 June 1994 (in MAE, May–June 1994, respectively pp. 90 and 360).

19. Address to the diplomatic press, 8 September 1993 in MAE (September–October 1994), p. 53, emphasis added.

20. Juppé referred to the domino effect theory for the first time in August 1993 and maintained it at least until June 1994. See MAE, July–August 1993, p. 115; January–February 1994, pp. 163 and 247; March–April 1994, p. 210; May–June 1994, pp. 90, 314 and 360.

21. Quoted in *Le Monde*, 6 August 1994.

22. See MAE (May–June 1994), p. 90.

23. Interview with Christophe Bigot (assistant to the deputy-director of the Maghreb-Mashreq department of the Ministry for Foreign Affairs), 21 April 1994.

24. In MAE (May–June 1994), p. 314. See also the declaration of the spokesman for the Ministry for Foreign Affairs in relation to the January 1994 'appeasement measures' (*Le Monde*, 22 January 1994) and Juppé's felicitations in relation to the transfer from jail to house arrest of the paramount leaders of the FIS in September 1994 (*Le Monde*, 16 September 1994).

25. In MAE (September–October 1994), p. 176.

26. See Juppé's statements on 5 September 1994 and 16 September 1994 in MAE (September–October 1994), pp. 35 and 104.

27. November 1993, August, September and November 1994.

28. *Le Monde*, 7 May 1994.

29. *Le Monde*, 2 September 1994.

30. This contradiction was underlined by F. Burgat in a personal conversation. Any error of interpretation is of course mine.

31. H. Roberts (1994), p. 27.

32. See the statements of the European affairs minister (*Le Monde*, 10 December

1993), of Mitterrand (*Le Monde*, 12 August 1994) and of Juppé in MAE (September–October 1994), p. 208.

33. Foreign firms must pay tidy 'commissions' to import directorates controlled by the Algerian military establishment if they want their export contract to be signed. On corruption and its foreign links, see A. Rouadjïa (1995).

34. *El Watan*, 17 June 1993 and *Le Monde*, 20–21 June 1993.

35. *El Watan*, 23 June 1994 and *Le Monde*, 25 June 1994.

36. *Le Monde*, 5 August 1994.

37. *El Moudjahid*, 10 July 1994.

38. See France's admonitions to the Algerian minister for economic affairs during his visit to Paris on 3 March 1994 in *Libération* and *Le Figaro*, 4 March 1994.

39. *Liberté*, 27–28 May 1994.

40. *MEED* (38)(29), 22 July 1994.

41. *Le Monde*, 16 November 1995.

42. *Le Monde*, 10 and 16 November 1994.

43. *Le Monde*, 14 December 1994.

44. On 4 June 1993 the FAF's newspaper was banned and on 9 August 1994 five publications were outlawed on the grounds of their anti-Western tonality and of their appeal to violence (respectively *Le Matin*, 17 June 1993 and *Le Monde*, 11 August 1994).

45. See *Le Monde*, 26 October 1993; 2 and 5 November 1993; 4 and 6 August 1994.

46. Juppé quoted in *Le Monde*, 20–21 June 1993.

47. *Ibid.*

48. Interview on 24 August 1993 in MAE (July–August 1993), p. 115.

49. Quoted in *Le Monde*, 12 November 1993.

50. *Ibid.*

51. *Europe Daily Bulletin* (6166 n. s.), 9 February 1994.

52. *Europe Daily Bulletin* (6241 n. s.), 1 June 1994.

53. Juppé recognised that violence had led to human rights violations on all sides (MAE (March–April 1994), p. 175) and Balladur affirmed that France was attached to the respect of human rights and tolerance in Algeria (*Le Monde*, 16 August 1994). However, the issue of human rights was raised only occasionally by the French government.

54. This ECU 400 million emergency loan for balance of payments relief was granted partly under the pressure of the Cresson government. It was signed by the EEC in September 1991, that is before the coup in Algiers.

55. *Le Monde*, 19 February 1992.

56. On Italy see *Le Monde*, 6 and 13 August 1994; on Portugal see F. Faria (1994) and on Spain see *The Times*, 15 September 1994.

57. On Germany, see V. Perthes (1994).

58. Quoted in *El Watan*, 21 June 1994.

59. Quoted in *MEED* 38 (24), 17 June 1994.

60. Robert Pelletreau, assistant secretary for Near Eastern Affairs, in R. Pelletreau, D. Pipes and J. Esposito (1994), p. 3.

61. *Ibid.*, p. 4.
62. *MEED* 38 (22), 3 June 1994.
63. *Le Monde*, 1 April 1994.
64. Speech reproduced in *Middle East Policy* (1994), III (2), p. 190. On US policy see also P. Golub (1994/95); C. Moore (1994) and P.M. Gorce (de la) (1993).
65. Quoted in *Le Monde*, 7–8 August 1994.
66. *Le Monde*, 6 August 1994.
67. *Le Monde*, 13 August 1994.
68. *Europe Daily Bulletin* (6097 n. s.), 30 October 1993.
69. *Europe Daily Bulletin* (6065 n. s.), 16 September 1993.
70. Quoted in *Le Monde*, 7–8 August 1994.
71. *Le Monde*, 8 August 1994.
72. *Le Monde*, 2 September 1994.
73. See *Le Monde*, 8 December 1994 and 15 December 1994.
74. See *Le Monde*, 4 March 1995 and 22 November 1995.
75. Reported in *Le Monde*, 11 October 1995.
76. See *Le Monde*, 20 May 1995 and 8 June 1995.
77. See *Le Monde*, 18–19 June 1995.
78. *Le Monde*, 8 December 1994.
79. *Le Monde*, 15–16 January 1995.
80. *Le Monde*, 4 February 1995.
81. Visits in May 1994 of the Algerian finance minister to Brussels and London, of the industry and energy minister to Madrid and of the trade minister to Bonn (*El Moudjahid*, 12 May 1994 and *El Watan*, 23 May 1994); visits in June 1994 of the Algerian prime minister to Brussels, Paris and Rome and of the foreign affairs minister to Washington (*El Watan*, 21 and 29 June 1994).
82. See MAE (March–April 1994), p. 119 and 189 and (May–June 1994), p. 90.
83. Following the Algeria–Belgium joint-commission meeting in April 1994, Belgium is to provide development assistance worth $8.3 million per year until 1997 in addition to balance of payments support and project financing (*MEED* 38 (16), April 22, 1994).
84. *MEED* 38 (22), 3 June 1994.
85. *MEED* 38 (32), 12 August 1994.
86. *Le Monde*, 18 May 1994.
87. *MEED* 38 (32), 12 August 1994.
88. *Le Monde*, 17 May 1995.
89. J. Cesari (1994/95), pp. 189-90.
90. In MAE (September–October 1994), p. 100.
91. Anti-riot police forces were deployed in Paris and major provincial cities. In Paris, over a period of twelve days, they proceeded to do about 27,000 identity checks and 10,000 car searches. About 500 persons were said to be liable for prosecution but none were arrested during these identity checks for their potential links with Islamist networks. Apart from drinking and driving offences or the like, the bulk of the arrested persons were illegal immigrants (*Le Monde*, 18 August 1994).

92. See notably Juppé's speech to the National Assembly, 11 October 1994 in MAE (September–October 1994), pp. 205-6; on economic aid linked to continued economic liberalization, see *Le Monde* 8 February 1995.

93. Interview, 5 September 1994, in MAE (September–October 1994), p. 35.

94. Interview, 16 September 1994, in MAE (September–October 1994), p. 104.

95. Interview, 14 September 1994, in MAE (September–October 1994), p. 87.

96. Interview, 5 September 1994, in MAE (September–October 1994), p. 35.

97. Hearing at the National Assembly, 5 October 1994, in MAE (September–October 1994), p. 179.

98. See his statements on 1 September 1994 and 11 October 1994 in MAE (September–October 1994), pp. 25 and 208 and on 8 December 1994 in MEA (November–December 1994), pp. 237-8.

99. Interview in MAE (November–December 1994), p. 114.

100. Interview, 8 December 1994, in MAE (November–December 1994), p. 237.

101. Interview in *Echarq Al Awsat* reported in *El Watan*, 5 February 1995.

102. Interview, 27 December 1994, in MEA (November–December 1994), p. 377.

103. Interview, 8 December 1994, in MEA (November–December 1994), p. 238. Emphasis added.

104. Interview, 27 December 1994, in MEA (November–December 1994), pp. 376-7.

105. *Le Monde*, 27 and 28 December 1994; *Le Nouvel Observateur* (1573), 29 December 1994–4 January 1995.

106. Quoted in *Le Monde*, 18 January 1995.

107. Respectively quoted in *El Watan*, 5 February 1995 and *Liberté*, 5 February 1995.

108. MAE (September–October 1994), p. 127.

109. *Le Monde*, 6 January 1995.

110. *Ibid.*

111. Quoted in *Le Monde*, 30 March 1995.

112. Pasqua quoted in *Le Monde*, 6 August 1994.

113. Interview in *Le Monde*, 15 October 1994.

114. Pasqua in *L'Heure de vérité*, France 2, 29 January 1995.

115. *Le Monde*, 26 October 1994 and 13 December 1994.

116. See *Le Monde*, 3 and 7 September 1994.

117. *Le Monde*, 5 November 1993.

118. *Le Monde*, 5–6 February 1995.

119. *Le Monde*, 8 February 1995.

120. *Le Monde*, 7 February 1995.

121. *Ibid.*

122. Juppé in La *France en direct*, France 2, February 27, 1995.

123. These elements of analysis draw upon an interview by the author with a high civil servant who expressed the wish to remain anonymous. As this civil servant is not named in the list of persons who brought a contribution to this work, I would like to thank this person now for the valuable insights I was provided with in the interview.

124. Leaked to *Le Canard enchaîné*, 5 April 1995.

125. Quoted in *Le Monde*, 11 August 1994.

126. *Ibid.*
127. Reported in *Le Monde*, 11 August 1994.
128. Quoted in *Le Monde*, 26 December 1994.
129. Quoted in *Le Monde*, 12 August 1994.
130. *Ibid.*
131. P. Euzière (1994), p. 73.
132. See the PCF's call for a demonstration in 'solidarity with the Algerian people', 13 October 1994 in *Les Cahiers du communisme*, 70 (11), 1994, p. 180.
133. Between the two rounds of the French presidential election, Jospin mentioned the Socialist Party's support to the Rome platform during his television debate with candidate Chirac. See *Le Monde*, 4 May 1995.
134. Up to Summer 1995, only one television broadcast partly avoided this flaw by having a relatively more diversified panel of intervening parties, including, however, no Islamists: 'Femmes courage', *Envoyé Spécial*, France 2, 29 June 1995.
135. For instance, Jacques de Barrin in *Le Monde*, 29 October 1993.
136. *Le Monde*, 17–18 October 1993 and 21 October 1993.
137. Jean Daniel, quoted by I. Ramonet in *Le Monde diplomatique* (December 1993). Ramonet was one of the first to ask in this article: 'Do the abominable killings committed by the religious extremists justify the excesses of the Algerian regime? Or the accomplice silence of the European democracies?'
138. See P. Bourdieu and J. Leca in *Le Monde*, 7 October 1994.
139. Among newly created associations the most well known is the CISIA (International Committee of Support to Algerian Intellectuals) created in June 1993 and headed by Bourdieu and Leca.
140. Three demonstrations were organized, out of which two specifically targeted the Balladur government's immigration and asylum policy. That of 11 October 1994 for which a 'Common platform for the hosting in France of Algerian asylum seekers and exiles' was elaborated and signed by many associations and that of 25 March 1995. See *Le Monde*, 16–17 October 1994 and 28 March 1995.
141. *Le Monde*, 6 December 1994.
142. Speech to the Centre d'analyses et de prévisions, 30 January 1995, quoted in *Le Monde*, 1 February 1995.
143. *Le Canard enchaîné*, 2 August 1995.
144. See *Le Monde*, 10 May 1995.
145. Remark of a former Commander reported in P. Dévoluy and M. Duteil (1994), p. 41.
146. For details on this affair, see e.g. M. Naudy (1993).
147. F. Burgat (1994), p. 205.
148. Kraouche was in custody after the November 1993 police operation because he was allegedly found in possession of copies of documents emanating from the GIA and, notably, of copies claiming the murder of the two first Frenchmen killed in Algeria and advising foreigners to leave Algeria. In January 1994, however, a policeman, having serious doubts as to the origin of the documents found in the flat of Kraouche, leaked to the press. A police inquiry into the matter concluded that it

was, indeed, possible that documents, thought to be in Kraouche's possession, had been introduced in his flat by the police at the time of the search (see *Le Monde*, 8, 10, 12 and 26 January 1994).

Chapter 3

The Meanders of French Policy Under the Right: The Chirac Presidency (May – November 1995)

French policy towards Algeria under Jacques Chirac's presidency can be read along different lines. It can be analysed in terms of the cyclical periods of cooling off and *rapprochement* that have characterised the Franco-Algerian relationship since Algeria's independence. It can also be read in terms of a pattern of continuity and change in relation to what the socialist and the Balladur governments did. Lastly, Chirac's policy on Algeria can be examined in the light of the shifting character of France's Algeria policy. As I have tried to underscore the shifting nature of French policy towards Algeria since 1992, it makes sense that I continue to follow this path in accounting for Chirac's policy. This, however, does not exclude reference to the other two lines of analysis.

During the first seven months of Chirac's mandate, French policy towards Algeria was marked by a slight shift, at least at the formal discourse level. The shift occurred in October 1995 as a result of the criticisms formulated by the French Socialist Party in relation to the prospect of a meeting between the French and Algerian presidents in New York. To answer the socialists' charge that the meeting amounted to support a military solution to the Algerian crisis, the Chirac administration was brought to develop a series of justifications for its decision to meet Zeroual. In the process, it introduced new elements in the policy it had hitherto advocated towards Algeria and, more generally, in France's policy *vis-à-vis* Algeria since 1992. As mentioned by the Juppé government, one of the new components of France's policy concerned a 'change in tactics' in order to push the Algerian regime into a political solution involving a wide political dialogue and democratization: the principle of strict non-interference was waived in favour of a political conditioning of French economic aid. Considering to tie economic aid to the opening of a dialogue and to the organization of free parliamentary elections in Algeria was a new attitude compared to what all French governments, including the Juppé government, had argued for since 1992. Another element of change which allows to talk about a shift in October 1995 relates to the issue of the FIS' inclusion within the political process. Until October 1995, the Juppé government openly maintained that the FIS should not be allowed back in the political process. Thereafter, it formulated no objection to an inclusion of the FIS within the political dialogue and to its participation in parliamentary elections.

Below, these two elements of change will be reviewed after France's official policy line towards Algeria before the October 1995 shift is spelt out. From May to September 1995, the Chirac administration upheld, as one of its central precepts, the principle of a 'double-distance policy' with regard to the Algerian Islamists as well as the Algerian regime. In practice, the Chirac administration proved tougher on the FIS than the Balladur government had in its last months in power. Relations between Paris and Algiers during that period were also lukewarm. However, to all appearances, this state of affairs arose less from a French decision to keep a distance from the Algerian regime than from the latter's manoeuvres. As a result, it can be questioned whether there was any substance in the search for a double-distance policy under President Chirac.

A double-distance policy (May – September 1995)

The official policy line

As indicated earlier, one of the main criticisms that had been formulated against the Balladur government's policy towards Algeria, particularly after Summer 1994, was its lack of balance. France, it was realized, had identified itself too closely with the repressive policies of the Algerian regime. It now needed to be positioned at a 'double distance' with regard to the Algerian regime and the Islamists. By operating his September 1994 shift, Foreign Minister Juppé did adopt a more balanced policy towards Algeria. Since he was appointed prime minister under Chirac, it came as no surprise that the double-distance principle was upheld as the guiding line of France's policy. Chirac's statement during the presidential debate with candidate Jospin is worth mentioning in this regard. Chirac then proposed two sets of principles for his future policy towards Algeria: (1) France would continue supplying Algeria with economic aid because, without it, Algeria would head for 'total collapse'; (2) However, France would back the 'party of democracy' in Algeria. The 'party of democracy' fitted well within the double-distance principle since it was defined as comprising those who 'reject all forms of fundamentalism and authoritarianism'.[1]

Continued economic aid and support to the 'party of democracy' were two policy tenets that, as Balladur's minister for foreign affairs, Juppé put forward after his September 1994 shift. In continuity with his past policy, Prime Minister Juppé also argued that, although France would refrain from interfering in Algeria's domestic affairs, it continued to see political dialogue and democratization in Algeria as the solution to that country's protracted crisis. In May 1995, Juppé thus declared that:

> It is through dialogue and free elections that the Algerians will be able to disentangle themselves from the meshes of violence and to come to a reconciliation around a [society] project that they themselves will have chosen for the future of their country.[2]

The facts

The Chirac administration's conciliatory discourse suggested that, in the pre-electoral period in Algeria, France might continue to support the Rome initiative and that it might be favourable to the reaching of a compromise with the FIS prior to the Algerian presidential election. It was precisely to cut off such speculations that, in late June 1995, Prime Minister Juppé stated that the FIS had not yet accepted the principles of democracy and, consequently, did not belong to the 'party of democracy' which Paris claimed to back in Algeria.[3] Juppé's declaration could be understood as a reversal of attitude with respect to his post-September 1994 stance in favour of conciliation. In this sense, it could be seen as yet another shift in France's Algeria policy. However, it must be recalled that, although Foreign Minister Juppé had agreed in principle to the FIS' reintegration in politics, he had also maintained that hostilities had to cease first and that the FIS had to give strong guarantees that it would respect the principle of political alternation. Because Juppé's 1994 shift was done only halfheartedly, he did not accept the reasons underlying the FIS' refusal to call for a cease-fire and did not see the FIS' signature of the Rome platform as giving sufficient guarantees with regard to the respect of democracy. Thus, Prime Minister Juppé's claim that the FIS did not belong to 'the party of democracy' did not constitute a wholesale questioning of his latest stance about conciliation. The question remains open as to whether Juppé would have been so categorical in excluding the FIS from the electoral competition if the Algerian election had been parliamentary rather than presidential.

What can definitely be regarded as a reversal of attitude under Chirac, however, was the return to the practice of viewing Islamism only through its violent fringe. Chirac's tough stand against Islamism in general, and against the FIS in particular, directly resulted from the breaking up of new networks operating in France for the Algerian armed groups[4] and from the wave of terrorist attacks by GIA support networks on French soil in Summer and Autumn 1995.[5] In response to the terrorist attacks, President Chirac warned that he 'would not allow France to become a sanctuary (...) for the fundamentalists and that [the Juppé government would] do everything in its power to eliminate them'.[6] Let us note the replacement of the term 'terrorists' by the more general term 'fundamentalists' in the French security discourse. In September 1995, on grounds of domestic security, the French Ministry for the Interior also banned the commercial distribution of a book dealing with state violence in Algeria. This *Livre blanc sur la répression en Algérie (1991– 1994)*[7] was written by the 'Committee of Free Militants for Human Dignity and Human Rights' which is presumed to be mainly comprised of FIS militants exiled in Switzerland. Reporters Herzberg and de Barrin described the book as a series of testimonies about state violence in Algeria (arbitrary arrests, torture, death sentences, imprisonment conditions in detention camps, etc.). The subject of violence perpetrated by the Islamist armed groups is said to be wholly excluded from the text.[8] This one-sided book may thus be categorised as a political publication or as propaganda. Its banning on grounds of domestic security, however, established a link between the FIS and the terrorist attacks in France whereas nothing had proved that the FIS was involved in, or even supported, such attacks. In fact, it condemned them all.[9]

If, in the first months of Chirac's presidency, the double-distance-policy principle gave way to a tough stand against the FIS, what about France's attitude towards the Algerian regime? We saw earlier that, under Balladur, relations between France and Algeria became somewhat strained as a result of Foreign Minister Juppé's September 1994 shift. The Airbus affair also contributed to a cooling off between Paris and Algiers. Under President Chirac, bilateral governmental relations showed no improvement. On the contrary, distrust and discord grew. However, from May to September 1995, the deterioration of relations between the two states did not result from any specific decision in Paris to keep at a distance from Algiers. Rather, it resulted from the Algerian government's manoeuvres seeking to turn the heat on the Juppé government prior to the Algerian presidential election.

Chirac's mandate opened with a conflict with the public *Air Algérie* company. In late June 1995, *Air Algérie* cut its flights from and to Paris in retaliation to the French authorities' decision – taken after the hijack of the French Airbus – to transfer the *Air Algérie* desk from the Orly airport to the Roissy-Charles-de-Gaulle airport in a special high security zone by the year 1997. In the meantime, the *Air Algérie* desk was transferred within the Orly airport in a high security zone separated from regular check-in areas. The

Algerian authorities claimed that these measures were 'vexatious' and 'racist' and that they expressed France's wish to ostracize Algeria.[10] France's airports were equipped with high security zones for other destinations than Algeria so that, to all appearances, the Algerian outcry was a means of protest against something other than this specific measure. Perhaps was it a means to put pressure on the Juppé government so that it would not denounce the expectable results of the Algerian presidential election?

After the *Air Algérie* dispute, the tension between Paris and Algiers grew as a result of the terrorist attacks in France. The French media and Algerian personalities in the opposition pointed out that some of the attacks could be the work of the Algerian Military Security as much as that of extremist Islamists linked to the GIA.[11] There were doubts about the murder of Sahraoui and about the Saint-Michel underground station bombing which had both been 'prophesied' by an Algerian newspaper said to be close to the Algerian Military Security. Franco-Algerian co-operation in the field of anti-terrorism led Paris to channel much of its attention on an Islamist activist exiled in Sweden and managing from there the GIA *Al Ansar* bulletin. As things turned out, the suspect had a good alibi for not having been involved in the bombing and the Swedish government later refused to extradite him to France. During a meeting with the French press, Interior Minister Debré questioned the value of co-operating with Algiers in matters of anti-terrorism. He declared that 'The Algerian Military Security wanted us to go on wrong tracks (...) so that we would eliminate people who bother them'.[12] Debré's dropping a brick did not contribute to warmer relations with the Algerian regime whose Embassy in Paris curtly 'took note of the formal denial'.[13]

It may be argued, then, that Chirac's policy from May to September 1995 was one of 'double distance'. However, this was less a chosen course of action than the result of the attitude of the Algerian government which, by trying to put pressure on the French authorities, in effect generated a feeling of distrust. The shift inaugurated by the Chirac administration in October 1995 brought Franco-Algerian relations to a crisis point.

The 'inopportune' Chirac–Zeroual meeting and its aftermath

The Juppé government was brought to reconsider some aspects of its policy as a result of a controversy that was sparked by the French Socialist Party about the prospect of a meeting between Chirac and Zeroual. Below follows an account of the terms of this controversy, the policy shift it induced, the crisis that this shift engendered in Franco-Algerian relations and, more briefly, subsequent attempts at *rapprochement* engineered by both governments.

The controversy

The Chirac–Zeroual meeting was planned to take place in New York during the celebration of the United Nations' fiftieth anniversary on 22 October 1995, coinciding with the opening of the electoral campaign in Algeria. For that very reason, the French Socialist Party's First Secretary, Lionel Jospin, described the meeting as 'inopportune'.[14] The Socialist Party's argument was that this get-together with President/candidate Zeroual could be understood as support for the Algerian military regime and that this could imply, in turn, that France favoured a military solution to Algeria's political crisis. On 9 October 1995, Gérard Fuchs, the National Secretary for International Relations at the Socialist Party, explained the Socialists' position in the following terms:

> Jacques Chirac must not meet Lamine Zeroual (...) Whereas the coming presidential elections in Algeria will unfold in material and political conditions that empty them of any signification, such a meeting would signify that the President of the Republic believes more in a military solution than in a political solution on the other side of the Mediterranean. Such a position is, from my viewpoint, wrong and dangerous.[15]

Let us note that the divisions within the Socialist Party as regards the policy to adopt towards Algeria had not yet disappeared in 1995. Indeed, both Cheysson and Chevènement disagreed with their party's position and brought their support to the Chirac–Zeroual meeting.[16] In Algeria, however, the French Socialist Party's stand was approved by the FFS and the FLN. Both parties 'deplored' Chirac's decision. The FFS added that the meeting would amount to a 'support to the policy of confrontation led by the [Algerian] regime'.[17] For its part, the FIS used both political talks and threats. It argued that, by meeting Zeroual, Chirac would 'forgo the requisite for true elections and formally abandon its favourites of the third way' – an allusion to the 'party of democracy'. Qualifying the meeting as a 'provocation', the FIS also warned France to change its decision if it did not want to expose the French people to 'adventures and consequences for which it [was] not responsible'.[18] And, indeed, the French National Police Union which did not directly condemn the decision to hold the meeting, nevertheless, expressed concerns about its potential impact on security in France.[19]

One might wish to argue that the French Socialist Party's line of argument was poorly constructed. By meeting Zeroual with a view to talking about the future of Algeria, the Chirac administration certainly showed that it expected Zeroual to stay in power. This implied that France had given up hoping for a truly democratic presidential election in Algeria. However, if one agrees with the contention that, although a military man, Zeroual was closer to the conciliators than to the eradicators, then meeting him suggested support for a political rather than military solution. In any case, the Juppé government which provided a series of justifications for the meeting to take place chose not to underscore that point. Among the government's justifications, only one is of interest to us. The Juppé government argued that the meeting would provide the opportunity to tell the Algerian leaders what France expected to see happening in Algeria after the presidential election – namely, the opening of a political dialogue encompassing all forces rejecting violence and the rapid holding of free parliamentary elections. Explaining in Madrid why he had agreed to see Zeroual, Chirac made this statement on 10 October 1995:

> I accepted this request in order to hear what he [Zeroual] has to tell me. (...) Concerning a country that is close to us, I have things to tell him [Zeroual]. First, there won't be any solution to the Algerian problem that is not a political one (...) it is my duty to inform him that the solution can be based only on a dialogue with all those in Algeria who reject violence (...) the essential step is to constitute a majority and thus to hold free, democratic parliamentary elections as soon as possible. From there, one can imagine that the democratic process will be reinforced and that civil peace will return. That is the message I would like to give President Zeroual.[20]

The shift

In discussing the content of the message Chirac would give Zeroual in New York, the French administration introduced two new components in its policy, thereby, inaugurating a shift. The two changes consisted of the inclusion of the FIS within the political process in Algeria and politically conditioned economic aid.

Officially, the French authorities remained ambiguous as to their position on the inclusion of the FIS within the political process. Chirac stated that the dialogue had to be held '(...) with all the economic, social, political, cultural [and] religious forces which exclud[ed] violence as a means of expression'.[21] However, the Chirac administration also argued that dialogue and future parliamentary elections needed to be concluded with a perspective for a return to civil peace. Now, one can hardly see how a dialogue and elections excluding the political forces having some form of control over violence could lead to such a perspective. With a good measure of certainty, it can be argued that Chirac was implicitly saying that the FIS should be included in the political process. And, indeed, the 11 October 1995 issue of *Le Monde* quoted authorised (but non-specified) sources which affirmed that what mattered to the Elysée was the holding of free parliamentary elections which would be opened to 'all the candidates who reject[ed] violence, which [did] not exclude the FIS'. Maintaining that the FIS should be included in the dialogue process and allowed to compete in parliamentary elections amounted to a shift in the position that the Juppé government had earlier adopted. This shift was given added weight by the claim that France might now be ready to tie its economic aid to democratization in Algeria. In early October, the Elysée, indeed, warned the Algerian authorities that '(...) if they [did] not take into account the demands [the French government] ha[d] put forward for the organization of a true democratic dialogue with all the forces rejecting violence, [it would] take appropriate action'.[22] After the meeting with Zeroual was effectively canceled (see below), Chirac clearly stated that it would be 'legitimate' to 'give French aid in proportion to the rapidity of the establishment of a democratic system in Algeria'.[23]

The 'change in tactics' adopted by the Chirac administration was a U-turn in the policy that the successive French governments had put forward since the cancellation of the Algerian parliamentary election back in January 1992. All governments had argued that, even though the Algerian regime left much room for improvement, economic assistance could not be used as a pressure tool. It was explained that French aid first of all benefited the Algerian people. Conditioning that aid would, therefore, prove unfair. It was also said that France could not add economic chaos to political chaos because it would reinforce the Islamists' popular appeal and spur emigration flows to the North. There were also economic reasons for not conditioning aid: tied economic assistance to Algeria was a mover in Franco-Algerian trade and, by lending money to Algeria, the French government made sure that Algeria paid its debt back to France. It is not very clear why suddenly these arguments were no longer of any value to the Chirac administration. It is possible that a sincere turn-about occurred and that the government saw no other solution than using aid as a pressure tool in order to speed up the return to a stable political situation in Algeria. However, it is somewhat puzzling that until the time of writing there was, to my knowledge, no report in the press announcing when the financial package for 1995 was signed and for what amount. Back in April 1995, during the two rounds of the French presidential election, a leak to the press intimated that France's 1995 financial assistance to Algeria might be reduced by FF1 billion to FF5 billion ($1 billion).[24] Since then, however, nothing has been said about what was effectively decided by the Chirac administration. When referring to the amount of French aid to Algeria in 1995, some reporters quoted FF6 billion.[25] Others, however, wrote (without comment) that Algeria received FF10 billion from France in 1995...[26] Be that as it may, since the October 1995 shift, there has been no report that France had in practice tied its aid to democratization in Algeria. To all appearances, the Juppé government was busier working at a *rapprochement* with Algiers.

Crisis and *rapprochement*

In October and November 1995, Franco-Algerian relations reached a crisis point as a result of the Chirac administration's new policy line. Chirac's message about democracy and his apparent determination to force democratization in Algeria quite expectedly displeased the Algerian regime. The Sifi government retaliated by canceling the meeting with Chirac on the very day it was supposed to take place, by initiating a controversy as to who had requested the meeting and by launching a media campaign against France. Soon, however, both states entered in the path of reconciliation.

In relation to the cancellation of his meeting with Zeroual, President Chirac explained that the Algerian party wished the meeting to be given media coverage – a request that Chirac rejected so as not to be accused of supporting candidate Zeroual. According to Chirac's account, he discussed this issue with Zeroual in a ten to fifteen minute conversation which took place in the presence of the UN General Secretary, Boutros Ghali. With both parties maintaining their positions, Zeroual decided to call off the meeting.[27] Chirac's account fits the justifications put forward by Algeria for canceling the meeting: Zeroual's spokesman declared that 'it [was] abnormal that relations between two sovereign states unfold on the sly' and that 'Algeria [was] not in the habit of conducting its diplomacy by hugging the walls'.[28]

The Algerian authorities then opened a debate as to which of the two states had first requested the meeting. The French always maintained that the request came from Algiers. Thus, in September 1995, the Elysée confirmed to the French press that Zeroual had made a request to see Chirac during the UN's festivities. On 22 October, Chirac was also careful to remind reporters that, since he had not sought to meet Zeroual in the first place, he had no particular regrets to express.[29] As to the Algerian authorities, they recalled that 'the principle of a meeting between the Algerian and French chiefs-of-state (...) was agreed upon in late July [1995] in Tabarka by the foreign ministers of the two countries at the suggestion of Mr. de Charette', the new French minister for foreign affairs.[30]

The cancellation of the meeting was followed by an Algerian media campaign accusing France of neo-colonial interference. The Sifi government which, until 22 October, had been quiet about the latest shift in French policy then strongly reacted. It maintained that Algeria did not need to be taught lessons in democracy and that it was not in its tradition to submit to conditions. The Algerian government further accused France's policy of flouting the dignity and sovereignty of the Algerian people.[31]   The Algerian press applauded 'Zeroual's snub' in the face of the old colonial power. The anti-French media campaign lasted up until after the November 1995 Algerian presidential election. In the wake of the election, the Chirac administration maintained the policy line initiated by the October 1995 shift. The communique of the Quai d'Orsay to Zeroual expressed the wish that the presidential election would 'open the way to a political dialogue and constitute the departure point of a democratic process leading to parliamentary elections'. 'In that perspective', Paris said it would be 'ready to pursue relations based upon friendship and co-operation with Algiers'.[32]   The French claim that the presidential election should be rapidly followed by a parliamentary one was denounced in Algiers as sheer neo-colonial interference.[33]

The storm, however, rapidly calmed down and both states made moves towards a *rapprochement*. In late November 1995, during the sixth summit of the French-speaking nations, Chirac declared that Zeroual was a 'legitimate president' and that he had, therefore, no problem meeting him.[34]   Philippe Séguin, president of the French National Assembly, went to Algiers on 20 December 1995. His visit was particularly important. It took place one month after the Algerian presidential election and was the first visit of a French official to Algiers since August 1994. It was reported that, although Séguin had been invited to Algeria for a long time by the head of the Algerian National Transition Council, the date of his trip had been brought forward at President Zeroual's request, thus, showing a willingness on the Algerian side to improve relations with Paris. In Algiers, Séguin made declarations to the same effect. He argued that 'Algeria and France ha[d] to co-operate, to get on well, to talk to each other.' and that 'If there [were] misunderstandings, they [had to] be relieved or cleared up'.[35]   Finally, 1996 opened with further prospects for a *rapprochement*: Hervé de Charette and Ahmed Attaf, the respective foreign ministers, met in Paris on January 11, 1996 on the occasion of Mitterrand's funeral and decided to reverse the 'abnormal course' of Franco-Algerian relations'.[36]

To conclude, it might be worth recalling that, since the cancellation of Algeria's first free parliamentary election back in January 1992, French policy towards Algeria shifted several times around the option of a conciliation with, or eradication of, the Islamist opposition. Quite unexpectedly, policy shifts did not follow the French electoral calendar: each governing administration was led at one stage or the other to revise its policy. Under Mitterrand's second mandate (1988–95), Cresson's socialist government (May 1991 – April 1992) promoted a compromise with the Islamist opposition and showed somewhat cool towards the new Algerian rulers who had taken office through a coup d'état. Cresson's successor, the socialist Bérégovoy (April 1992 – March 1993), also followed a conciliatory policy until January 1993. Then, however, he changed his mind. By now he backed the Algerian regime's eradication strategy which implied a tough repression policy. The socialists were defeated in the French parliamentary election of March 1993. The new right-wing Balladur government (March 1993 – May 1995), operating under Mitterrand's presidency, followed the path opened by Bérégovoy. It was, however, given more time to fully develop France's eradicator stance on Algerian politics. The Bérégovoy government had moved towards eradication only three months before being defeated in the election. It did not have time to give a significant substance to its new eradicator line otherwise than by a political discourse of support to Algiers and increased economic aid. The Balladur government, on the other hand, had plenty of time to also establish a tight police and intelligence co-operation with Algiers, to offer military assistance and to campaign in Algeria's favour in international organizations. Although of all the French governments the Balladur one gave the strongest approval to the Algerian regime's eradication policy, it eventually moved away from its support for eradication. In September 1994, under the pressure of the Ministries for Foreign Affairs and Defence, the Balladur government realized that a compromise with the Islamist opposition might be the solution to Algeria's political crisis and protracted armed conflict. Through the voice of Foreign Minister Juppé, the Balladur government subsequently adopted a more balanced policy with regard to the Algerian authorities and the Islamists. The French May 1995 presidential election brought an end to cohabitation: right-winger Jacques Chirac entered the Elysée and appointed Balladur's foreign minister, Juppé, in Matignon. Within the framework of a rather conciliatory policy, the early months of the Juppé government were also marked by a shift in emphasis towards a greater support for conciliation. In October 1995, the government made a clear move from opposing the reintegration of the FIS into politics to supporting such an option, albeit in a controlled manner. By warning that it considered to condition its economic aid to Algeria to the return to democratic life, the Juppé government also showed some determination in pushing the Algerian regime to find a political solution to the crisis.

Since 1992, French policy towards its ex-colony, thus, shifted several times. From promoting conciliation with the Islamist opposition, it shifted to supporting its eradication and reverted again to advocate compromise. Does the wavering of the French policy-makers indicate that they did not know what they wanted? Or were they each time trying to adjust their policy to the fluctuations of Algerian politics? The key to understanding the shifting character of French policy towards Algeria seems to lie in the fact that what mattered to French policy-makers was not the issue of conciliation / eradication in itself but the way in which each of these two strategies was perceived by them as affecting political stability in Algeria. The concern for political stability more than any commitment to democratization is, indeed, what led French policy-makers to make the choices they made. The socialists' cool reaction to the cancellation of the Algerian 1991/92 parliamentary election was not, in the last analysis, prompted by the anti-democratic nature of the coup d'état. The socialists were concerned by the risks involved in wiping off the Islamist current from the political map of Algeria. They considered that the Algerian authorities could have sought better ways than sheer force to find a solution that could have been accepted by the Islamists. True as well, the socialists did not like the fact that the coup was bringing back old nationalist enemies to power. Towards the end of the socialists' mandate (1993), however, the security situation in Algeria had grown worse. A FIS take-over by violence was thought within the odds while the Algerian regime, then still unified in its eradication strategy, was unwilling to talk about conciliation. Supporting a compromise with the FIS was, consequently, no longer seen in Paris as the best way to protect political stability. Hence, the socialists' shift of January 1993. Under Balladur, political stability was also equated with regime stability until it was realized that the eradication strategy had not proved the right answer to curb down violence and to tackle the political and social problems at the root of the success of Islamism. The security situation had become disastrous but, at the same time, the Islamist armed groups did no longer seem in a position to overthrow the regime and the FIS had made political overtures. It was time, therefore, to advocate some form of compromise, however reluctantly this decision had to be made. Hence, the hesitant change of heart of both the French ministers for foreign affairs and for defence in September 1994. Similarly, the Juppé government's firmer support to conciliation in October 1995 stemmed not from its desire to promote democratization for its own sake, but from the view that allowing the FIS to compete in parliamentary elections but not presidential ones was the way to put some order back into Algerian affairs without taking too many risks. The concern for political stability more than for democracy was, thus, the yardstick of French policy towards Algeria during these years. This still leaves one question unanswered: for what reasons did the various French governments believe that a FIS takeover, or a compromise with the FIS in Algeria, would breed an unstable situation? This is a question that Part Three will attempt to answer.

Notes

1. See *Le Monde*, 4 May 1995.
2. Parliamentary speech about the general policy orientations of the new Juppé government, quoted in *Le Monde*, 25 May 1995.
3. In *Géopolis*, France 2, 25 June 1995.
4. *Le Monde*, 30 June 1995.
5. From July to October 1995, seven terrorist attacks took place: (1) Sheik Sahraoui was murdered in his mosque in Paris on 11 July; (2) a bomb blew up in the Paris underground at the busy Saint-Michel station on July 25 (7 dead, 85 casualties); (3) in a public square near the Champs-Elysées, a bomb placed in a rubbish bin exploded on August 17 (17 wounded); (4) another (defective) bomb went off in a Parisian street market on 3 September (4 wounded); (5) a car bomb, parked close to a Jewish primary school, blew up in a suburb of Lyon on 7 September (14 casualties); (6) in retaliation to the killing by the French police of one of the suspects (the Kelkal affair) in the Maison Blanche village in the Rhône *département*, a bomb exploded in the Maison Blanche underground station of Paris on 6 October (13 lightly wounded); (7) a bomb exploded in the St Michel - Musée d'Orsay metro station in Paris on 17 October (28 casualties). There were also four failed terrorist attacks. One of them aimed at the high-speed train (the TGV) on the Lyon-Paris line on 26 August. Another was meant to target a market in Lille but was frustrated by the arrests of suspected Islamists on November 2, 1995.
6. Quoted in *Le Monde*, 14 July 1995.
7. Editions Hoggar: Geneva, 1995.
8. *Le Monde*, 14 September 1995.
9. See *Le Monde*, 15 September 1995.
10. See *Le Monde*, 21, 28 and 30 June 1995.
11. See e.g. *Le Monde*, 19 August 1995. In an interview with *Le Figaro*, 19 October 1995, Abdelhamid Brahimi did not exclude that the terrorist attacks might be performed or inspired by the Algerian special services. He suggested infiltration and manipulation (see *Le Monde*, 20 October 1995).
12. Quoted in *Le Monde*, 23 September 1995.
13. *Le Monde*, 26 September 1995.
14. See *Le Monde*, 19 October 1995.
15. Quoted in *Le Monde*, 11 October 1995.
16. See *Le Monde*, 20 October 1995.
17. See *Le Monde*, 14 October 1995.
18. See *Le Monde*, 13 and 16 October 1995.
19. See *Le Monde*, 13 October 1995.

20. Quoted in *Le Monde*, 18 October 1995.

21. Quoted in *Le Monde*, 22 October 1995.

22. Quoted in *Le Monde*, 18 October 1995.

23. In *Le Journal*, France 2, 26 October 1995.

24. *Le Monde*, 29 April 1995.

25. See *Le Monde*, 24 October 1995.

26. See *Le Monde*, 16 November 1995.

27. See Chirac's declaration in New York, 22 October 1995 in *Le Monde*, 24 October 1995.

28. Quoted in *Le Monde*, 24 October 1995.

29. See respectively, *Le Monde*, 29 September 1995 and 24 October 1995.

30. Official communiqué, 22 October 1995 in *Le Monde*, 24 October 1995.

31. *Ibid.*

32. See *Le Monde*, 19–20 November 1995.

33. See *Le Monde*, 22 November 1995.

34. *Le Monde*, 5 December 1995. Algeria never participated in these summits which it condemned as perpetuating neocolonialism.

35. See *Le Monde*, 22 December 1995.

36. See *Le Monde*, 21–22 January 1996.

Part Three

Opposing the FIS

Introduction to Part Three

The first and second sections of this study were concerned with confronting discourse with deeds so as to understand what the successive French governments did as opposed to what they said they were doing. The purpose of Part Three is to identify the French political establishment's underlying reasons or motives for opposing both a violent FIS take-over and the FIS' inclusion in the political process in Algeria. Much of this study concerns the Balladur government since it was under its mandate that opposition to the FIS was most patent. However, this inquiry into the motives for opposing the FIS also applies to the socialist governments and to the Juppé government under the Chirac Administration. Indeed, under Bérégovoy, France's policy shifted towards a support to the eradication strategy of the Algerian regime and Chirac's presidency opened with an opposition to the FIS' integration in the political game. The socialists' and Chirac's motives for opposing the FIS were in all points similar to those of the Balladur government. It must be strongly emphasised, however, that the motives underlying the French governments' opposition to the FIS did not hamper them from eventually calling for conciliation in Algeria, even though conciliation would not necessarily have solved the foreseen risks implied by a FIS take-over or by its re-integration into politics. In this sense, however strong concerns about a FIS victory were, they did not constitute a stumbling block to a rethinking of the Algerian quandary.

The coming chapter deals not only with French opposition to a violent FIS take-over but also to its coming to power through negotiations. Until September 1994, Balladur's foreign minister (Juppé) always argued that the FIS' coming to power would be a 'catastrophe'. But he was never precise, when saying so, whether he was thinking of a take-over through violent means or through a negotiated settlement. Christophe Bigot, assistant-deputy to the head of the Maghreb-Mashreq department of the Quai d'Orsay, made the point that, in assessing the consequences of a possible FIS take-over, the issue as to how it came to power had to be taken into account. If the FIS seized power violently, revolutionary ardour had to be expected. The Franco-Algerian relationship might be questioned by the new regime, at least in the short- to medium-term. On the other hand, if the FIS was part of a coalition government, its radicalism might be tempered and conciliation lay perhaps ahead. Yet, Bigot also mentioned that, even if a negotiated settlement occurred, not all problems would be solved.[1] Obviously, this was also Juppé's viewpoint. For, when he argued that an Islamist regime in Algiers would be a 'catastrophe', it was already thought since Summer 1993 that the FIS was unable to take power through warfare.

What were then the envisaged consequences of a FIS take-over or of an inclusion of the FIS within the political process? French officials never greatly expanded on the issue as to how Islamists in government would prove to be a 'catastrophe'. Nevertheless, from Juppé's speeches and interviews with members of the political establishment, it appears that there were two types of concern. One corresponded to the perceived risks of a FIS take-over or of its inclusion in government as they were foreseen by the French political establishment: the domino effect that a FIS victory might have throughout the Mediterranean, the negative consequences that such a victory might have on Franco-Algerian relations as well as on France itself through the issues it raised in the fields of immigration, national security and economic relations. In addition to these issues, opposition to the FIS was justified on ideological grounds: a FIS victory needed to be resisted because it was inevitably perceived as bringing Algeria back to 'seventh century Medina'.

Regarding perceived risks, one of the French authorities' overriding concern was the domino effect that a FIS take-over or inclusion in government might have throughout North Africa. It was argued in Paris that, were the neighbouring Islamist movements to climb on the bandwagon, instability with risks of intra-regional conflicts might become acute. Second, and perhaps most importantly, with falling dominoes, the negative consequences of a FIS victory on Franco-Algerian relations would be multiplied on a larger scale, thus rendering the situation 'unmanageable'.

The FIS' coming to power was thought to have several negative effects on France. Here we group such effects under three headings: immigration, national security and economic relations. Immigration issues raised by a FIS take-over or an inclusion of the FIS within the political process dealt with the risk of a massive influx of refugees from Algeria and with the risk of re-Islamisation within the Muslim community living in France. Such issues played a crucial role in the French governments' hostility to the FIS, first, because it was forecast that they would be raised even if the FIS was included in government through negotiations and, second, because they entailed profound tensions in France's socio-political system. National security issues (revolving around terrorism) as well as economic considerations did have a role to play in the French political establishment's opposition to the FIS but essentially as contributing factors. Indeed, issues of state-sponsored terrorism were most likely to occur if the FIS came to power by toppling the regime. As it was rapidly understood that the FIS was not able to do so, the problem was not of the highest salience. Nevertheless, the FIS' ambiguous attitude towards violence, notably against France, contributed to the view in Paris that France would be better off without Islamists in government in Algiers. In the economic domain, the reasoning was similar. It was assumed that a FIS regime would not question Algeria's economic relationship with France. If it did, it was assessed that, while incurring a cost, this would not constitute a major blow to France's economy. However, if avoiding a change of regime allowed the maintenance of the economic relationship intact, all the better.

In addition to these perceived risks, the prospect of the FIS coming to power (by violence or not) stirred concern because its political project, based upon the restoration of a supposed divine will, was understood as profoundly regressive and intolerant. French opposition to the FIS on ideological grounds did not, however, merely correspond to France's more general hostility towards Islamism. The very fact that the FIS was an Algerian party reinforced the French political establishment's hostility. We enter here within the realm of what we have termed 'psychological' motives. Franco-Algerian relations cannot be fully understood if it not realised that Algeria has remained a part of France in the French collective imaginary. With the exception of 1954, never before did this view have such a wide impact on France's policy towards Algeria. Indeed, because Algeria has always been seen in some way as France's sister, the FIS' vote was lived in France as a 'psychological trauma'. The FIS' vote implied that part of the Algerian people did not recognise itself in France and its values. This disturbing fact was simply not accepted. Was it so because it amounted to a symbolic loss of Algeria for a third time – the first at political Independence and the second when Algeria nationalised French interests in oil? Still in connection with 'Franco-Algerian closeness', it is also important to note that the French political establishment was led to oppose the FIS in its defence of the Algerian gallicised elite with whom bonds of understanding and friendship had been woven through the years.

Deconstructing French policy-makers' perceptions as to the risks involved by a FIS take-over leads us somewhat into the realm of political fiction. Political fiction does, however, have real implications for policy-making. Indeed, it was a series of hypotheses as to the consequences of the FIS' coming to office which led Paris to decide on its Algeria policy. In addition, on the basis of these hypotheses, the various French governments took practical steps to limit the effects of a potential change in regime. This was particularly perceptible in the field of immigration but also in France's promotion of the EU 'partnership policy' in the Mediterranean and its involvement in various initiatives dealing with 'comprehensive security' in the Mediterranean. It is thus important to comment on these specific policies when dealing with the issues they were responding to. Moreover, in relation to the ideological and 'psychological' aspects of French opposition to the FIS, it is necessary to review briefly the existing academic literature on the rise of Islamism in Algeria in order to contrast it to the views of the French political establishment on that question.

Note

1. Interview with Christophe Bigot, 21 April 1994.

Chapter 1

Opposing the FIS: Perceived Risks

When trying to drum up international support for Algiers, the major argument put forward by the Balladur government was the risk of falling dominoes. Even well after it was thought in Paris that the FIS was unable to topple the Algerian regime, it was argued that the FIS should be contained because its coming to power might have spillover effects throughout the Muslim world and notably, from the viewpoint of France's immediate concerns, in neighbouring countries prey to Islamist agitation: Morocco and Tunisia. Libya, Egypt and the Occupied Territories were, however, also identified as potentially falling dominoes.[1] French policy-makers never made a (public) detailed treatment of the risks entailed by their hypothesis of falling dominoes.[2] The reconstruction of their projections, however, points to two major connected concerns. First, the region could become highly unstable with risks of intra-regional tensions. Second, anti-Western Islamist regimes could eventually emerge on Europe's doorstep, multiplying the problems generated by the presence of a FIS regime in Algiers. The view that a FIS victory might generate turmoil elsewhere and, especially, in Morocco and Tunisia was a central factor in leading Paris to support the Algerian regime's eradication strategy. At the same time, together with Southern European countries, France supported initiatives for an inter-shore political dialogue as well as the EU's 'Euro-Mediterranean economic area' policy with a view to promoting economic development and political stability in the Mediterranean.

Falling dominoes and their foreseen consequences

As mentioned above, the risk of falling dominoes in North Africa generated two major concerns. One was that the region would become highly unstable with risks of intra-regional tensions. This hypothesis drew attention to the fact that North Africa could become a theatre for violence. Their morale boosted by a FIS victory, muzzled Islamist movements would conclude that violence could pay, if not in overthrowing regimes, at least in forcing an overture of the political game. If, switching from having been the 'leader of the Third World' to being 'the light of Islam', Algiers attempted to export its revolution by supporting like-minded movements, inter-state conflicts might emerge. Increased intra-regional tension – already illustrated by Algeria's closure of its border with Morocco from August to September 1994[3] – could be accompanied by destabilising arms races in a context where the proliferation of non-conventional weapons is becoming an acute issue on the world stage. In this respect, Algeria's interests in chemical technology and its development of nuclear power, purportedly for civilian use, could become a more worrisome concern than it has been until today.[4] This dramatic scenario was never brought to its possible conclusion, namely the direct involvement of foreign powers in regional conflicts with a view to containing Islamist expansion. Certainly, Juppé maintained that 'Naturally, France will not economise on its help to preserve the security and stability of [Morocco and Tunisia]'.[5] But French policy-makers were advised to keep current state to state arrangements in case of changes in regimes across the Mediterranean, precisely to avoid feelings of ostracism and risks of confrontations.[6]

In addition to intra-regional instability, the other major concern generated by cascading dominoes was their 'multiplier effect': whereas the foreseen negative consequences on France of a coming to power of the FIS could be faced, a generalisation of these problems to the entire North African region would become 'unmanageable' for France and perhaps for other European countries.[7] With a view to counterchecking falling dominoes, particularly in the Western Mediterranean, France parallelled its support to the Algerian authorities with bilateral aid to Morocco and Tunisia. Most importantly, however, it encouraged regional initiatives aimed at fostering economic development in the Maghreb in order to favour political stability and to undercut radical Islamism.

Promoting regional initiatives for stability

Concerns about stability in the Western Mediterranean did not simply grow out of the Algerian crisis. In the late 1980s, despite a slackening of tensions resulting from the end of the Cold War and the creation of the Arab Maghreb Union (AMU),[8] France as well as Southern European states were worried about the destabilising effects both for Europe and the Western Mediterranean of the widening socio-economic development gulf between the Northern and Southern shores of the Mediterranean. In the early 1990s, two initiatives were sponsored by the Southern European states in order to deal with socio-economic development problems and their implications for political stability and security in the Mediterranean: 1) the Conference on Security and Co-operation in the Mediterranean (CSCM) which applied to North Africa and the

Middle East and 2) the '5+5' which specifically focussed on the Western Mediterranean by gathering together the four Latin European states (France, Italy, Portugal and Spain), Malta and the five AMU members. Both initiatives, however, failed to produce any results. Because the field of application of the CSCM extended to the Middle East, it generated hostility from the USA and from France which preferred the 5+5 framework. The latter, however, collapsed after only two meetings in 1990 and 1991 where proposals for socio-economic co-operation and for the promotion of mutual trust were brought forward. The 1992 coup d'état in Algiers and mounting tensions between Brussels and Tripoli following Libya's suspected involvement in the Lockerbie and UTA affairs explain the freeze of the activities of the 5+5.[9]

After the Algerian 1991/92 parliamentary election, however, the link between socio-economic problems, the rise of radical Islamism and political instability was considered all the more relevant. The Lisbon European Council's meeting in June 1992 was, indeed, concluded by the following statement: 'Demographic growth, repeated social crises, large scale emigration and the rise of religious fundamentalism are all problems which threaten the stability [of the Maghreb]'.[10] The idea that the Western Mediterranean should be 'anchored' to Europe in a stable and long-term relationship thus continued to inspire Euro-Mediterranean initiatives. Two main types of framework were used to try to answer the problems caused by political developments in the Mediterranean. One was the Mediterranean Forum. It gathered the foreign ministers of eleven Mediterranean countries with a view to providing a framework for informal discussions on economic, political and cultural issues concerning the region.[11] The other was the EU's 'Euro-Mediterranean economic area' proposal which aimed at transforming the 'co-operation agreements' signed with Mediterranean countries in the late 1960s or 1970s into 'partnership accords'. Exploratory negotiations for the conclusion of partnership accords were conducted, notably, with Morocco and Tunisia for three years before being successfully concluded in 1995. As to Algeria, informal exploratory talks began in June 1994.[12]

In addition to traditional issues of financial, technical, social and cultural co-operation, partnership accords revolved around the creation of bilateral free-trade zones and the institutionalisation of a political dialogue. The latter was seen by the EU as a means of discussing issues pertaining to regional security (e.g. proliferation of weapons of mass-destruction) and to domestic politics. Indeed, political dialogue was geared towards the establishment of democratic systems of government, based upon the rule of law and the respect of human rights.[13] As noted by George Joffé there was a tendency in Europe to conceive democratic systems of government in strict European terms and to encourage the simple reproduction in North Africa of the European political model.[14] In the main, talks between the EU and its Maghrebi partners essentially focused on the establishment of free-market areas. The contentious issue of political dialogue was, during this time, reduced to 'defining the areas of mutual interests that could be included in the dialogue'.[15] If the EU was willing to relegate political dialogue to the background, it was because its priority was to integrate the Maghreb and the Mediterranean as quickly as possible into the European context, partly as a means to struggle against the rise of radical Islamism.

In addition to the Mediterranean fora and the EU Mediterranean policy as regional instruments to undermine the development of radical Islamism, it is worth mentioning the January 1995 meeting of the interior ministers of the four Latin European states and of Algeria and Tunisia who set out to co-ordinate actions to struggle against 'terrorism, fundamentalism, extremism and fanaticism' and who intend to meet every year.[16]

France's involvement in this series of regional frameworks which were more or less directly meant to contain the rise of radical Islamism (the borderline as to when Islamism becomes 'radical' being still relatively obscure in official discourse) partly stemmed from its concerns about the multiplication on a regional scale of the problems that might arise from a FIS victory. The foreseen impact on France of the FIS coming to power are reviewed in the three following sub-sections dealing with immigration, national security and economic relations.

Immigration issues

One central explanatory factor for France's opposition to a FIS take-over and, then, to an inclusion of the FIS in the political process in Algeria, relates to the immigration issues raised by such prospects. There were two major kinds of concern. One was linked to the potential immigration to France of Algeria's Western-oriented elite as a consequence of a coming to power of the FIS. It was feared that, even though these Europeanised, middle/upper class, new immigrants would have a different profile from that of traditional Maghrebi immigrants (blue-collar workers joined by their families), their arrival in France would exacerbate existing anti-Arab/Muslim feelings and, thus, favour social and political tensions. At the same time, an inflow of refugees could possibly hinder relations with a new regime encompassing the FIS, since it would represent a pool of potential political opponents to Algiers. The other main concern raised by the potential coming of the FIS to office dealt with the

Algerian community and, more generally, the Muslim community living in France. In relation to this issue, there were two major worries. First, that the pro- or anti-FIS attitude of the Algerian (and Muslim) community be a constraint on French foreign policy and, second, that the FIS attempt to control the Muslim community at large by encouraging a process of re-Islamisation.

All these concerns were reinforced by the fear of falling dominoes, notably as Morocco and Tunisia were concerned. They explain, in part, French support to the Algerian eradicators. In addition, the French government took measures to limit the impact of a potential FIS arrival in power. Under Balladur and Juppé, immigration inflows stemming from political violence in Algeria were restricted. By keeping entries from Algeria within tight bounds, the French authorities sought to hamper permanent settlement in France, should the FIS be accepted back into the political game. Also, through a restrictive position on the wearing of headveils at school, the French government showed tough on the issue of re-Islamisation in France.

Politically-driven immigration from Algeria: concerns and restriction

An immigration wave: governmental hypotheses and concerns

In the Quai d'Orsay's view, a sudden immigration wave from Algeria could have resulted from a FIS take-over as well as a political settlement between the Algerian government and the FIS. In September 1994, Foreign Minister Juppé, indeed, argued that a political compromise would lead to an Islamisation process that not all Algerians would accept.[17] Logically, this meant that, despite a lull, some would still be candidates for emigration. However, it was not very clear whether the French government had a sound estimate of the proportion such a movement could take on. Government members gave significantly different projections. In April 1994, whereas Juppé advanced a high hypothesis of hundreds of thousands of people, Pasqua 'bet' on tens of thousands.[18] In addition, the Quai d'Orsay made an about-face in October 1994: Juppé, who had hitherto argued that there was a real risk of seeing an immigration wave to France,[19] then minimised the risk, claiming that to expect a massive exodus was part of a 'psychosis' and 'catastrophism' which he did not share.[20] Whether or not the Balladur government had a precise idea as to how many Algerians might effectively have been candidates for immigration if a political compromise was struck with the FIS,[21] it was vocal in claiming that France would not adopt a lax policy. Pasqua, indeed, stated:

We would not be able to host several tens of thousands of persons. (...). We would evidently accept those who have the French nationality. Bi-nationals will have to justify of their quality [as bi-nationals]. For the rest, we have absolutely no obligation (...). Besides, this issue, if it were to be raised, should be examined not within the framework of our own country, but within that of the Mediterranean countries, at the level of the European Union. (...) We cannot be the natural receptacle of all the oppressed, all the persecuted, all those who are in opposition.[22]

What were the French government's concerns explaining its refusal to open at large its border?

The French political establishment put forward three main reasons explaining why it considered a mass influx of Algerian refugees as a major trouble. First, there were practical problems to cope with welcoming a significant number of Algerians, if only in terms of lodging, schooling for children, employment and diploma recognition.[23] Second, especially when it was criticised for its restrictive Algeria immigration policy, the French political establishment emphasised that 'Algerian democrats' needed to stay in their country if they wanted their political ideas to triumph there. Pasqua went somewhat out of his way when recalling that he did not 'clear off' when the Nazis invaded France.[24] But a civil servant expressed the government's concern by asking: 'Is it in our interest to empty Algeria of its modernist substance? A million and half Iranians left after the Revolution; the sole result was to reinforce the power of the ayatollahs'.[25] Third, it was argued that an immigration wave would cause 'domestic politics complications' and would upset the 'social equilibrium'.[26]

Without denying that the first two problems were important, it seems that the overriding concern related to these 'domestic politics complications' and, notably, to the fear that anti-Arab/Muslim sentiment might be boosted by a sudden immigration wave. For that reason, what follows will focus on this concern rather than on the others. The analysis will suggest that French policy-makers were preoccupied with the impact that sheltering Algerian would-be political opponents might have on France's future relations with a government encompassing the FIS. Although never publicly mentioned, this concern about the future of Franco-Algerian relations was most certainly on the policy-makers' minds.

The protest actions undertaken by the French intellectual community in order to denounce the Balladur government's policy of 'non-assistance to endangered persons' did not have much influence on French public opinion which expressed a certain anxiety about a massive inflow of new 'boat-people'

– a suggestive mediatic idiom. According to a September 1994 opinion poll, only 11% of the French people thought that political refugee status should be granted easily to Algerians if the FIS came to power. 34% argued that entry should be limited to those who had family in France and no less than 29% thought that the frontier should be sealed.[27] Besides the specific Algerian issue, since the 1980s, public opinion increasingly expressed its anti-foreigner feeling which, it must be stressed, was directed against alien citizens but also French citizens of foreign – usually non-European – origin. North Africans and their children were in the line of fire because they constituted the most important non-European community in France.[28]

Following the French government's mid-1970s decision to cease importing foreign labour, Maghrebi immigrants settled in France and were joined by their families, whereas they used to go to France in order to work mostly as blue-collar workers and then to return to their homelands. This settlement process occurred in a context of deepening economic crisis and of social upheavals, which favoured racist sentiment. The Maghrebi community thus increasingly came to be seen as either competing for jobs or as draining Social Security benefits. With the increase in violent protest in the suburbs, recurrent since the mid-1980s, the *Beurs* were increasingly perceived as disrupting law and order.[29] In the eyes of many, they were the 'new dangerous class'.[30] Settlement also generated a focus on cultural and behavioural differences. The view that Islam was, in itself, a stumbling block to integration into French society gained currency throughout the 1980s. The Gulf War raised fears of a lack of allegiance of the *Beurs* to their own state, that is France. Similar national security concerns were raised by the Islamic revival in the Maghreb.[31] In short, Maghrebi immigrants and their French children were perceived as a threat.

Whether it was right or wrong that they should be so perceived – and there is ample literature showing that this sense of threat partakes of a collective fantasy[32] – people behave according to their perceptions. Radicalisation about immigration and 'foreignness' was reflected in the growing success of Jean-Marie le Pen's extreme-right party, the National Front (FN).[33] The FN's electoral platform revolved around the discriminatory concept of 'national preference' and the idea that the survival of 'Frenchness' was threatened by the presence in France of Arab Muslims. Rising anti-Arab/Muslim feeling[34] and the subsequent success of the extreme-right led all political parties to advocate tougher immigration policies throughout the 1980s and 1990s in order to minimise social tensions and to thwart the drawing power of the FN. The French government's concern about an immigration wave from Algeria and, eventually, from Morocco and Tunisia must, therefore, be read within this general context of rising 'populist anti-Muslimism'.[35] That an immigration wave might have occurred before the French presidential election was certainly an additional source of concern because of its possible direct impact on the le Pen vote. Indeed, one might be tempted to explain Juppé's baffling change of heart about the reality of a mass exodus (see above) merely as a means of reassuring anxious voters. Fundamentally, however, the French government's concern was motivated by the view that, in the long run, a massive influx of Algerian refugees might provoke socio-political tensions in France.

Thinking ahead

An immigration wave sparked off by the FIS coming to power would result in France sheltering likely political opponents of the new regime in Algiers. There were few doubts that, once in France, some refugees would seek to structure a political opposition. Such political activism might prove a hindrance to France's relations with the new regime in two ways. First, depending on how good relations between the two states would be, Algiers could quite easily accuse Paris of seeking to destabilise the new Algerian regime by hosting opposition movements. Second, the political activism of some opponents to the new regime in Algiers could turn into a threat to territory security in France and, thus, generate tensions between France and Algeria. In exactly the same way as the FLN regime eliminated major political opponents abroad, so could a regime comprising the FIS. In the current situation where both Islamist and secular Algerians had found refuge in France to escape political violence in Algeria,[36] there were signs indicating that France could become an arena of confrontation between Algerians. It was reported that complaints to the French police had been filed by some Algerians in self-exile who had received threatening telephone calls and visits presumably by self-exiled Islamists reproducing the GIA's intimidation methods in France.[37] The murder of Sheik Abdelbaki Sahraoui in July 1995 in his Paris-based mosque also showed that France might be turned into a hunting arena for political adversaries.[38] The killing of political opponents, while in itself affecting national security, could lead to further complications. For instance, in 1980, the attempted murder of Shahpur Baktiar (last prime minister of Iran's Shah regime) in Paris led to the imprisonment of the head of the commando, Anis Naccache. The release of Naccache became one of the demands of pro-Iranian terrorist groups which took French hostages in the Middle East and carried out bomb attacks in France.

If relations between Paris and Algiers were difficult for a variety of reasons, the very fact that France would be hosting potential political opponents to the new regime in Algiers might prove a hindrance to a normalisation of political relations between the two states. It is very unlikely that this scenario did not strike French policy-makers when they assessed the various consequences of a mass influx of Algerian refugees. In view of the potentially unsettling effects that an immigration wave would have in terms of France's 'social equilibrium' and in terms of its future relations with a new Algerian regime including the FIS, the French governments backed the High State Council and then the Zeroual regime, hoping to avoid being faced with an exodus from Algeria. In addition, the Balladur government and, in its wake, the Juppé one, adopted a restrictive immigration policy towards Algeria. By making it harder for Algerians to enter France and to stay there, the French government sought to limit inflows and to hamper the permanent settlement of those who already left Algeria, in case the FIS came to power.

Restricting entry

Immigration to France generated by political violence occurred, although not on a scale that would justify alarmist rhetoric. According to press records, between 1992 and 1994, 10,000 Algerians would have benefited from a 'territorial asylum' status which granted a renewable three-month residence permit.[39] The Interior Ministry's data also showed a trend of immigration from Algeria for political reasons. The number of asylum-seekers, indeed, increased from 1992 even if the numbers involved remained low: 144 in 1990, 191 in 1991, 618 in 1992, 1,098 in 1993[40] and 2,385 in 1994.[41] In the main, Algerians seeking protection abroad belonged to the Westernised *intelligentsia*. Many were threatened with death by the Islamist armed groups. Some might also have been threatened by the regime for their conciliatory views. Among the Algerians who left Algeria for France, however, there were also some Islamists, although they were far less numerous.[42]

In order to prevent (in case a compromise was reached with the FIS in Algiers) the long-term settlement in France of those who already left Algeria, the Balladur government took three main measures which were not reversed under the Juppé government. To begin with, the Balladur government adopted a restrictive interpretation of the Geneva Convention on political asylum, arguing that asylum status could be granted exclusively to people persecuted by their own government. This implied that persons claiming to be victimised by Islamist armed groups could not benefit from this status. This stance on political asylum explains why very few applications were approved: 15 in

1992, 14 in 1993, and 18 in 1994.[43] The French government's refusal to consider as political refugees individuals persecuted by Islamists was a gesture of political support to the Algerian regime: it implied that the regime was capable of protecting its citizens and that it was in control of the security situation. But the French government's refusal was fundamentally motivated by its unwillingness to create a precedent and so ease the long-run settlement of these new immigrants. By merely providing momentary shelter through a renewable three-months' 'territorial asylum', the French government attempted to answer protection needs while at the same time avoiding permanent settlement.

The government also made it harder for Algerians to come to France. A policy of tourist visa restriction was adopted under the socialists as early as 1990. However, between 1993 and 1994, issued visas dropped from 300,000 to 100,000 (less than 20% of the demand).[44] In December 1994, an immigration agreement was signed with the Algerian authorities. It abolished the preferential treatment hitherto granted to Algerians in matters of visa issuance. This accord had two effects. First of all, it toughened entry conditions: Algerian tourists had to hold a letter confirming that they would be hosted in France. This letter had to be signed by the host and the French mayor of the host's town. In the second place, this accord restricted the possibility of changing status once in France: Algerians could no longer go to France with a tourist visa and then ask for either a lengthening of stay or a change in status. The authorities maintained that 'endangered persons' may be granted a derogation to the rule, but such a derogation was not regulated by law.[45] This December 1994 agreement was in negotiation for about two years and brought Algeria in line with Tunisia and Morocco which signed similar accords with France in 1992 and 1993 respectively. Nevertheless, the fact that the French government pushed for its conclusion in the particular context of violence in Algeria showed a deliberate will to restrict inflows from Algeria as much as possible.

Lastly, in Summer 1994, the Balladur government reached a secret agreement with the Algerian authorities over the expulsion of clandestine immigrants. This agreement provided that the Algerian authorities had to accept back all persons who were held to be Algerian citizens by the French government and who were to be deported. For this agreement to be reached, the Algerian authorities had to recognize the persons concerned as their citizens before they could be expelled to Algeria.[46] The agreement obviously sought to counter the clandestine migrants' tactic of destroying their identity papers and, thus, to guard against a wave of immigrants.

The FIS and the Muslim community in France

Events such as the Rushdie affair or the Gulf War raised the issue of the impact that conflicts within the Arab/Muslim world and conflicts between the West and the Arab/Muslim world might have on Arab/Muslim communities established in Europe. The attitudes of Arab/Muslim communities towards such conflicts were important both because they might prove a constraint on foreign policy and because they might generate social tensions within the domestic arena. Considering the size of the Algerian community in France and of the Muslim community at large (about 4 million people),[47] it is not surprising that the French government expressed concern about the effect that the Algerian conflict and a possible FIS victory might have on such communities.

Regarding this problem, there were two major concerns. First, it was feared that the Algerian community and, more generally, the Muslim community in France, would become involved in the Algerian conflict. This risked a transposition within the French borders of the Algerian conflict and, depending on which sides these communities stood, the risk that French foreign policy-making might be constrained. In practice, the Algerian community and the Muslim community installed in France showed no interest in becoming actively involved in the Algerian political game despite the efforts of the Algerian political parties to bring them to do so. In addition, in their great majority, these communities expressed no special attraction for the FIS even though they encompassed elements which were ready to go far to support the advent of an Islamic state in Algeria.

The French political establishment's second source of anxiety concerned the wider phenomenon of 're-Islamisation' which appeared in France in the early 1990s, particularly among young French Muslims, and which referred to a focus on the Muslim dimension of identity. It was feared that, once in power by force or compromise, the FIS might encourage this process of re-Islamisation. The FIS' primary objective might not have been re-Islamisation for its own sake but for political control of the Algerian (and Muslim) community living in France. However, by encouraging re-Islamisation to that end, it might transform what were only signs of re-Islamisation into a trend. Re-Islamisation was a source of concern for the French government primarily because it was seen as threatening national cohesion and as undermining allegiance to the French state.

Opposition to a FIS takeover thus reflected the French political establishment's desire to limit the effects of re-Islamisation, even though keeping the FIS from power would not ensure that re-Islamisation did not progress in France. Under Balladur, the French government also found its own responses to the foreseen threats engendered by re-Islamisation through the 1993 reform of the Citizenship Code and its tough 1994 decision on the wearing of head-veils in public schools.

Attitudes towards the FIS

The Algerian conflict has generated concerns about its possible impact on the Algerian community and, more generally, on the Muslim population living in France. It was feared that these communities might become involved in the conflict and mobilise against the French government's own policy. There were particular anxieties about a support for the FIS. In four years' time, however, these concerns have rapidly been undermined because there have been no sign of massive militant involvement in the Algerian conflict in the immigrant milieu, despite Algerian political parties' attempts to mobilise the Algerian community. In addition, attitudes towards the FIS have proved to be rather negative, thus lessening fears about massive FIS support.

When Algeria got on the path of democratization, the Algerian community in France became an electoral stake for Algerian political parties which attempted to arouse interest in their political ideas. The Algerian Brotherhood in France (FAF), while not having any organic link with the FIS, was created in February 1991 in France with the specific aim of inciting Algerian immigrants to vote for the FIS in the 1991/92 parliamentary election. Similarly, all Algerian political parties or movements created an immigration branch in France and tried to mobilise voters. On January 5, 1992, responding to Aït Ahmed's call, 2,500 – 3,000 FFS supporters demonstrated in Paris in echo of the January 2, 1992 'demonstration for democracy' in Algiers which was meant to incite people to vote in the second round and, thus, to limit the FIS' success.[48] In some Parisian newsagents, Saïd Sadi's electoral platform, which had been prepared for the second round of the parliamentary election, was on sale even well after the election was cancelled.[49]

After the coup, all Algerian political parties continued to seek the support of the Algerian community in France. Associations having direct links with Algerian political movements were created in France. The association 'The Friends of Alger Républicain in France' was, as its name indicates, a relay of *Alger Républicain* – a communist, eradicator newspaper. This association published an information bulletin which accounted for 'its' victims of terrorism in Algeria and denounced dialogue with the Islamists.[50] In May 1994, the association 'Algeria in our Hearts' (*L'Algérie au cœur*) was created in the Parisian northern outskirts of Saint-Denis. It showed all the signs of being a direct expression of the MRP. One of its meetings (organized with other associations in Saint-Denis) actually took place on the very day the MRP was demonstrating in Algiers: June 29, 1994. In its first publication, *L'Algérie au cœur* legitimised the 1992 coup, recognized the Algerian Army as an institution acquired to democracy, denounced dialogue with the Islamists and enjoined the Algerian community in France to mobilise in solidarity with the Algerians who struggled for 'a republican, modern, democratic and progressive Algeria'.[51] The FAF, which directed its militancy towards the Muslim community at large, organized support for the FIS and its cause, essentially through propaganda. It set up 'information meetings' across France and distributed a news bulletin at the entrance of mosques in major French cities. This – by now outlawed – bulletin brought news of the 'jihad in Algeria', denounced the Algerian regime and foreign support for the 'junta'.[52]

This militant activism which had several objectives (creating housing networks for self-exiled Algerians, raising funds, 'informing' French public opinion, etc.) did not seem to have had much success.[53] There were some 'information meetings' organized by associations supporting democracy and denouncing the risks involved in Islamism. Mention can be made, for instance, of the meeting set up by the Young Arabs of Lyon and its Suburb (*Jeunes arabes de Lyon et sa banlieue*, JALB) in April 1994. This association, which had no direct connection with Algeria, directly concerned the *Beurs*. It played a militant role for the integration of *Beurs* into French society along a secular path. JALB's advertising statement for its meeting read: 'We have the duty and the responsibility to understand and to manifest an active and concrete solidarity for peace and democracy in Algeria'.[54] However, there was no massive participation in public demonstrations. In April 1994, the Federation of Algerian Associations (*Collectif des associations algériennes*) called for demonstrations throughout Europe in order to 'denounce violence in Algeria'.[55] But *Le Monde* did not report any demonstration on April 9, 1994, suggesting that it was either cancelled or that it did not attract much of a crowd. The December 1994 demonstration of 'solidarity with the people and the democrats of Algeria' was organized by French political parties, trade unions and associations even though the immigration branches of Algerian political parties participated. It brought together only 10,000 people in Paris.[56] In Nantes (where the visa service for Algeria was transferred following the August 1994 attack on French consulate agents in Algeria), the March 1995 demonstration which was intended to protest against France's restrictive immigration policy towards Algerians gathered only 3,000 people.[57]

Insofar as the FAF is concerned, it had to curb its militant activities as it had been under police surveillance since the November 1993 police raid. Its president, Djaffar el Houari, was actually expelled to Burkino Faso in August 1994 (he then moved to Britain) and its spokesman, Moussa Kraouche, was under judicial surveillance from November 1993. The discovery of FIS and GIA networks in France, the wave of terrorist attacks against France in Summer–Autumn 1995, the involvement in such networks and attacks of Muslims who had been living in France for a long time and especially of young *Beurs* contributed to the view that the FAF and, more generally, Algerian Islamists had woven a network of influence within the Muslim community in France. In fact, cases of direct involvement in the armed struggle were proportionally very few and, most importantly, the FAF and other Islamist networks did not manage to convey a positive image of the FIS within the Muslim community in France. Indeed, a September 1994 poll showed that there was no major support for the FIS among Muslims living in France, although many (on average 22%) showed a certain prudence by declining to express their views on the various questions about the FIS. The results of this survey indicated that only 9% of the Muslims living in France had a 'very good or a quite good opinion of the FIS', whereas 69% had a 'rather bad or very bad opinion of the FIS' (with 50% opting for the 'very bad'). Among the youngest (16 to 24 years of age), 72% had a 'rather bad or very bad opinion of the FIS'. 70% of the whole Muslim population said they disagreed with the proposition that 'the FIS represents the values of Islam as I see them' (8% agreed); 62% agreed with the idea that 'the FIS threatens democracy' (15% disagreed) and 57% agreed with the proposition that 'the FIS signifies regression' (21% disagreed). Lastly, whereas 9% of the whole Muslim population said they 'personally wish[ed] the coming to power of the FIS in Algeria', 68% said they did not wish so. However, 48% thought that negotiations with the FIS were required while 28% disagreed with the principle of negotiations.[58] These results were similar to those of a December 1993 survey which polled *Beurs* aged 18 to 30. 63% showed a negative attitude towards 'Islamic fundamentalism' (*intégrisme musulman*); 20% an indifferent attitude and 14% a positive attitude.[59]

Generally speaking, there was thus a hard core of about 15% of Muslims in France supporting the religio-political ideas advocated by the FIS. It comprised an extremist fringe ready to use violence for the cause of political Islam. Although the existence of this radical fringe was problematic for the French authorities, the government's freedom in terms of foreign policy-making seemed to be guaranteed. However, the way in which the French government conducted its policy towards Algeria and, more generally, towards Islamism might generate tension and antagonism with the Muslim community in France. In this respect, both concern and anger were the responses of the

Muslim community when faced with an equation that became more and more accepted within the political discourse: 'Arab/Muslim = fundamentalist = terrorist'.

The FIS and Islamisation

The conjunction of the Algerian conflict with the phenomenon of re-Islamisation in France was also one of the factors contributing to French opposition to the FIS: it was feared that, once in power, the FIS would seek to extend its influence among the Muslim community in France and encourage, to that effect, the re-Islamisation process. Before turning to the issue of the concerns generated by re-Islamisation, a word must be said on re-Islamisation itself and on the objectives that the FIS might have been seeking in encouraging re-Islamisation.

Numerous surveys on the Muslim community in France conducted in the mid-1980s and early 1990s showed that, for the majority of young French so-called 'sociological' Muslims, Islam did not play a significant role in their process of identity construction. The majority neither endorsed nor rejected Islam, which was seen primarily as a cultural and family heritage and, eventually, as an ethical code of behaviour.[60] Nevertheless, from the early 1990s, there emerged signs of an identity assertion along Islamic lines (re-Islamisation) among the 16 to 24 years of age group, even though re-Islamised young French Muslims remained a minority within their own age-class. Re-Islamisation was reflected in a more assiduous religious practice compared to their elders.[61] Re-Islamisation also appeared through a greater will to have Islam allotted a wider place in the public space: according to a 1994 survey, 34% of young Muslims in the 16-24 age-class favoured the call to the prayer by means of a loud-speaker, as opposed to 23% for the 25-34 age-class and 28% for the national average (Muslim population). Similarly, whereas 56% of young Muslims in the 16-24 age-class stood for minarets as visible as bell towers, percentages were lower for the 25-34 age-group (37%) and the national average (45%). In addition, although the demand for a distinct Muslim status regulating civil life remained low among the youngest (21%), it was higher than among the 25-34 years of age (12%) and higher than the national average (17%).[62] Re-Islamisation also transpired through the head-veil-at-school issue which has periodically turned up at the forefront of France's social debates since 1989. Re-Islamisation was a phenomenon that had its roots in the conjunction of several factors: reaction to 'anti-Muslimism'; socio-economic marginalisation; a decline in the popularity of secular, anti-racist and 'assimilationist' associations such as *SOS-Racisme* and *France-Plus* which failed to deliver the goods for many and which have subsequently been supplanted, notably, by Islamic associations. The Islamic associational fabric developed in France since the 1980s as a result of both the settlement process of primary-migrants and a looser legislation on foreigners' associations. Through their social work structured around the neighbourhood mosque/prayer room, local Islamic associations were mainly concerned with rebuilding communitarian bonds defined in religious terms.[63]

Islamisation: the FIS' objectives

It is doubtful that, once in power, the FIS would seek, as an end in itself, the re-Islamisation of the Algerian community or, indeed, of the Muslim community settled in France. Its primary goal was to build an Islamic state in Algeria, not elsewhere. However, re-Islamisation could become a by-product of other aims. Charles Pellegrini has thus argued that the enrolment of *Beurs* by FIS networks in France would correspond to the long-run objective of creating pressure groups with the ultimate aim of constraining the French government's international and domestic policy. With a population under its influence, it was argued, the FIS in Algiers could, by remote control, transform the suburbs of French major cities from a state of social peace to one of unrest and try to influence the course of France's policy through this means.[64]

Perhaps more realistically, in attempting to control the Algerian (and Muslim) community in France by encouraging the process towards 'Islamic assertion', the FIS could just be reproducing the FLN regime's past strategy.[65] In order to protect the Algerian community in France from unwanted political influences, the FLN regime had, indeed, sought to 'officer' this community through secular networks (*Amicale des algériens en Europe*) and religious ones (Paris Mosque).[66] Particularly if FIS opponents were to find refuge in France, it was likely that a FIS regime would strive to prevent competing political formations from holding sway over the Algerian and Muslim community. In order to curb their influence, the FIS might encourage re-Islamisation and support Islamic associations operating in immigrant circles in France.

Islamisation: French concerns

The prospect of re-Islamisation was a source of concerns for the French government essentially because it was perceived as a threat to national cohesion and to allegiance to the French state. These concerns have been articulated around two issues: the foreign influence that might be exercised on 'born again Muslims' and the demand for a minority status possibly deriving from re-Islamisation.

Regarding the first issue, it was feared that once brought back on the path of God, young French Muslims might be permeable to Islamism while the latter asserted itself against Western political culture. That some French citizens might not abide by the ideologico-political substratum of French society was viewed as threatening national cohesion as well as national security: 'born-again Muslims' might feel they primarily belonged to the Islamic community rather than to the French one. Such a sense of belonging could raise questions about their allegiance to the French state. In this regard, the 1993 reform of the Nationality Code restricting the automatic acquisition of French nationality for foreigners born in France was not innocent. By requiring foreigners who were born in France and who had been living there all their lives to explicitly request French citizenship, the state implicitly asked for an oath of loyalty and allegiance.[67]

Second, it was feared that re-Islamisation might be accompanied by demands for the recognition of Muslims in France as a minority which should be granted specific rights.[68] As opposed to Britain where immigration was structured in terms of community-based relations, the French 'republican model' of immigrant absorption (inspired by the very process through which the French Nation was built after the Revolution) has traditionally been based on the negation of minorities. Instead, it has promoted individual citizenship as a means of integration to French society.[69] The assertion of a collective identity, eventually leading to claims for the recognition of a minority status, thus challenges the very system through which national integration had always been performed. It naturally partakes of the debate on the 'crisis of national identity' and on the 'crisis of the republican model' which has taken place in France in recent years.[70] Public confidence in the capacity of the republican model to culturally integrate foreigners and their children and, thus, to maintain social cohesion is declining. As a result, many French people (84%) thought that 'cohabitation' between the French of 'old stock' and foreigners (and their French children) would become tense in the future[71] – another reason for the government to be wary of re-Islamisation.

The view that re-Islamisation was a threat to national cohesion both because it might engender obedience to a foreign ideology and question the national integration model was particularly apparent in the *hijeb* affair. The wearing of head-veils at school by some Muslim girls[72] was understood as an assault on the secular character of the French state, organized by foreign Islamists waging an 'insidious jihad'[73] against France. Philosopher André Glucksmann thus depicted the head-scarf as a 'terrorist sign by itself'.[74] As concerns about the establishment of FIS and GIA networks in France grew, François Bayrou, Balladur's education minister, made an about-face. In

October 1993, Bayrou supported the 1989 ruling of the Constitutional Council which, in the wake of the first *hijeb* affair, had allowed the wearing of head-veils in public schools on the ground that the wearing of religious signs by individuals was not in contradiction with state secularism. A year later, Bayrou recommended the exclusion of veiled pupils from public schools on two main grounds. First, because the head-veil was an 'ostentatious religious sign', implying that, in Bayrou's view, there was something wrong in publicly showing that one was a Muslim. This stand can be understood only if the assertion of one's 'Muslimness' was equated with support for a religio-political ideology. And, indeed, Bayrou maintained that 'One has to be blind not to see the fundamentalist movements behind the young girls who wear [the head-veil]'.[75] Second, Bayrou justified banning head-veils in schools on the ground that 'the choice of the Republic is not to let France evolve into separate communities'.[76] He thus cut short the debate on whether the republican model, by denying the social reality of minorities, proved obsolete.[77]

As a concluding note, it may be worth recalling that the eventuality of a FIS take-over (by force or compromise) in Algeria was perceived as generating significant problems for France. In particular, it was thought that a FIS regime would encourage re-Islamisation within the Muslim community living in France whereas re-Islamisation raised issues about existing societal arrangements. That the re-Islamisation process might be encouraged from outside the national realm was also thought to be wholly unacceptable because of the allegiance issue to which it gave rise. The prospect of a massive influx of Algerian refugees sparked off by a FIS take-over was deemed to endanger France's 'social and political equilibrium' while at the same time possibly undermining political relations with the new regime in Algiers. In addition, the presence in France of would-be political opponents to a FIS regime raised concerns about national security. The following section will focus on national security concerns although from a different angle.

National security: the terrorist issue

One of the issues raised by the Algerian conflict and the potential arrival to power of the FIS dealt with terrorism. As suggested above, although the French political establishment expressed no overt concern about it, it seems quite plausible that it was worried about the potential hunt for political opponents that a FIS regime might undertake on French soil. Such state-terrorism would be a blow to French national security inasmuch as the French state is supposed to ensure physical protection to the persons residing within its borders. This section deals with another type of threat to national security: the undertaking of terrorist acts against the French state.

It is not wholly certain that, in opposing a FIS take-over and then a compromise with the FIS, the French government was primarily motivated by the fear that, once in power, the FIS might resort to terrorism against France. Nevertheless, it can quite logically be argued that the ambiguous attitude of FIS leaders in exile, notably as regards the killings of French nationals in Algeria, and the AIS' threats against France (in addition to the GIA's), reinforced the negative perceptions that the French political establishment had about the FIS. In a context where the government feared terrorist attacks in France by Algerian Islamist armed groups – attacks which eventually took place under the Chirac Administration – the fact that the FIS was understood to back violence against France logically led to the view that France would be better off without Islamists in government in Algiers.

Threats against France

The support lent by the Balladur government to the Algerian regime quite rapidly backfired partly because the strategy of the Algerian Islamist armed groups (particularly the GIA's) had shifted in Spring 1993 from aiming at the security forces to also aiming at civilians who were suspected of active or passive collaboration with the Algerian authorities. French nationals (and, more generally, foreigners) thus became the target of murderous attacks in Algeria as of September 1993 on the ground that they were 'Christian crusaders' or that they brought a support to the regime by working for state companies. France's rounding-up of Islamist activists in France, as well as the killing of the four hijackers of the *Air France* Airbus – the hijack being itself a terrorist act – by the French *gendarmerie* elite unit triggered threats of retaliation not only from the GIA but also from the AIS, the FIS' armed-wing. As a response to the August 1994 round-up of twenty-six Islamist militants who were held in Folembray and expelled to Burkina Faso or put under house arrest, the AIS demanded freedom for the 'internees of Folembray' and declared that 'The French government must renounce its aggressive policy or it will endorse the responsibility of what the mujahidins of the Islamic Salvation Army will inflict on it.'[78] The GIA also threatened to 'violently hit French interests in Algeria'.[79] After the December 1994 hijack, the AIS stated that 'war against France [was] legal' and that it would 'return a hit for a hit' in order to 'revenge the Faithful'.[80] As to the national structure of the GIA, it was reported to have sent ultimatums to the French, German, British and American governments enjoining them to evacuate their nationals and to break diplomatic relations with Algiers.[81]

Not all of these communiqués clearly mentioned the extension of terrorist actions against France to its own territory and, when they did, they were later denied. After the AIS' threat of retaliation about the Folembray affair, Abdelbaki Sahraoui maintained that terrorist attacks on French soil were not part of the AIS' objectives.[82] Similarly, after the hijack, while a group claiming to belong to the AIS warned that 'The AIS' mujahidins [were] able to hit France in its own house',[83] the AIS as well as the FIS denied that *jihad* was to be extended to French territory and denounced this communiqué as counter-propaganda.[84] The Balladur government was, nevertheless, extremely worried about the very possibility that violent acts might be carried out on French soil.

From fearing terrorist attacks in France ...

The Balladur government's fear that French territory might become a target for terrorism was perceptible when it cracked down on the Islamist nebula in France. In chapter two of Part Two, it was argued that such crackdowns were part and parcel of the Balladur government's political support to Algiers.[85] They allowed the government to curb the FAF's political militancy as well as to break up networks which organized concrete support for the AIS and the GIA in Algeria. But they also aimed at minimising the risk of terrorist attacks in France: once a network had been built, its original aim could, in principle, always been altered. Pasqua was perfectly clear on this point when he said:

> I do not believe that there is a risk of a wave of attacks in France, but one can never exclude it. One day or the other, terrorism can perfectly be carried out in our country. What do I have to do: to wait for bombs to blow up in our country and for people to be assassinated here, or to intervene before in order to dismantle networks? That [the second option] is what I am doing.[86]

In practice, none of the police raids supervised by Pasqua brought evidence of planned terrorist actions in France (or they were not revealed to the public). From press reports, the results of the round-ups and the various arrests tended to demonstrate two things. First, that the FAF has never really been involved in anything else than political militancy. Its propaganda has certainly revealed itself strongly anti-French, but, to all appearances, it has not been implicated in concretely supporting the armed struggle in Algeria. Following Sahraoui's stance, Kraouche condemned the undertaking of illegal actions in France and claimed that the FAF was 'against the killing of innocents and foreigners in Algeria.'[87] The contention that the FAF has not been a support network for guerrilla action in Algeria seems to be confirmed by the fact that, in the wake of Sahraoui's murder, Kraouche was offered police protection by the French authorities.[88] Second, the various police operations showed that, as Algerian Islamist activists fled their country for France, they built support networks to help guerrilla action in Algeria. The activities of such support networks revolved around legal or illegal fund-raising, arms, explosives and equipment transfers to Algeria, provision of fake ID papers to the guerrillas, and infiltration/exfiltration of '*mujahidins*'. Some of these networks operated under the cover of Islamic associations or of firms.[89] Maghrebi nationals installed in France for a long time and, in some cases, young *Beurs* and French converts were involved in such networks. Prior involvement in petty criminality was a recurring feature of these recruited activists.

Under the Chirac Administration, bomb attacks were eventually carried out on French soil. The results of the police investigations tended to show that the various attacks were planned by GIA leaders exiled abroad who relied on several structures implanted in France in order to carry out the operations. It is thus not surprising that, even though until Summer 1995 none of the police raids indicated that the objective of Islamist networks had shifted from organizing support to the armed struggle in Algeria to carrying out terrorist attacks in France, the Balladur government was worried about this very possibility.

... to opposing the FIS

As underlined in the introduction to this section, it is not certain that in opposing a FIS takeover the French government was motivated by the vision that, once in power, the FIS might resort to state-sponsored terrorism against France, thus turning Algeria into a threatening 'terrorist state'. Actually, despite a strong concern about 'Islamic terrorism', the idea that a FIS regime might turn to terrorism as a means to bring pressure to bear on its external environment never transpired in public interviews nor in my own discussions with members of the political establishment or of the Administration. Of course, this silence does not mean that such a possibility never crossed policy-makers' minds. It rather shows that the hypothesis, while perhaps in the background, was not given prime importance. This may be explained by the fact that, as of the Summer of 1993, Paris believed that if the FIS came to office this would be by compromise, not by toppling the regime.

Nevertheless, French opposition to a FIS takeover and to a compromise with the FIS can be explained by the fact that the FIS' ambiguous relationship with violence added to the French political establishment's negative perceptions of this religio-political party. As mentioned in chapter two of Part Two,[90] FIS leaders in exile had an equivocal attitude towards the violent course of action adopted by the armed groups. Until the February 1994 FIS declaration which made a distinction between the 'armed struggle' and 'terrorism', not all FIS leaders in exile condemned violence systematically and clearly. Even after this declaration, while some terrorist attacks were strongly condemned, others were condemned but at the same time justified. For instance, reacting to the killing of the five French consulate agents in early August 1994, Kebir condemned the act but added that 'he who sows the wind shall reap the whirlwind'.[91] These justifications were understood in Paris as clear FIS support for violence against France. The reprisal threats of the FIS' military wing reinforced this view. Inasmuch as there were strong concerns about the potential transformation of AIS and GIA support networks into cells undertaking terrorist action, no longer from, but against France, the view that the FIS was backing violent acts against France (even though it was not necessarily involved in them) was certainly a contributing factor to French opposition to the FIS.

Economic relations: limited risks

In general, members of the French political establishment expressed no anxiety about the eventuality of a questioning of the Franco-Algerian economic relationship by a FIS regime. As of Summer 1993, it was thought that only compromise could lead the FIS to power and that, as part of a coalition government, the FIS would not bring Algeria's economic relationship with France under review. As a result, economic concerns cannot explain French opposition to a re-integration of the FIS into the political process. To a certain extent, it was also believed that, even if the FIS seized power by force, it would not fundamentally question economic relations because, Algeria being more dependent on France than France on Algeria, doing so would cause more damage to the Algerian economy than to the French one. In the hypothesis where a FIS revolutionary regime would despise economic realities, a questioning of the economic relationship would not bring about a collapse of the French economy – France having much less important economic interests in Algeria than is usually thought. However, a diversification of trade away from France, a questioning of French investments and perhaps a non-reimbursement of the debt owed to France would have a cost. This would all the more be true if radical Islamist regimes emerged in Morocco or Tunisia and endeavoured to do the same. It may thus be argued that, up to the point it was feared that the FIS might take office through warfare, the impossibility of predicting exactly how a FIS revolutionary regime might behave and the fear of cascading dominoes contributed to the French government's opposition to the FIS. In the face of such a potential risk, it was concluded that the status quo would be better than the FIS.

To demonstrate that economic concerns did not play a crucial role in the French government's opposition to the FIS – or only as a contributing factor – we examine the arguments brought forward by members of the French political establishment for believing that a FIS regime would not question economic relations with France. We then give credence to their viewpoint by proceeding to an analysis of the Franco-Algerian economic relationship. Three aspects of this relationship are reviewed: trade, investments and finance.

No foreseen questioning of the economic relationship

Members of the French political establishment argued that it was unrealistic to think that a FIS regime would resort to an ending of its economic relationship with France. Their argument was based on two main considerations. Firstly, at the very beginning of the 1990s, FIS leaders gave assurances that France's economic interests in Algeria would not suffer from a coming of the FIS to government.[92] Later, spokesmen for the FIS warned that, once in power, the FIS would review international agreements signed since 1992, such as import contracts, oil exploration deals and the IMF agreement.[93] Yet, at the same time, they argued that an Islamist government would be attached to good-neighbourliness and open to foreign co-operation. Anwar Haddam also maintained that 'whether one wants it or not, the French and Algerian people will continue to have relations in the future (...)'.[94] These contradictory statements were part of the FIS' carrot and stick strategy, aimed at bringing the international community to end its support for the Algerian regime. The French political establishment was apparently quite aware of that. It remained convinced that a FIS regime would not implement drastic measures in the realm of its economic relations with France because – and this is the second consideration – Algeria's economy was more dependent on that of France than *vice-versa*.

Trade relations are significantly asymmetric and Algeria needs foreign capital in the form of both foreign direct investments and economic aid. Consequently, whichever way the FIS came to power, it was very unlikely that it would resort to 'punitive' acts which would cause damage to the Algerian economy more than to the French. It was reckoned that the FIS was more likely to take measures in the symbolic field of cultural relations[95] (total Arabisation, removal from the political vocabulary of Western political wording, etc...) since one of its central claims was to replace Western political culture by the indigenous Muslim one in order to organize society, economy and political power.

By examining trade relations, investments and the debt, it appears that, indeed, it would not be in the interest of a FIS regime to question economic relations with France. In addition, the French economy would not be greatly disturbed by such an event.

Table 5: **Algeria's share in France's world imports and exports and France's share in Algeria's world imports and exports, 1960–92 (in %)**

	1960	1970	1980	1990	1992
France					
Imports from Algeria	8.0	3.4	1.3	0.8	0.8
Exports to Algeria	16.0	2.9	2.4	1.3	1.0
Algeria					
Imports from France	83.0	42.0	23.2	23.1	24.2
Exports to France	92.0	53.5	13.4	17.3	18.3

Source: I. Brandell (1981), p. 168 and UN, *International Trade Statistics Yearbook.*

Trade relations

The analysis of trade flows between France and Algeria shows that, in the main, Algeria is more dependent on its exports to France than France on its exports to Algeria. It also shows that, as regards consumption, France was not dependent on Algerian supplies, even in the sensitive case of natural gas. As a result, the Algerian economy would suffer most from a deterioration of trade.

On top of being consistently asymmetrical since Independence (Table 5), the Franco-Algerian trade relationship also shows another striking feature: it had lost much of its importance since 1962, although only relatively. Indeed, although France's share in Algeria's trade activities decreased, it remained significant. With a market share of 24.2% in 1992, France was Algeria's prime supplier before Italy (14.4%) and the USA (11.5%). France lost its rank of prime client to Italy after 1989. But it still bought 18.3% of Algeria's exports in 1992, thus ranking second behind Italy (21.7%) and ahead of the USA (13.9%).[96] In parallel, although Algeria accounted for merely about 1% of France's trade since the latter part of the 1980s, it was France's prime trade partner in the developing world for many years. Today, it remains France's first client in the developing world. It has, however, lost its prime supplier rank since 1992. Morocco took on the title, confirming the long-run trend of redistribution of France's trade within the Maghreb to the benefit of Morocco and Tunisia (see Table 6). French exports to and imports from Algeria must be reviewed in greater details in order to demonstrate that if a FIS regime had attempted to divert its trade flows away from France this would certainly have incurred a cost but not caused great damage to the French economy.

French exports to Algeria

French exports to Algeria, although not negligible, were not particularly important (Table 6). They had been cut by half since the 1986 oil countershock and since Algeria went into financial troubles. The downward trend was reversed in 1993 and particularly in 1994, as a result of France's continued granting of tied commercial credits to Algeria. Yet, mid-1990s levels did not compare with those of the mid-1980s.

Despite its relatively low imports from France, Algeria remained an interesting export market for numerous French service companies, constructors, manufacturers and, increasingly, the agribusiness sector.[97] Small and medium enterprises located in Southern France and for which Algeria is a significant outlet, would be quite seriously hit by a diversion of Algeria's import flows. Nevertheless, and however troublesome it would be, a cut in Algerian imports from France or a diversification of suppliers would not generate a catastrophe for the French economy as a whole.

While a FIS regime could question the place of France as prime supplier, it could not abruptly put an end to some of its imports from France.

Table 6: French trade with the Maghreb, 1980–94 (in French francs, million)

	1980	1985	1990	1991	1992	1993	1994
French imports							
World	570,778	962,730	1,266,789	1,297,042	1,263,964	1,094,831	1,214,600
Maghreb	12,361	30,553	26,136	28,411	26,382	24,739	26,825
In % of World	*2.2*	*3.2*	*2.1*	*2.2*	*2.1*	*2.3*	*2.2*
Algeria	7,431	20,754	10,556	11,996	9,933	7,782	8,285
In % of Maghreb	*60.1*	*67.9*	*40.4*	*42.2*	*37.7*	*31.5*	*30.9*
Morocco	3,252	6,053	10,319	10,848	10,547	10,860	11,862
In % of Maghreb	*26.3*	*19.8*	*39.5*	*38.2*	*40.0*	*43.9*	*44.2*
Tunisia	1,677	3,746	5,260	5,567	5,902	6,097	6,678
In % of Maghreb	*13.6*	*12.3*	*20.1*	*19.6*	*22.3*	*24.6*	*24.9*
French exports							
World	469,694	870,873	1,142,183	1,200,923	1,228,241	1,185,183	1,302,371
Maghreb	20,017	37,431	33,937	31,474	32,112	32,404	35,236
In % of World	*4.3*	*4.3*	*3.0*	*2.6*	*2.6*	*2.7*	*2.7*
Algeria	11,078	21,798	14,770	12,271	11,780	11,901	13,355
In % of Maghreb	*55.4*	*58.2*	*43.5*	*39.0*	*36.7*	*36.7*	*37.9*
Morocco	5,011	9,178	10,655	10,962	11,276	11,393	12,035
In % of Maghreb	*25.0*	*24.5*	*31.4*	*34.8*	*35.1*	*35.2*	*34.2*
Tunisia	3,928	6,455	8,512	8,242	9,056	9,110	9,846
In % of Maghreb	*19.6*	*17.3*	*25.1*	*26.2*	*28.2*	*28.1*	*27.9*

Source: Ministère du Budget, *Statistiques du commerce extérieur de la France.* Percentages: my calculations.

This was the case, notably, for spare parts for 'ready for use' imports or French vehicles. In addition, by challenging France's prime supplier status, Algeria would come in for retaliation: France could decide to buy less. Indeed, as shown below, France was not dependent on its imports from Algeria for its consumption – natural gas being a sensitive case but not one of complete dependence.

French imports from Algeria

France imports almost exclusively hydrocarbons. In 1994, hydrocarbons accounted for 96.1% of French imports from Algeria. France primarily buys natural gas (56.3% of French imports of Algerian hydrocarbons). Refined petroleum products come second (26.2%) and oil last (17.5%).[98] Hydrocarbon exports remain central to the Algerian economy providing 95% of foreign exchange revenues, with gas exports accounting for about a third, and crude oil and refined products for less than a quarter each (the balance being made of condensates and liquefied petroleum gas exports).[99]

The oil trade was thus at the heart of the Franco-Algerian relationship in the 1960s. The 1971 nationalisation of the French oil companies operating in Algeria led to a clear disengagement from the Algerian market throughout the 1970s. In the 1980s and 1990s, oil imports from Algeria continued to decrease (see Table 7). Two reasons for this decrease can be put forward. One is related to France's energy policy which sought to substitute oil by nuclear energy, leading to reduced world oil imports. The other is directly related to Algeria whose potential as a crude oil exporter is limited.[100] Algeria has relatively limited reserves of oil (9.2 billion barrels).[101] As domestic consumption of oil rose, oil exports represented a declining share of output.[102] At the beginning of the 21st century, Algeria was expected to use most of its oil for domestic purposes.[103]

French imports of Algerian crude oil concern very small quantities. In 1993, they amounted to 746,000 metric tons (Table 7), which was less than France's domestic production.[104] Imports of Algerian crude oil represented a low share of France's world crude oil imports: 1% in 1993, placing Algeria as fourteenth supplier (Table 7). France imported more than 95% of its total supply of crude oil.[105] Algerian crude oil thus provided a low share of French oil consumption. France was, thus, not dependent on Algeria for its supplies of crude oil.

As regards Algeria, an end to its crude oil exports to France might not have had dramatic consequences on its foreign exchange receipts considering the small volume involved. Algeria could easily find alternative clients on the generalised spot market. Yet, inasmuch as an end to exports to France would not provoke problems for the French economy, one does not see why an Algerian government would take the trouble of shifting its crude oil exports away from France.

Refined petroleum products

Just as for oil, France was not dependent on its Algerian supplies of refined petroleum products. In the 1970s, French imports of Algerian refined products were low both because of Algeria's low offer and because France had its own refining industry. The late 1970s deregulation, and notably the waiving of the obligation for French oil companies to refine 50 % of their oil in France, led to increased imports throughout the world. In 1980, French world imports of refined products were twice as high as in 1970.[106] In 1993 they were about double their 1980 level, covering a quarter of French consumption (see Tables 8 and 9).

Algeria did not wholly benefit from this growth. After significantly increasing in the early 1980s, French imports of Algerian refined products stabilised thereafter, varying between 1.2 millions of metric tons (Mmt) and 2.4 Mmt. As France's world imports grew faster than Algerian supplies, Algeria lost its rank of second supplier since 1983 (with the exception of 1992), and was relegated to fourth, fifth or even sixth place. Since 1986 (except for 1992), France's imports from Algeria accounted for less than 7% of its world refined products imports. After 1980, they never covered more than 3% of France's consumption of refined products. With imports accounting for 15.3% of Algeria's exports of refined products in 1993, France was Algeria's fourth client after the USA (25.8%), the Netherlands (18.2%) and Italy (15.7%).[107] By ceasing its exports to France, Algeria would thus hurt itself more than it could hurt France.

Natural gas

France imported natural gas (only in a liquefied form) from Algeria from the 1960s. Algeria was its first foreign supplier. As other providers, it has benefited from the growth in French demand which resulted from a rising consumption and a low domestic output.[108] In the 1990s, France's imports of Algerian liquefied natural gas (LNG) were regulated by four contracts (Table 10) which provided for imports amounting to 10.15 billions of cubic metres (Bcm) per year at least until 2002.

Table 7: French crude oil imports by selected countries of origin, 1980–93 (in 1000 metric tons)

	1980	1985	1990	1991	1992	1993
World	109,495	67,043	69,566	72,964	71,003	75,370
Algeria	4,218	1,994	1,850	2,612	1,735	746
In % of world	*3.9*	*3.0*	*2.6*	*3.6*	*2.4*	*1.0*
Rank	*6*	*13*	*14*	*9*	*10*	*14*
Saudi Arabia	38,277	5,232	14,878	20,469	20,145	22,068
In % of world	*35.0*	*7.8*	*21.4*	*28.1*	*28.4*	*29.3*
Iran	1,212	4,076	8,949	8,355	7,263	11,879
In % of world	*1.1*	*6.1*	*12.9*	*11.5*	*10.2*	*15.8*
Norway	1,793	4,171	5,755	5,724	6,349	8,165
In % of world	*1.6*	*6.2*	*8.3*	*7.8*	*8.9*	*10.8*
(Former) USSR	6,296	2,970	4,997	1,893	5,721	6,136
In % of world	*5.8*	*4.4*	*7.2*	*2.6*	*8.1*	*8.1*
UK	2,694	14,897	5,755	5,724	6,349	8,165
In % of world	*2.5*	*22.2*	*6.7*	*6.2*	*5.6*	*8.0*
Nigeria	11,065	8,083	3,111	4,210	4,491	5,586
In % of world	*10.1*	*12.1*	*4.5*	*5.8*	*6.3*	*7.4*

Source: IEA, *Annual Oil and Natural Gas Statistics* and IEA, *Oil and Gas Information*. Calculated percentages.

Table 8: **French imports of petroleum refined products by selected countries of origin, 1980–93 (in 1,000 metric tons)**

	1980	1985	1990	1991	1992	1993
World	12,678	16,703	24,466	26,826	24,865	21,888
Algeria	382	1,391	1,206	1,654	2,320	1,415
In % of world	*3.0*	*8.3*	*4.9*	*6.2*	*9.3*	*6.5*
Rank		4	9	6	2	5
UK		1,917	2,797	4,919	4,356	4,444
In % of world		*11.5*	*11.4*	*18.3*	*17.5*	*20.3*
Germany		884	1,224	1,076	1,523	2,646
In % of world		*5.3*	*5.0*	*4.0*	*7.0*	*12.1*
Belgium		872	1,626	2,087	2,138	2,467
In % of world		*5.2*	*6.7*	*7.8*	*8.6*	*11.3*
Netherlands		1,910	2,365	2,688	1,887	1,466
In % of world		*11.4*	*9.7*	*10.0*	*7.6*	*6.7*

Source: IEA, *Annual Oil and Gas Statistics* and IEA, *Oil and Gas Information.* Calculated percentages.

Table 9: **France's dependence on world and Algerian supplies of refined products, 1980–93 (in 1,000 metric tons)**

	1980	1985	1990	1991	1992	1993
Consumption	106,268	81,360	83,356	88,579	88,405	87,269
Dependence on World Imports (%)	11.9	20.5	29.3	30.3	28.1	25.1
Dependence on imports from Algeria (%)	0.4	1.7	1.4	1.9	2.6	1.6

Source: IEA, *Oil and Gas Information* and my calculations from Table 8.

Although French LNG imports from Algeria were, in effect, lower than the contracted volumes (Table 11), they were still significant in relation to both France's world imports and its consumption of natural gas. From 1982, imports of Algerian gas accounted for about 30% of France's total imports, placing Algeria as prime or second supplier after the Netherlands or Russia. Thereafter, they also covered between a quarter and a third of French consumption (Table 12). At first sight, this high rate suggests a certain dependence on Algeria's supplies because of the rigidities inherent in natural gas trade.

Table 10:   Gaz de France's LNG contracts with Sonatrach

Contract	Yearly volume, Bcm	Validity period	Renewal	Ending date	Total yearly volume, Bcm
1	0.50	1962– 1987	December 1991	2002	0.50
2	3.50	1971– 1987	December 1991	2013	4.00
3	5.15	1982– 2002	December 1991	2013	9.15
4	1.00	1991– 2002	-	2002	10.15

Source: GDF (1990) and *Le Monde*, 27 December 1991.

Despite an emerging spot market, natural gas trade is mostly regulated by long-term bilateral contracts (10 to 25 years) which allow both parties to plan the particularly heavy investments required to explore, produce, process, transport and store natural gas and to wait until they are paid off. If suppliers can always be switched, this is an experience that any purchaser would like to avoid. New supplies, indeed, cannot be obtained at short notice. Because of the difficulties in storing gas and because of the long-term contracts tying suppliers to their clients, producers do not hold huge reserves of gas immediately available for sale. In addition, diverting import flows may involve new investments in infrastructures. While incurring a loss over former investments, this implies new costs and a time lag. For the gas producer, diverting its export flows may also prove difficult: new clients must be found and supplying them may require new investments.

Table 11: French natural gas imports by selected countries of origin, 1980–93 (in million cubic meters)

	1980	1985	1990	1991	1992	1993
World	20,700	25,700	28,197	30,038	31,640	29,500
Algeria	2,159	8,070	8,712	8,620	8,796	8,400
In % of World	*16.9*	*26.6*	*30.9*	*28.7*	*27.8*	*28.5*
Rank	*4*	*2*	*2*	*2*	*2*	*2*
(former) USSR	3,492	6,830	9,891	10,639	11,268	10,757
In % of World	*16.9*	*26.6*	*35.1*	*35.4*	*35.6*	*36.5*
Netherlands	11,686	8,250	4,111	5,003	5,506	4,520
In % of World	*56.6*	*32.1*	*14.6*	*16.7*	*17.4*	*15.3*
Norway	2,306	2,510	5,483	5,776	6,070	5,823
In % of World	*11.1*	*9.8*	*19.4*	*19.2*	*19.2*	*19.7*

Source: IEA, *Annual Oil and Gas Statistics* and IEA, *Oil and Gas Information.* Calculated percentages.

Table 12: **France's dependence on world and Algerian natural gas supplies, 1980–93 (in terajoules)**

	1980	1985	1990	1991	1992	1993
Consumption	971,505	1,132,529	1,177,018	1,313,290	1,305,620	1,347,674
World imports	758,456	963,215	1,174,554	1,217,725	1,281,068	1,200,654
Imports from Algeria	85,436	317,611	375,836	371,779	379,361	364,957
Dependence on World Imports (%)	78.1	85.0	97.5	92.7	98.1	89.1
Dependence on imports from Algeria (%)	8.8	28.0	31.9	28.3	29.1	27.1

Source: Oil and Gas Information. When necessary, teracalories were converted into terajoules according to the following rate: 1Tcal = 4.1868 Tj. Calculated percentages.

Table 13: Structure by type of credits of Algeria's medium and long-term debt, 1987–92 (in US$ million)

	1987	1988	1989	1990	1991	1992
Multilateral credits	921	1,169	2,064	2,233	3,187	3,124
As % of total debt	*3.8*	*4.8*	*8.3*	*8.4*	*12.1*	*12.4*
Bond issues	995	1,293	1,435	1,465	1,454	1,281
As % of total debt	*4.0*	*5.3*	*5.7*	*5.6*	*5.6*	*5.1*
Bilateral credits	12,271	12,033	12,283	14,743	14,776	13,543
As % of total debt	50.0	49.7	49.2	56.0	56.3	53.7
Direct Government credits	*4,900*	*5,214*	*5,076*	*4,656*	*4,981*	*5,205*
As % of total debt	20.0	21.5	20.3	17.7	19.0	20.6
Guaranteed buyer credits	*7,371*	*6,819*	*7,207*	*10,087*	*9,795*	*8,338*
As % of total debt	30.0	28.2	28.9	38.3	37.3	33.1
Financial credits	6,670	6,409	5,649	5,265	4,866	5,026
As % of total debt	27.2	26.5	22.6	20.0	18.5	19.9
Syndicated credits and leases	*6,613*	*6,304*	*5,494*	*5,024*	*4,680*	*3,575*
Down-payments financing	*57*	*105*	*155*	*241*	*186*	*203*
Bank reprofiling operations	*0*	*0*	*0*	*0*	*0*	*1,248*
Non-guaranteed commercial credits	3,668	3,309	3,541	2,640	1,975	2,242
As % of total debt	15.0	13.7	14.2	10.0	7.5	8.9
Supplier credits	*2,568*	*1,924*	*1,915*	*1,502*	*1,340*	*1,768*
Other credits	*1,100*	*1,385*	*1,626*	*1,138*	*635*	*474*
Total medium and long-term debt	24,525	24,213	24,972	26,346	26,258	25,216

Source: Maison Lazard et Compagnie et. al. (1993), pp. 70-1 and Addendum, pp.7-8.

From the early 1990s, the French gas utility's concerns over the security of foreign natural gas supplies grew steadily because 60% of its imports came from two countries – Russia and Algeria – both of which represented a risk, although of a different nature. From the creation of the Commonwealth of Independent States in 1991, the issue of the security of

Russian supplies was no longer related to the context of the Cold War, but linked to the fact that gas pipelines crossed several states before reaching Western Europe. The risk was that gas supplies to Western Europe might be disturbed by, or used as, a pressure tool in a quarrel between two or more neighbouring states. Insofar as Algeria was concerned, the issue of the security of supplies was wholly different since imported LNG arrived by tankers directly to French gas terminals. Actually, the late 1950s decision to import gas in a liquefied, rather than in a gasified, form was taken both for technical and security reasons.[109] The option of a submarine pipeline linking France to Algeria was excluded because of the distance and depth of the Mediterranean Sea. Two other possible routes had, however, been identified: either a pipeline crossing Tunisia to Sicily via the Tunis Canal, and then crossing Italy, or a pipeline crossing Morocco and linked to Spain via the Straits of Gilbratar. Both these options were waived not only because of the difficulties in crossing the Alps or the Pyrenees, but also because, at the time, Morocco and Tunisia supported Algeria in its War of Liberation.[110]

In the 1990s, the potential risks concerning the security of Algerian supplies derived primarily from the uncertainties as to the future political evolution of the country. However, the context of guerrilla warfare did not, apparently, affect the regularity of LNG supplies. France's imports of Algerian natural gas decreased by 10% in 1994, but this was an expected development resulting from the revamping of the Skikda liquefaction facility[111] – a modernising operation in which GDF took part.[112] The major factors linked to the security situation that could have led to irregular supplies did not occur. When the armed rebellion started in the 1990s, it was thought that Islamist armed groups might resort to sabotage operations against hydrocarbon infrastructures in order to strike at the regime's export earnings. However, the available information indicates that very few sabotage operations were carried out from 1992. In October 1994, the GIA claimed responsibility for the destruction by fire of some equipment at an oil-drilling base.[113] A year later, it was reported that a gas pipeline had been sabotaged, severing supplies to Tizi-Ouzou.[114] The infrequency of events on this front means either that these infrastructures were so well protected that they were beyond reach or that their sabotage was not an essential part of the Islamist armed groups' strategy. The regularity of LNG supplies could also have been affected by strikes. Algerian oil and gas workers went on strike several times, but not long enough to unsettle export flows.[115] Whereas Algerian workers protested against their government's domestic economic policy, their French counterparts, when striking, did so in relation to the lack of security in Algeria. Thus, after the Airbus hijack in December 1994, the crew of one of GDF's gas tankers refused to take the gas supply in Skikda, arguing that the French government ought to increase protection in Algerian waters and harbours.[116] The strike in itself was not long enough to disturb trade.

From the angle of political changes in Algeria, the hypothesis of a complete cut of Algerian LNG supplies to France, in the case of a FIS take-over, was rightly judged to be improbable. In the mid-1990s, France imported 24.2% of Algeria's natural gas exports and was the country's second client after Italy (37.2%).[117] Whether or not the Islamists would have held the reins of power on their own or with others, they quite certainly would neither have sacrificed important export revenues, nor taken the risk of having to switch clients, just to annoy the French. They could, on the other hand, have delivered the supplies irregularly as a means of retaliation against France's specific acts showing hostility to the new regime. If this had happened, the consequences for France would still have been less important than might at first be feared because of the existence of security stocks. According to GDF's official data, storage capacities amounted to 9.6 Bcm[118] and, thus, wholly covered France's annual imports from Algeria. In the event of frequent and significant disturbances or even in the unlikely event of a complete cut in deliveries, GDF would have had at least a year to find another supplier. Despite difficult relations with Libya, the Quai d'Orsay considered it as a potential alternative supplier.[119] This is probably best explained by the fact that Libya exports LNG. Consequently, imports from Libya would neither cause a waste of invested capital nor would it require new investments in infrastructures.

The analysis of trade flow between France and Algeria shows that, in the main, Algeria was more dependent on its exports to France than France on its exports to Algeria. It also shows that, as regards its consumption, France was not dependent on Algerian supplies. As a consequence, the Algerian economy stood to suffer most from a deterioration of trade. The same conclusion could be reached if one was to think of Morocco and Tunisia as falling dominoes. For the same asymmetrical pattern characterised their trade relationships with France.[120] In addition, compared to Algeria, they had the disadvantage of exporting products like clothing, vegetables and manufactured goods (notably electrical appliances) which are easily replaced in world markets.[121]

French direct investment

Just as for trade, the Maghreb was a marginal partner in France's direct investment activities. In 1992, France's direct investment stock in the Maghreb merely amounted to FF3.1 billion (about $585 million). This accounted for

0.4% of France's world stock. Unlike trade, however, French direct investments in the developing world are not mostly channelled to the Maghreb. Indeed, France's direct investment stock in the Maghreb accounted for just 5% of its stock in the non-OECD countries in 1992. Within the Maghreb, France's foreign direct investments are mainly located in Morocco (stock of FF2.3 billion in 1992) and only marginally in Tunisia (FF648 million) and Algeria (FF196 million).[122] In terms of flows, France's direct investments to the Maghreb were multiplied by four between 1990 and 1993, mostly as a result of greater investments to Morocco. Yet, totalling FF791 million ($139 million) in 1993, they accounted for just 1% of France's world outflows.[123]

From the Maghrebi countries' viewpoint, foreign direct investment (FDI) is being actively sought as a means to save foreign exchange and create employment. Encouragement to FDI is also required by the IBRD's restructuring programmes in force in each of the Maghrebi states. Despite the adoption of flexible investment codes, FDI, which was the most dynamic in Morocco and Tunisia, was not as high as expected. In these two countries, advantageous legislation did not produce its effects before the early 1990s.[124] Two main factors played against Morocco and Tunisia. First, cheap labour, which is their main comparative advantage, was in cutthroat competition on the world labour market. This made it harder for them to attract production delocalisation. Second, financially solvent demand was low as a result of the austerity economic policies carried out under the guidance of the Bretton Woods institutions. As a consequence, import substitution FDI was also constrained.[125] In Morocco, France's contribution as a foreign investor grew throughout the 1980s and 1990s. In 1993, French direct investment ($114.7 million) accounted for 22% of world FDI to Morocco. By contrast, French investors did not contribute to the growth of FDI in Tunisia. In 1993, with $14.4 million of investment, they accounted for a mere 6% of Tunisia's total inflows.[126]

Algeria is quite a special case since it was closed to FDI throughout the 1970s as a result of extensive state monopolies and unfavourable legislation. Throughout the 1980s, however, Algeria progressively opened its economy to FDI and, in October 1993, an advantageous new investment code was adopted. In accordance with the 1994 structural adjustment programme, privatisation was opened to foreign investors.[127] Nevertheless, Algeria's efforts to attract FDI were not crowned with much success. This essentially resulted from the dangerous security context. Guerrilla warfare and the killing of foreigners made operating in Algeria a difficult task, indeed. Besides this unfavourable security context, FDI was constrained by three other factors: governmental instability, lack of guarantees for investment protection and vested interests. Since the April 1990 money and credit law which definitively opened Algeria to FDI, governmental turnover was high. Foreign investors adopted a wait-and-see attitude in the face of government instability because changes in fiscal, pricing or foreign exchange regulations might significantly alter the profitability of their investment projects. The abrogation of some provisions of the money and credit law under Abdesselam's premiership is a case in point. FDI was also hampered by the fact that Algeria did not move to reassure investors: it signed the New York Convention on international arbitration only in April 1993 and did not ratify international conventions on the protection of foreign investments in the early 1990s.[128] As previously mentioned, it was not until 1993 that a bilateral accord for the protection of investments was signed with France. Last but not least, opening the economy to FDI threatened domestic vested interests in production and distribution as well as commissions pocketed on import contracts. FDI projects (concerning tyres, pharmaceuticals or vehicles, for instance, in the case of France) were never carried through because of these problems.[129] French direct investment to Algeria involved very low amounts but showed a significant growth in the early 1990s. They amounted to $400,000 in 1990, $4.8 million in 1991, $9.4 million in 1992 and $9.6 million in 1993.[130] In 1991, French direct investment to Algeria accounted for 40% of total FDI inflows in Algeria ($12 million). Considering the growth of French outflows to Algeria, on the one hand, and Algeria's unattractive environment for FDI, on the other, France may well have remained an important contributor.

As a concluding note, it may be underlined that, in the hypothesis of inimical Islamist regimes taking power in the Central Maghreb, these regimes, like the current ones, could not spare foreign capital in the form of foreign direct investment. If they were to discriminate specifically against French enterprises, this would not generate a profound alteration of France's FDI strategy. In addition, if French subsidiaries operating in the Maghreb were forbidden to continue their activities there, this would not cause much damage to the French economy as a whole.

Financial relations

If Algeria was marginal to France's world trade and foreign direct investment activities, what about the financial links between the two countries? As seen in Parts One and Two, France's financial transfers to Algeria (together with its drumming up of support from the Bretton Woods institutions and the EU) were a central element in its political backing of the Algerian regime. Through the financial protocol established in 1989, the French state also became an active agent in the financial relationship with Algeria. Algeria's official debt was owed in great part to the French state and there may have been concern in French policy-making circles that a revolutionary FIS regime would decide not to repay it.

Before addressing this issue, it must be underlined that, from published data, it is impossible to know exactly how much was transferred annually to Algeria from 1992. It is also impossible to know exactly what amounts were due to France and how much of Algeria's total debt was accounted for by Algeria's debt to France. The impossibility of conducting a personal audit is due to the French Central Bank's practice of retaining information on short-term financial operations. This practice made it impossible for the public to know exactly how much was lent by France to foreign governments each year and exactly how much was owed by these foreign governments. One is, therefore, forced to rely on what the French government was willing to say.

Regarding Algeria, the Quai d'Orsay stated that Algeria's total short to long-term debt due to France amounted to FF35 billion (about $7 billion),[131] which implies that France held about a quarter of Algeria's total debt. The debt due to France was made up of official and private debts. The official debt comprised debts due to the French state and debts due to the Coface. According to the Quai d'Orsay, the official debt amounted to FF31 billion (i.e. about 46% of Algeria's total official debt).[132] The private debt comprised non-guaranteed debts to the French banking and non-banking sectors. It amounted to FF4 billion (i.e. about 11% of Algeria's private debt).

Relying on the French government's data, it appears that the debt due to France was significant. The agent most involved in the financial relationship was the French state, although this situation arose only indirectly *via* its engagement to finance the deficit of the Coface if guaranteed credits were not returned. It is possible that in opposing a FIS takeover, the French government was motivated by the fear that a revolutionary FIS government might not recognize the previous regime's debt and thus might decide not to repay it. Nevertheless, it could not be disregarded in Paris that, by adopting such a course of action, a FIS regime would put itself in a very difficult situation as its access to international finance would most probably be seriously constrained. Again, in face of the unlikelihood of the hypothesis, one is tempted to say that if concerns about the debt played a role at all in the French government's opposition to the FIS this would have had to result from a preference for minimising risks and not from an objective threat. In addition, the moment it was realised that a FIS in government would necessarily be a FIS in a coalition government, there were no grounds to believe that, specifically for political reasons, Algeria's debt to France might not be honoured.

On the whole it thus seems that economic issues were not at the heart of French opposition to a FIS take-over or to its integration in the political process in Algeria. Indeed, it was thought that even if the FIS took power violently it would not fundamentally question its economic relationship with France for the simple reason that Algeria is structurally more dependent on French goods, services and capital than *vice-versa*. Of course, if taken in a revolutionary whirl, a FIS regime did review economic links with France, this would have had a cost and this cost would have been even greater if the Moroccan and Tunisian dominoes fell. In this sense, up to the point when it was no longer feared that the FIS might overthrow the Algerian regime, economic concerns may have contributed to French opposition to the FIS merely because the French government wished to avoid risks. But after Summer 1993, when it was assumed that the FIS could come into office only *via* a compromise, there were no reasons to believe that the economic relationship would come under review – although there may today be concerns that Algeria will not be able to pay back its debt because of economic problems, not political ones.

In justifying its opposition to conciliation with the FIS, the French political establishment not only put forward immigration concerns and fears about the domino effect, but also ideological motives. Particularly under the Right, the religio-political ideology conveyed by the FIS was described as an ideological ill that needed to be combatted. The socialists did not insist on ideological views in their public statements. This must be understood in terms of the policy they sought to promote in Algeria until January 1993. In the main, however, the socialists also saw the FIS' political project as regressive although some recognized that secular authoritarianism was not a panacea. The next chapter examines this dimension of French hostility to the FIS.

Notes

1. See Juppé's press conference in Washington, 12 May 1994 in MAE (May–June 1994), p. 90. The domino theory was also mentioned by Jean Audibert (interview, 7 June 1995) and Christophe Bigot (interview, 21 April 1994).
2. Juppé's declarations dealing with falling dominoes were, indeed, of the following type: '(...) [Algeria] 'matters to us'. I think there is no need to explain why: history, geographic proximity and the importance for France to have in Algeria a stable partner because instability in Algeria, the destabilisation of the Maghreb, I shall not follow on, we can see the consequences' (in MAE (January–February 1994), p. 247).
3. In late August 1994, Algeria closed its land, air, and maritime borders with

Morocco as a protest against Morocco's decision to reintroduce entry visas for Algerians. Such a measure followed the murder of two Spanish tourists in a Marrakech hotel and the arrest of several persons having, in most of the cases, the dual French and Algerian nationality (see *Le Monde*, 31 August 1994 and 24 September 1994). Several cases of arms trafficking from Morocco to the Algerian Islamist armed groups have increased the tension between the two states which periodically accuse each other of intended destabilisation.

4. Although the *Asmidal* chemical plant in Annaba is reported to have stopped its research activities in Summer 1992 under American pressure (A. Charef (1994), p. 71), it is estimated that Algeria has the industrial infrastructure and basic technology to acquire a chemical offensive capacity (R. Aliboni (1993), p. 49). Algeria also bought two small nuclear reactors. The *Nour* reactor (low power of 1 megawatt) was built in co-operation with Argentina. In operation since 1989, it is regularly visited by the IAEA. The *Es Salam* reactor (15 megawatts), constructed with the help of China, was inaugurated on December 21, 1993 at Birine. An IAEA visit occurred in 1991 after American satellite images revealed the construction of this nuclear plant. Western experts estimate that the Algerian *Es Salam* reactor could produce plutonium for military use (*Le Monde*, 23 December 1993). Up to the present day, however, the French authorities have considered nuclear developments in Algeria as an issue of secondary importance compared to the more urgent problems of underdevelopment and political instability (Interviews with Jean Audibert, 7 June 1995 and Christophe Bigot, 21 April 1994).

5. Interview in *Réalités*, 30 June 1994 in MAE (May–June 1994), p. 360.

6. See Commissariat Général du Plan (1993), pp. 90-1.

7. Christophe Bigot, interview, 21 April 1994.

8. The AMU (*Union du Maghreb Arabe*) was founded on 17 February 1989 between Algeria, Libya, Mauritania, Morocco and Tunisia. Its formal aim was political and economic integration. From its creation, however, the AMU made little progress towards these goals. For details, see G. Joffé (1993b), pp. 203-12 and C. Spencer (1993), pp. 46-8. See as well J. Damis (1993) for details on the AMU and the resolution of regional disputes in North Africa.

9. For details on these two initiatives see e.g. T. Niblock (1993), pp. 251-5; M. Ortega (1993), pp. 75-6 and M. Bonnefous (1992), pp. 79-85.

10. In MAE (May–June 1992), p. 194.

11. Two meetings occurred in the mid 1990s. The first was held in Alexandria, on July 3–4, 1994 (*Europe Daily Bulletin* (6266), July 4–5, 1994). The other took place in Sainte-Maxime (France) on April 8–9, 1995 (*Le Monde*, 11 April 1995). The following states participated in the Mediterranean Forum: Algeria, Egypt, France, Italy, Greece, Malta, Morocco, Portugal, Spain, Tunisia, and Turkey.

12. *Europe Daily Bulletin* (6257), 23 June 1994.

13. D. Engelis (1994).

14. G. Joffé (1994b).

15. D. Engelis (1994).

16. Morocco did not participate in this Tunis meeting, arguing that its subject was of

no interest to Morocco (*Le Monde*, 24 January 1995).

17. Press communiqué of Juppé's address to the Senate, 15 September 1994 in MAE (September–October 1994), p. 102. The point that a political settlement with the FIS would not solve the problem of potential immigration was also raised by Christophe Bigot, interview on 21 April 1994.

18. See the interviews of Juppé and Pasqua, respectively in *Le Point* (1126), 16 April 1994 and *Le Figaro*, 18 April 1994.

19. See his interview in *Le Point* (1126), 16 April 1994 and in *Jeune Afrique* in MAE (May–June 1994), pp. 314-5.

20. See his speeches to parliament in MAE (September–October 1994), p. 207 and (November–December 1994), p. 16.

21. By arguing that a precise evaluation of the Algerian migratory risk was still needed, high civil servants suggested that the French government did not know exactly what to expect (see Notes de la fondation Saint-Simon (1995), p. 25).

22. Interview with *Le Figaro*, 18 April 1994. Juppé said the same thing in his interview with *Le Point* (1126), 16 April 1994. The number of persons having dual citizenship and living in Algeria is evaluated between 25,000 and 50,000 (*Le Monde*, 5 August 1994).

23. Interview with Christophe Bigot, 21 April 1994. In Autumn 1994, *MEI* reported that senior government representatives (*préfets*) had been asked to draw up a list of sites in which refugees could be installed and that the Red Cross contemplated using the Albertville Winter Olympic facilities (*MEI* (485), 7 October 1994).

24. In *L'Heure de vérité*, France 2, 29 January 1995.

25. Quoted in *Libération*, 29 June 1994.

26. Respectively, Christophe Bigot (interview, 21 April 1994) and Alain Juppé (in *Le Point* (1126), 16 April 1994).

27. *Le Monde*, 13 October 1994.

28. Maghrebis and their French-born children amount to about 3 million persons. According to the 1990 census, the number of Maghrebi nationals amounted to approximately 1.5 million (620,000 Algerians, 585,000 Moroccans and 208,000 Tunisians). Accounting for 17.2% of the total foreign population in France, Algerians were the second largest community after the Portuguese (17.9%). Moroccans (16.2%) were the third largest foreign community (A. Lebon (1992), p. 92 and my calculations). Children of Maghrebi nationals account for an estimated 1.5 million people. The Algerian community is the most important and counts about 1.5 million people. It is made of three main groups of about half a million each: 1) Algerian nationals, 2) the *Harkis* and their children (the *Harkis* are Algerians who fought on the French side during the War of Liberation and who expatriated to France at Independence) and 3) the generation of *Beurs* (French children of Maghrebi nationals) (A. Hargreaves, 1994).

29. Because of cheap housing in the suburbs, immigrants and their children are mainly located there. Throughout the 1980s and increasingly in the 1990s, the 'suburb issue' has become a major social problem in France as riots, often sparked by bad relations with the police and, eventually, by the death of a young *beur*, became more and more

frequent. Stone throwing against police forces was readily identified as a new form of *intifada* in the French suburbs. For details on the 'suburb issue' see e.g. A. Jazouli (1992).

30. J. Cesari (1994b), p. 159.

31. See section on the FIS and the Muslim community in France, below.

32. See e.g. C. Withol de Wenden (1992a) and (1992b) on the problem of collective images on Maghrebi immigrants and their French-born children and (1991) on the issue of the Beurs and the Gulf War. See also C. Jelen (1991) on the issue of the economic threat and, more generally, on the assimilation of *Beurs*. For references on the issue of religion, see *infra*.

33. In the first round of the 1995 presidential election, the FN secured 15% of the vote (*Le Monde*, 28 April 1995), which was in line with previous scores varying between 10% and 15%. In addition, in the 1995 local elections the FN was in the run for the second round in over 150 towns. FN mayors won the towns of Marignane (37.3% of the vote), Orange (36%) and Toulon (37%). The FN realised this score in many other towns (*Le Monde*, 20 June 1995).

34. Anti-Arab/Muslim sentiment is reflected in the results of an opinion poll led by the National Consultative Commission on Human Rights (1994 Report): 65% of those polled admitted to be harbouring some element of racist prejudice; 62% judged there were too many Arabs in France and 59% too many Muslims (*Le Monde*, 22 mars 1995).

35. Fred Halliday uses the concept of 'anti-Muslimism' to depict Western hostility to the Islamic component of Muslims' identity. He makes a distinction between: 1) 'strategic anti-Muslimism' which is articulated around strategic issues (nuclear power, oil, terrorism, etc.) and directed against states and 2) 'populist anti-Muslimism' which is directed against Muslim immigrants in the West and which is one component of xenophobia and racism (F. Halliday (1993)).

36. See section on restricting entries, below.

37. *Libération*, 30 June 1994.

38. Sahraoui was shot point-blank on 11 July1995. The inquiries of the French police suggest that he was killed by one of the GIA support networks involved in the various terrorist attacks undertaken in France in the Summer and Autumn of 1995. Sahraoui was a FIS founding-member. As a *salafiyyist*, he was marginalised after the FIS Batna Congress in July 1991 and left for France where he obtained the position of *imam* of the *Khaled-ibn-Walid* mosque thanks to the World Islamic League (Saudi obedience). Sahraoui was an interlocutor of the French authorities: he called for the liberation of the three French consulate agents held hostage in Algeria in late September 1993 as well as for an end to the killing of foreigners in Algeria (*Le Monde*, 5 November 1993). In August 1994, following the internment of suspected Islamist activists in Folembray which triggered the AIS's retaliation threat against France, Sahraoui claimed that the AIS '[was] only opposed to the puppet regime in Algiers and (...) hit only the forces of repression in Algeria'. His declaration implied that the French territory was not a target for terrorist attacks as it was then feared (see *Le Monde*, 11 August 1994). In addition, Sahraoui was opposed to the undertaking of illegal

activities by Algerian Islamists on French soil which, in his view, had to be kept as a safe haven for fleeing Islamists (see H. Terrel (1994), p. 362).

39. *Le Monde*, 24 December 1994.

40. A. Lebon (1994), p. 26.

41. *Le Monde*, 23–24 April 1995.

42. Only 1% of the Algerian asylum-seekers are Islamists (*Le Monde*, 6 December 1994). This does not imply, however, that only 1% of the persons who came to France as a result of the slaying in Algeria are Islamists.

43. *Le Monde*, 6 December 1994 and 30 March 1995.

44. *Le Monde*, 3 February 1995.

45. *Le Monde*, 24 December 1994.

46. *Le Monde*, 22 October 1994. However, Algeria is reported not to respect this secret agreement (*Le Monde*, 24 August 1995).

47. As a result of the 1978 Information and Freedom Law which prohibits the listing of religious denomination, there are no official data on the number of Muslims in France. Estimates vary between 3 and 4 million people. Maghrebis and their children, by far the most numerous, account for about 3 million. Others come primarily from Black Africa. Islam is France's second religion after Catholicism. See J. Cesari (1994b), pp. 21-22 and Haut conseil à l'intégration (1992), p. 40.

48. *Le Monde*, 7 January 1992.

49. As late as Winter 1992/93, Sadi's *Plate-forme pour l'Algérie républicaine. Réinventer novembre* (dated 11 December 1992) was still displayed with dailies in some Parisian newsagents.

50. Les Amis d'Alger Républicain en France, *Bulletin nº 2*.

51. *L'Algérie au cœur* (1994).

52. On the FAF, see N. Beau (1995), pp. 280-7 and G. Kepel (1994b), pp. 291-7. The FAF's twin in Britain is the Algerian Community in Britain (ACB) which controls two other organizations, the Algerian Brothers in Britain and the Algerian Community Association. Their activities revolve around propaganda. Leaflets distributed, for instance, by the Algerian Brothers in Britain at the lecture of Dr. M. Bedayoun (a FIS-member, visiting lecturer in Leeds University) on 'The Revival of Islam in Algeria' (4 November 1993, SOAS, London) are similar to those of the FAF.

53. My conclusion is akin to L. Belaïd's (1995).

54. Advertising statement reproduced in *Algérie Actualité* (1487), 12–18 April 1994.

55. *Algérie Actualité* (1485), 1–7 April 1994.

56. *Le Monde*, 6 December 1994.

57. *Le Monde*, 28 March1995.

58. Size of the sample: 535. See *Le Monde*, 13 October 1994.

59. The exact result of this survey (500 persons polled) were: 'I take part in Islamic fundamentalism' : 5%; 'I approve ...': 9%; 'I am indifferent to ...': 20%; 'I am worried about ...': 37%; 'I am hostile to ...': 26% and 'I have no opinion': 3%. See *Le Nouvel Observateur* (1517), 2–8 December 1993.

60. For details on the role of Islam for primary-migrants and their children see J. Cesari (1994b); P. Balta (1991); A. Hargreaves and T. Stenhouse (1991); G. Kepel

(1991); A. Krieger-Krynicki (1988) and R. Leveau (1988).

61. In the main, religious practice by Muslims in France is low and declining. Only 27% declare themselves 'practicing Muslims' against 37% in 1989. Daily prayer is performed by 31% (41% in 1989) and only 16% follow the Friday prayer. The Ramadan is respected by a majority (60%). Alcohol consumption (39%) is relatively high. The pilgrimage to Mecca was done only by 4% but 55% (and 65% among the youngest) intend to go to Mecca at one stage or the other. See *Le Monde*, 13 October 1994.

62. See *Le Monde*, 13 October 1994.

63. J. Cesari (1994/95), pp. 184-6 and G. Kepel (1994b), pp. 210-1.

64. C. Pellegrini (1992), pp. 105-6.

65. This was a concern expressed by Georges Morin, interview, 29 June 1994.

66. The Paris Mosque was founded in 1926 under the sponsorship of the French Third Republic. Stemming from an Algerian association, the Paris Mosque has always had an unclear status. In 1982, the effective control of the Mosque shifted from Paris to Algiers. The Paris Mosque has since then become an 'ancillary embassy' to channel official religious policy to Algerian immigrants. This became overt with the appointment of the Mosque's rector, Tijani Haddam, to the HSC in 1992. Haddam was eventually forced to resign. On the Paris Mosque see e.g. A. Boyer (1992).

67. Until January 1994, the children of Algerian nationals (as opposed to the Moroccan or Tunisian ones) were often entitled to become French citizens automatically. Article 23 of the Nationality Code provided, indeed, that children born in France of parents who were born in Algeria when it was a French department were entitled to French citizenship at birth. On the other hand, children born in France of foreign parents (e.g. Tunisian or Moroccan) were entitled to French nationality at 18 if they had been permanently living in France since they were 13 (article 44). The Nationality Code was amended by parliament in June 1993. One of the major effects of this reform was to suppress the automatic acquisition of French nationality. Article 23 was changed to the effect that children of Algerian parents who were born in Algeria before Independence benefit from the so-called double *jus soli* only if their parents have been living in France for five years before the birth of their children. Article 44 now reads that children born in France of foreign parents must willingly ask for the French nationality between the ages of 16 and 21. Criminal records are taken into account. For details, see *Le Monde*, 1 January 1994.

68. G. Kepel (1994b, p. 272) thus maintains that the ultimate goal of the federating Union of Islamic Organizations of France is to obtain a minority status for Muslims in France.

69. On the French and British models of integration see P. Weil and J. Crowley (1994).

70. For details, see J. Cesari (1994b), pp. 257-65 and D. Schnapper (1994), pp.132-5.

71. 1994 Report of the Consultative Commission for Human Rights, reported in *Le Monde*, 22 March 1995.

72. According to the Education Ministry, 2,000 girls were concerned at the beginning of the 1994 school year (*Le Monde*, 26 November 1994).

73. Some MPs portrayed the wearing of head-scarves in these terms, in *Le Monde*, 28 October 1993.

74. In *Le Point* (1163), 30 December 1994.

75. Quoted in *Le Monde*, 22 November 1994.

76. Quoted in *Le Monde*, 11–12 September 1994.

77. See Bayrou's October 1993 circular (in *Le Monde*, 28 October 1993) and September 1994 circular (in *Le Monde*, 21 September 1994).

78. Quoted in *Le Monde*, 9 August 1994.

79. Quoted in *Le Monde*, 13 August 1994.

80. Quoted in *Le Monde*, 1–2 January 1995.

81. See *Le Monde*, 5 and 6 January 1995.

82. See footnote 38.

83. Quoted in *France-Soir*, 31 December 1994.

84. *Le Monde*, 4 and 7 January 1995.

85. See the discussion of bilateral and multilateral support in Part 2, chapter 2.

86. Respectively quoted in *Le Monde*, 13 August 1993 and 2 September 1994.

87. Interview in *Le Figaro*, 12 April 1994.

88. *Le Monde*, 13–14 August 1995.

89. All these activities can be judged from press reports on the round up of November 8, 1994 which led to the imprisonment of 77 Islamists. See *Le Monde*, 9,10 and 15 November 1994.

90. See the section on the Rome Conference.

91. Quoted in *Le Monde*, 6 August 1994.

92. Interview with Georges Morin, 29 June 1994.

93. See Anwar Haddam's interview with *Libération*, 6 May 1994 and Rabah Kébir's with *The Financial Times*, 20–21 August 1994.

94. Interview with *Al Hayat* reproduced in *Le Courrier international* (198), 18–24 August 1994.

95. Interview with Jean Audibert, 7 June 1995.

96. UN (1994), volume I, p. 8.

97. In 1992, 2 745 French firms exported to Algeria (Chambre de commerce et d'industrie de Paris (1993), p. 68). French exports of agricultural products (mainly cereals and dairy products) have increased significantly since the latter part of the 1980s as a consequence of Algeria's growing food-dependency. Whereas in the early 1980s French exports of agricultural products accounted for less than a tenth of French total exports to Algeria, they now represent almost a quarter. The remaining three-quarters consist almost entirely of finished manufactured products (capital goods, vehicles, spare parts and consumer goods). See DREE (1995), p. 163.

98. *Ibid.*

99. Maison Lazard et Compagnie *et. al.* (1993), p. 22.

100. This point was emphasised by J.P. Brevost (Total), interview 9 December 1993.

101. OPEC (1994), p. 10.

102. Whereas in 1973 90.5% of crude oil was exported, this share dropped to 41.2% in 1993 (my calculations from *ibid.*, pp. 14 and 24).

103. A. Hirèche (1989), p. 109.

104. IEA (1994b), p. 270.

105. *Ibid.*, p. 269.

106. IEA (1987), volume I, p. 397.

107. My calculations from OPEC (1994), p. 88.

108. France's natural gas consumption tripled between the early 1970s and the early 1990s (IEA (1994b), p. 91). France's domestic output accounts for only 10% of its total natural gas supplies (GDF (1994) p. 14) and the biggest gas field is expected to run dry in the first decade of the next century.

109. Interview with Sadek Boussena, 26 July 1993.

110. These two projects have, nevertheless, materialised. The Trans-Mediterranean pipeline, supplies mainly Italy whereas the Euro-Maghreb pipeline supplies primarily Spain and Portugal from Morocco and Algeria.

111. *Le Monde*, 9 February 1995.

112. GDF (1994), p. 14.

113. *Le Monde*, 25 October 1994.

114. *The Times*, 2 October 1995.

115. See *The Financial Times*, 29 November 1994.

116. *Le Monde*, 31 December 1994. After the hijack, the French-managed air and maritime passenger services to Algeria were cut. This did not include commercial transport (*Le Monde*, 28 December 1994).

117. Calculated from S. Cornot-Gandolphe and M.F. Chabrelle (1995), Table 35.

118. GDF (1994), p. 15. In reality, France's security stocks are said to be equivalent to a year's supply of its two major suppliers.

119. Interview with Christophe Bigot, 21 April 1994.

120. In 1993 France accounted respectively for 23% and 33.2% of Morocco's imports and exports (UN (1994), volume 1, p. 632). For its part, Morocco accounted for 1% of both France's world imports and exports (calculated from Table 5). As for Tunisia, France represented 26.9% and 30% of its imports and exports (UN (1994), volume 1, p. 970). Tunisia accounted for 0.6% and 0.8% of France's imports and exports (calculated from Table 5).

121. See DREE (1995), pp. 190 and 209.

122. For all these figures see BDF (1994b), pp. 75 and 87.

123. Calculated from BDF (1994a), p. 219 and annex, p. 35.

124. See IMF (1994), pp. 458 and 716.

125. L. Tahla (1993), pp. 927 and 932-4 and B. Khader (1992), pp. 99-107.

126. Calculated from: IMF (1994), p. 458 and 716 regarding world FDI in Morocco and Tunisia; bilateral balance of payments between France and these two countries (document obtained from BDF). IMF's exchange rates.

127. For details on Algerian legislation regarding FDI see R. Abdoun (1989) (1982 and 1986 laws); R. Zouaimia (1991) (1990 money and credit law); *Petroleum Economist* (58), December 1991 (1991 hydrocarbon law); *Algérie Actualité* (1481), 4–10 March 1994 (October 1993 investment code).

128. *Algérie Actualité* (1469), 7–13 December 1993.

129. See Audibert's interview with *Jeune Afrique* (1742), 26 May–1 June 1994.
130.   Bilateral balance of payment France-Algeria, obtained from BDF. IMF's exchange rates.
131. Interview with Christophe Bigot, 21 April 1994.
132. Calculated on the basis of Table 13. IMF's exchange rate.

Chapter 2

The Ideological and 'Psychological' Dimensions of French Opposition to the FIS

Much has already been written about the ways in which Westerners' images of a threatening, militant and fanatical Islam were formed and reproduced from the time of the Crusades to contemporary threats against Salman Rushdie or Taslima Nasreen and terrorist attacks against foreigners in Algeria or elsewhere. It therefore is not part of the analysis that follows.[1] The point to be made here is that the French government's opposition to the FIS, while certainly nourished by pre-determined presumptions of Islamism as a necessarily intolerant force, partly derived from its feeling of repulsion towards a political force that asserted itself against France. The anti-French outlook of the FIS or, for that matter, of all the Islamist movements in Algeria, was not understood merely in terms of their (violent or not) protests against the fact that 'France made itself a party to the conflict in Algeria by standing by the exclusionist forces [the eradicators]'.[2] It was also understood in terms of the challenge that the FIS and, more generally, Islamism represented for the hegemony of Western thought to which the French Revolution made its contribution – a challenge which was perceived as anti-Western and anti-French because its potential legitimacy was denied from the start. The French government and, in particular Balladur's, did not hide the view that, in addition to its concrete worries about immigration, terrorism, economic relations and falling dominoes which led it to oppose the FIS, it also did so on ideological grounds.

To a certain extent, the 'ideological confrontation logic' into which the French government allowed itself to settle is representative of the West's general hostility towards political Islam. At the same time, however, it would seem that such confrontation would not have occurred if the FIS was not an Algerian party. In this sense, the ideological element in the French opposition to the FIS would not have taken root if the 'psychological' dimension of the Franco-Algerian relationship was not so peculiar in itself. For, basically, if the FIS' religio-political ideology had been felt as an attack against one of France's most cherished values – secularism – what was most badly received was the

FIS vote, that is, the fact that part of the Algerian people did not recognise themselves in France and in what the French think France represents.

Before actually looking into the French political establishment's ideological and 'psychological' motives for opposing the FIS, it is important to deal with the issue of the French political establishment's understanding of Islamism. It is important because questioning the French political establishment's understanding of this political phenomenon eventually leads us to the issue of French perceptions of Algerian society. And entering the realm of French perceptions of Algerian society is essential to understand the 'psychological' aspect of French opposition to the FIS.

Misunderstanding Islamism or Algerian society?

The French political establishment has been criticised by some in France for holding an economistic view of the Algerian crisis and more specifically of the rise of Islamism. It was argued that the French government failed to see the Islamic resurgence otherwise than as a response to economic hardship and that this failure could be inferred from French policy which consisted in believing that, by pouring money into Algeria, the force of political Islam would be held in check.[3] It is true that the French political establishment as a whole attached great significance to the socio-economic determinant in the rise of Islamism. Although the Left also viewed the lack of socio-economic development in Algeria as a major contributing factor to political instability and to the rise of Islamism, this was particularly obvious in Juppé's speeches. They, indeed, often emphasised that 'underdevelopment [was] a fertile ground where bad ideologies proliferate'[4] and that, therefore, Algeria needed foreign help while proceeding with its transition to market economy:

> It is evident that Algeria's political stabilisation will depend on its success in its economic recovery programme, notably in improving the people's plight. (...) When people are housed, when they can decently get supplies and when they have jobs, they do not have the same inclination for political agitation as when misery and underdevelopment are acute.[5]

Despite the centrality of socio-economic thinking in the French political establishment's view of the success of Islamism in Algeria, it is a simplification to argue that, in its eyes, political Islam came down to a question of bread and butter. The analysis of Islamism put forward by the French political establishment was, indeed, more comprehensive in scope and, in fact, very close to the content of the academic production on that subject. Nevertheless, despite its 'theoretical tools', the French political elite was unable to appreciate the extent of the success of the Islamist discourse in Algeria because its contacts with Algerian society were (and remain) restricted to the secular Western-oriented elite. As a result, French perceptions of Algerian society were truncated: Algerian society at large was, in some way, seen as a mirror image of France.

Islamism in Algeria: explanations

The political establishment's view

As indicated above, for all its stress on the socio-economic dimension of the FIS' success in Algeria, the French political establishment did not hold a completely reductionist or economistic view of political Islam. Juppé, for instance, always argued that Algeria's socio-economic crisis was an important, but not an exclusive, explanatory factor of the FIS' success. In his 11 October 1994 speech to parliament, he also pointed to 'political' and 'moral' factors.[6] The administration of the Quai d'Orsay also had a non-reductionist analysis of Algeria's crisis and of Islamic revivalism. Bigot argued that Islamism was not a new phenomenon in Algeria: it had its roots in the anti-colonial struggle against France and, if at Independence the secular nationalists got the upper hand, movements drawing upon the Islamic idiom emerged again particularly in the 1970s and 1980s. Bigot further argued that the FIS' success in the late 1980s was to be explained by the combination of economic, political and socio-cultural factors. The socio-economic crisis allowed the poor strata to jump on the Islamists' bandwagon and thus to swell the ranks of the FIS' sympathisers. Political factors also contributed to the FIS' success. First and foremost among them, was the legitimacy crisis of the Chadli regime which was associated with economic mismanagement and widespread corruption, thus generating a tremendous popular feeling of injustice. Other political factors were also identified by Bigot, notably, the lack of a structured secular opposition. Lastly, it was recognized that the attractiveness of the FIS' discourse resulted from the identity crisis of the Algerian nation.[7] The Quai d'Orsay's analysis of Islamism in Algeria basically incorporated all the ingredients that can be found in the academic literature dealing with this subject or with Islamism more generally.

The academic view

In the main, although academics might disagree about what they saw as the overriding factors explaining the existence and success of Islamism in Algeria, there was a general consensus around the following issues. First, that the origin of the contemporary Islamist movement in Algeria had to be traced back to the *salafiyya* movement incarnated by Sheik Ben Badis's Association of the Reformist Ulema (1931).[8] Partly as a reaction to French colonialism, the Association of the Reformist Ulema called for an Islamic revival, a reinterpretation of the original text to find answers to the state of subjugation of Algeria. Islamic revivalism, through Arab and Islamic self-assertion, was seen as going hand in hand with liberation from colonial rule. Ben Badis, indeed, argued in 1936 that 'this Muslim Algerian nation is not France, (...) it is not possible for her to be France. (...) this is a nation totally removed from France, by her language, her customs, her ethnic origins, and her religion'.[9] During the anti-colonial war (1954–62), the Association of the Reformist Ulema (as all the nationalist movements) joined the wartime FLN. When the latter transformed itself into a state machine at Independence, the *ulema* were co-opted through the establishment of official Islam and, at the same time, marginalized because their project for building an Islamic state was not part of the secular nationalist elite's agenda. However, this dual process of co-optation / marginalization generated resentment among some *ulema* who, as early as 1964, founded an independent Islamic organization: the Association *Al Qiyam* (The Values). *Al Qiyam* developed as a religious 'soft-opposition', placing its own religious discourse between 'fundamentalism' and 'Islamism'. It did not restrict its religious activism to the moral sphere of private life. Although careful not to directly challenge the authority of the Ben Bella and Boumediene regimes, it developed themes that contested both the social and political order of Algerian society: it advocated re-Islamisation and the implementation of the *shari'a*; demanded official support for religious observance; denounced the laxity of morals and reliance on non-Islamic cultural manifestations; it also criticised imported foreign ideologies (secularism, socialism and communism) for being 'un-Islamic'. Among the members of *Al Qiyam* who had been befriended with Ben Badis's Association, there were such personalities as Ahmed Sahnoun (1908–) and Abdellatif Soltani (1902–84). Both played a significant role in organizing the Islamist movement in Algeria. Abassi Madani (1931–) also joined *Al Qiyam*. Although *Al Qiyam* was banned in 1970, religious currents continued to operate more or less undercover outside the sphere of official Islam, notably through 'free mosques' in the student and popular milieu. Throughout the 1970s, new figures emerged, disappeared and were to re-appear in the 1980s: Abdullah Djaballah (MNI) created and animated the mosque of the University of Constantine and Mahfoud Nahnah (Hamas) protested against the 1976 National Charter's secular and socialist content.

The present day Algerian Islamist movement can thus be seen as the offshoot of the counter-society that grew out of the co-optation of the *ulema* and out of the original rift between the nationalist elites as to their political project for independent Algeria. As it developed, the Algerian Islamist movement became indebted to varied sources of inspiration and became itself more diversified in terms of its approach to politics (greater emphasis on predication or on political activism, greater emphasis on a legalist approach or a violent one to political power) and in terms of what 'the Islamic solution' was meant to bring to Algeria (a fundamentalist or modernist Islamic state).

Second, there was a general consensus among academics as to the factors that contributed to the success of the FIS in the 1980s (even if there was sometimes a tendency to take these factors as an explanation of Islamism *per se* whereas they merely explained its success). Basically, there were three agreed hard-core elements of explanation for the success of Islamism in Algeria: socio-economic marginalization, political exclusion, and the 'crisis of identity'. Whether theorised in the concept of 'the crisis of the authoritarian rentier state'[10] or not, there was a wide acknowledgement that the faltering economy allied to corruption and nepotism favoured political protest on the part of all those – that is the majority – who were economically and politically marginalized, both often working in tandem. In this sense, socio-economic and political exclusion prepared the ground for dissent.[11] It was also recognized that, if the FIS managed to capitalise on these 'economic and political frustrations', it was not only because it addressed the people's grievances against a failed political establishment, but also because its discourse responded to a 'quest for authenticity'. The quest for authenticity was generally seen as being ultimately rooted in the 'identity crisis' of the Algerian nation which resulted from contradictory cultural and political dynamics. Whereas emphasis was put on the Arab-Islamic character of the Algerian nation ever since the anti-colonial struggle, the post-independence state relied on Western models of socio-economic and political organization: secular nationalism, French-designed state-capitalism through the 'industrialising industries' model and then economic liberalism. The contradiction between the maintenance of a traditional value system through official Islam and the introduction of a radical modernisation policy involving rapid social change inevitably created tensions in national identification processes and, thus, fuelled a deep sense of bewilderment and alienation.[12] The Islamist discourse, by tapping into the reservoir of the norms and categories of what appears to be a lost indigenous culture, resolved the contradiction and thus appealed to those in search of an identity.

In addition to these core explanatory factors (socio-economic and political exclusion and crisis of identity/quest for authenticity), some also argued that if Islamism had been better at mobilizing the masses than other opposition forces it was because: (1) it had benefited from a 'logistical advantage' over secular forces since 'free mosques' and social activities provided an independent political space for opposition that non-religious forces could not enjoy under authoritarian rule;[13] (2) Algeria's secular forces showed complete disorganization;[14] and (3) to come full circle, the discourse of these opposition forces did not appeal because it relied on the same political paradigms as the FLN's.[15]

This brief literature review thus shows that the French political establishment had much the same analysis of Islamism in Algeria as academics did. In defence of a policy that sought to undermine the success of Islamism by financially backing the Algerian regime, the assistant-deputy to the Maghreb-Mashreq department argued that there was not much France could do otherwise, at least in the short-run: it could not help towards the lack of legitimacy of the Algerian regime and could not really intervene in matters of identity crisis.[16] Despite its comprehensive view of the rise of Islamism, the French political elite, nevertheless, failed to properly gauge the success of the FIS' discourse because it wore blinkers when looking at Algeria.

French truncated perceptions of Algerian society

The French political establishment failed to understand that the FIS phenomenon was not ephemeral, and not just the result of a 'sanction vote' against the FLN, because it did not realise that in Algeria, as in many other parts of the Muslim world, Islam as an ideational system permeates popular culture as well as social and political life. Islamic categories, values and norms have remained central features of culture in Algeria, not because they would derive from a trans-historical transposition of an unchanging Islamic tradition permeating the Muslim psyche,[17] but because they were given particular salience historically. The anti-colonial struggle against the French occupier played a crucial role in this process because it was by reaction to colonialism that the definition of the Algerian national identity along an Arab-Islamic line emerged – somewhat at the expense of history and diversity.[18] The way in which the war-time FLN was formed (by co-optation or elimination of competing nationalist movements) and the way in which it survived in the post-Independence era also played a role in the reproduction of Islamic culture because the integration of part of the *salafiyya*-orientated nationalist movement within its fold implied that the *ulema's* Islamic project had to be accommodated in some way. Since the FLN never split over ideological disagreements,[19] it found an accommodating solution in a hybrid system of 'Islamic secularism', as coined by Henri Sanson.[20] The state was neither Islamic nor secular: with the exception of personal status,[21] state policies were not governed by Islamic jurisprudence.

Yet, Islam was consecrated as the state religion in all the Constitutions promulgated since 1963, and the state had the duty to encourage religious practice. Islamic principles thus inspired, in part, the organization of public and private life: definition of the Algerian nationality by reference to religion (1963); compulsory religious education at school (1963); prohibition of gambling and of the sale of alcohol (1976); weekly holy day on Fridays (1976); forbidding of pig breeding (1979) and regulation of personal status according to the *fiqu* (1984). In addition, while controlling the *ulema* by turning them into civil servants, all Algerian regimes used the vocabulary of Islam to legitimise their polities – the typical example being the justification of socialism on religious grounds: Algeria's socialism was deemed to be Islamic because it responded to the Islamic tradition of social justice.[22] Official Islam, thus, reproduced the centrality of Islamic categories, values and norms and did not allow any effective secularisation of religion.

This was a process of which Westerners, and more particularly the French, were not markedly aware because the FLN regime presented a secular face when addressing the rest of the world. But Boumediene, for instance, could very well defend the Third World in terms of imperialist exploitation in international conferences and, at home, launch a 'campaign against the relaxation of morals' (1970)[23] or have officials cultivate the theme of the need for authenticity in the journal of the ministry for religious affairs, *Al-Asâla*.[24] This relative unawareness in France was reinforced by the contacts of the French political elite which, in most cases, were limited to the Algerian gallicised *intelligentsia*. The secular, Western-oriented elites (in power or in opposition) simply projected a replica image of France and, thus, promoted the creation of an incomplete vision of Algerian society in French perceptions of that country. Bernard Guetta, a French radio commentator on international news, perfectly illustrates this French view about Algeria:

> For more than three decades Algeria has been independent (...).
> Algeria is Algerian, completely Algerian and, yet, Algeria is France.
> It is no longer, of course, a piece of the French territory or State, but

it is still France because French is being spoken there, because a culture and values (...) are shared with France, because the great city, mirage or lighthouse (...) remains Paris, because the big newspapers there are called *Le Monde*, *Le Figaro*, *Libération*, because Radio-France is being listened to and French television channels are being watched. (...)

Algeria is France, like a relation, even a distant one, is part of the family. Algeria is France because there is not a single Algerian to consider that France is [just] a foreign country among others and not a single Frenchman either who does not know that Algeria is closer to us than Spain, the Netherlands or Norway.[25]

Because, when looking at Algeria, the French elite saw only what they knew and what was similar to themselves, they could not realise the appeal of a discourse revolving around the simple formula 'Islam is the solution'. They could not accept it either.

Ideological and 'psychological' motives

Ideological and psychological motives played their part in the French political establishment's opposition to the FIS. Opposition on ideological grounds was linked to the fact that the FIS challenged France's political legacy by rejecting the principle of secularism, which made it, in the eyes of the French, an inherently regressive political force. This attitude was similar to the more general Western reaction in face of a new type of nationalism. However, the ideological dimension would not have found its place in French public discourse if Franco-Algerian relations had not been tainted with a closeness that hampers France from 'letting Algeria go'.

Islamism and the challenge to Western ideological and cultural hegemony

If Islamism is a vehicle for political opposition to the regimes in power, it indirectly relates to the West since its chief criticism against ruling regimes is to have adopted Western modes of government and Western modes of socio-economic development which are perceived as the root of Muslim societies' ills. Islamism may be understood as the product of disillusionment with the ideologies underpinning the models adopted in the post-independence period. However, it is often too rapidly concluded that Islamism rejects all these models at once. In reality, if there has, indeed, been a disillusionment with models that did not bring about 'true' independence, the original goal (independence from Western hegemony) remains alive. As a result, 'It is in the soil of the old dynamics of decolonisation that, for the main part, 'Islamism' finds its profound roots'.[26] Islamic self-assertion and the re-appropriation of the Islamic idiom can, thus, be viewed as a 'cultural nationalism' meant to repel Western continued ideological and cultural hegemony. As several scholars have argued, more than a break with nationalism, Islamism is its natural development to the ideological and cultural sphere.[27] The contention that Islamism is a 'new-wave nationalism'[28] or the 'supreme stage of nationalism'[29] was well reflected in the FIS' discourse which accused the secular FLN regime of betraying the call of November 1, 1954 for 'the restoration of the sovereign, democratic and social Algerian state within the framework of Islamic principles'.[30] Indeed, Abassi Madani, who received primary education in the *medersa* of the Association of the Reformist Ulema and who joined the FLN's insurrection (and was jailed by the French throughout the Independence War as a result), indicated very clearly that the FIS did not repudiate nationalism as such, but rather the secular form it took at Independence:

> The Algerian state in 1962 did not correspond whatsoever to the state about which we were dreaming on November 1, 1954 and for which we took up arms: an independent state based upon Islamic principles. The state that saw the light under our eyes was grounded on secular and socialist principles. This was a grave deviation, the opened door to ideological and intellectual misleadings with, as a consequence, their inevitable backlash effects from the political and economic viewpoints. (...) We were entering into the era of despair, failure and disaster'.[31]

Ali Benhadji quite clearly demonstrated the symbiosis between nationalism and Islamism when he commented that:

> If my father and my brothers physically expulsed oppressive France from Algeria, I with my brothers and the arms of faith devote myself to intellectually and ideologically banish them [the French]'.[32]

By transposing nationalism onto the ideological and cultural sphere, Islamist movements oppose the inroads of Western culture which, incidentally, have often been referred to as '*world* culture' in the West. The rejection of Western political paradigms for Islamic ones is not comprehensible to the West. There is nothing really odd about this, since the Revolutions that brought about the West's value systems were lived as extremely positive experiences for progress. The Islamists' rejection of the principle of secularism – more than their supposedly anti-democratic agenda[33] – was at the core of the West's profound unease. Indeed, to Westerners, secularism incarnated the freeing of human reason from a supposed God's will and the guarantee of freedom for individuals and minorities. To reject secularism was, thus, equated with repudiating modernity, subordinating Man to God and enforcing a medieval human-made law seen as the word of God.[34] This made the Islamists' agenda particularly reactionary and retrograde in Western eyes. It was particularly so in France where secularism achieved a purist form as a result of the long battle between republican secularists and (often monarchist) clericalists. It is actually noteworthy that if, traditionally, the French Left has been readier than the French Right to defend secularism, the rise of Islamism on the southern shore of the Mediterranean led the Right to champion secularism, indicating a reactive resort to the value system of the Republic.

As argued by Lahouari Addi, the religio-political vocabulary used by the most radical Islamists (in the Algerian case, by Ali Benhadj) generates puzzlement because it does not correspond to the landmarks of modern Western political thought.[35] It also generates a feeling of repulsion perhaps less because this religio-political language revives negative images created by the conflicts between Christendom and Islam than because it recalls Europe's dark Middle Ages against which modern thought triumphed. The replacement, in radical Islamists' discourse, of the vision of an opulent North exploiting the South by the image of a Christian crusader campaign against Islam is greeted in the West as irrational and, as a result, as threatening. But, at the bottom-line, were not Islamists saying exactly the same thing as their secular nationalist opponents, albeit in another form?

As the frontal attack on secularism is generally lived in the West as an aggression, it is also seen as something that must be fought. Juppé clearly demonstrated that, along with all the concrete concerns that the FIS' coming to power would cause, he also opposed the FIS on ideological grounds:

> (...) we have explained that we will show no leniency towards those who struggle against us, against what we represent, against our values, our philosophy of History and Man (...)'[36] and that '(...) we shall combat ideologies that combat us.[37]

There is little doubt that such responses were understood in Islamist circles as further proof of the West's 'crusader mentality' or of the most pernicious aspect of its neo-colonialist scheme: 'depersonalisation'.[38] It is also quite obvious that, as a result, such a language is an engine for self-fulfilling fears about confrontations.

By entering the field of the 'ideological war', with its simplifying logic, the French political establishment was led mistakenly to consider Islamism as a threatening monolith. As any other social and political movement, Islamism has its radicals and moderates who differ not only in terms of the means they intend to use to reach their aims but also in terms of their final objectives (what an Islamic state should be, how the *shari'a* should be understood and implemented, and so on). In this respect, if Islamism was to be part of the indigenous political equation of the Muslim world, as all indicators suggested, the question to be addressed was which of the Islamist movements, or which of their factions, would get the upper hand. Also, since Islamism was born in the late 1960s, it was characterised by an internal evolutionary dynamic to the effect that some Islamist movements did not just seek to return to a mythical past but wished to make their tradition fit into the framework of modernity. It is this internal flexibility and process of change that now needed to be recognized.[39]

It must be suggested that the French political establishment would not have advanced itself through the minefield of ideological confrontation if the new 'voice of the South'[40] had not come from its ex-colony. The psychological component, indeed, played a central role in French opposition to the FIS.

The FIS vote: a 'psychological' trauma for France

Relations between France and Algeria have always been complex, passionate, marked by an attraction/repulsion dynamic. The colonial venture and the atrocities of the war of decolonisation left their stamp on the 'mental universe'[41] of the bilateral relationship and locked both countries in a face-to-face posture from which they have not yet managed to liberate themselves. After the June 1990 elections in Algeria, Benjamin Stora, who analysed the French collective memory/amnesia regarding Algeria, argued that, through the FIS vote, 'Algeria [was] about to become truly independent and to break its attachments with the old colonial power' and that 'the French ought to understand that.' He concluded that the FIS vote allowed Algeria to become a truly foreign country to France.[42] As the events were to show, the French have not really accepted that Algeria, which in the 'French psyche' has always remained a part of France, might assert itself against 'the only good things' of the colonial legacy.

Generally speaking, the reaction of the French (including the political and intellectual elite) to Islamism in Algeria worked along three lines. For the partisans of 'French Algeria' who never accepted de Gaulle's 'treason', the reaction was to say in substance: 'they wanted independence; they got it; they want the FIS; let them have it; it is their problem and they should face its consequences'. It was the 'revenge reaction', common in extreme-right circles.[43] For those who supported Independence or the socialist adventure of the new independent state, the failure of the FLN regime was felt as a personal one. One sentence that turned up often at the time among leftist Frenchmen belonging to the 'Algerian generation' (that is all those who whatever their age confronted the 'Algerian question' at the time of the war of decolonisation) was: 'all this for just that'. By saying this, they expressed their shattered hopes of a Revolution that turned sour and their puzzlement in discovering in Algeria a 'new' country that did not correspond to 'their' Algeria. Lastly, for others, and notably the *pieds-noirs*, the FIS vote was simply felt as a personal loss, as a heartbreak. More generally, one could say that, in a diffuse way, the advent of an Islamic state in Algeria would be felt in France as the third and final severing of the umbilical cord between the French metropole and its former colony. Earlier severings were, in sequence: (1) political Independence under de Gaulle in 1962 and (2) the so-called 'normalisation of bilateral relations' declared by President Pompidou in the wake of Algeria's attempts at achieving economic independence through the highly symbolic oil nationalisation measures in 1971.

In addition to these collective attitudes, it is also worth underlining the crucial role played by the bonds of understanding and, sometimes, of friendship that were woven through the years between the French and Algerian political elites. As shown in Part One, the fact that Dumas was acquainted with Taleb Ibrahimi, who represented the Islamic trend of the FLN party, played a role – even though it might not have been the determining one – in designing a policy that sought to promote a compromise that might have satisfied Islamist challengers without having them in control of the wheels of government. In general, however, bonds of friendship were more often with the gallicised Algerian political elite which was threatened, first politically and then physically, by the Islamist movement and its extremist fringe. In respect to those deep trans-Mediterranean bonds of friendship, Cheysson's comment deserves to be quoted in full. In this interview, Cheysson was not giving an explanation of his reaction to the FIS in particular. However, his memories are precious to the scholar because they provide the keys to understanding much about the French political elite's reaction to the FIS:

> I cannot be objective when it comes to the Maghreb and most particularly to Algeria. I had the pleasing surprise of being asked by General de Gaulle to be in charge of the Sahara at the time of the signature of the Evian accords. [It was a] fascinating co-operation, with a country that just got out of a war against France, on a major

subject of economic independence. I am very Algerian in my reactions all the more because, out of the politicians of the last few years in Algeria, more than half had been my collaborators or advisers during that period. So, I am not impartial.[44]

Cheysson may represent the case *par excellence* of the 'closeness' of the relationship between the Socialist Party and the FLN. Nevertheless, his testimony of the impact that close relations with the Algerian elite had on the French establishment's view of political developments in Algeria remains valid. Indeed, in its vast majority the French political elite reacted negatively to the FIS because of the reasons mentioned throughout Part Three but also because of a sense of solidarity with its peers in Algeria. FIS militants were exaggerating but were not wide of the mark when they said that if the French opposed the FIS it was because 'they cannot accept an Islamic government which would not be under the Elysée's orders'.[45] They were exaggerating in the sense that none of the Algerian governments had ever been 'under the Elysée's orders' even if they encapsulated pro-French elements. But they were not far from the mark either, because a FIS team in Algiers would certainly imply many changes in the way personal relations had operated until then.

To conclude, the main arguments of Part Three may be quickly recalled. We have shown that the French political establishment forecast that the FIS' coming to power would have direct negative consequences on France because of its immigration, national security and economic impact. Of these three types of concern, only immigration problems, in fact, satisfactorily explain France's opposition to both a violent FIS takeover and a compromise between the Algerian regime and the FIS. Indeed, an immigration wave consisting of Algeria's 'modernist' substance and an encouragement to re-Islamisation within the Muslim community living in France were thought possible whichever way the FIS came to power. It was assessed that these events would create tremendous tensions in France's socio-political system. By contrast, apprehensions about a possible questioning of the economic relationship were very low. It was thought unlikely that the FIS would fundamentally review this aspect of the Franco-Algerian relationship, even if it seized power. Nevertheless, economic concerns probably contributed to the French government's opposition to a FIS takeover because, if against all odds the FIS reviewed economic relations, this would have a cost for the French economy (without, however, being catastrophic). But economic concerns played no role at all in the French government's opposition to conciliation in Algeria inasmuch as it was estimated that, within a coalition government, the FIS would not have the power to question economic relations with France. National security concerns presented, as it were, an intermediate case. Anxiety about the possible resort to state-sponsored terrorism by a FIS regime explained France's opposition to a violent FIS takeover and, to a certain extent as well, to conciliation in the sense that the FIS' ambiguous attitude towards violence probably contributed to the view in Paris that France would be better off without the FIS included in government in Algiers.

A FIS victory (by violence or not) was also opposed by France because of the snowball effect it might have throughout North Africa and, in particular, in France's ex-protectorates: Tunisia and Morocco. It was feared that, by demonstration effect and 'revolution export', the end result of a FIS victory might be the emergence of radical Islamist regimes on Europe's southern flank after a period of turmoil. If the Tunisian and Moroccan dominoes fell, the foreseen consequences of a FIS takeover on France, it was said, would be multiplied and thus more difficult to face. The domino effect argument, however simple at first sight, must not be overstated. For, insofar as the French political establishment recognized that the way in which the FIS came to power had different implications for Franco-Algerian relations, it probably also recognized that the way in which the Maghrebi dominoes might fall also mattered. The domino effect theory, in fact, raised some unanswered questions: would Islamist challengers in the Central Maghreb try to overthrow their governments or would they favour an accommodation strategy? If they chose the course of violent action, could they in effect topple their regimes? What kind of strategies would current regimes adopt in face of a more active Islamist challenge? How radical and anti-French might Islamist regimes prove to be? Did the French government have sound answers to all these questions? If not, then one cannot truly understand why domino thinking was so central to the French government's opposition to the FIS unless one were to argue that the French government relied on the mere view that it was within the odds that neighbouring Islamist movements might take power violently, thus bringing about potentially radical regimes which would be likely to question the past relationship with France. The realm of the possible may, indeed, be a basis upon which foreign policy is decided. This may be all the more so when ideological motives are involved.

As demonstrated in chapter two, ideological hostility to the Islamists' political project played a role in the French political establishment's opposition to a FIS takeover and to conciliation because the FIS' rejection of secularism made it a necessary anti-modernist political force to French observers. Beyond the issue of whether the FIS should be considered as regressive or not, French ideological opposition to the FIS would not have arisen if the relationship between France and Algeria had not been so complex in itself. A century of colonisation and the War of Liberation have marked collective attitudes on both sides. In France, Algeria has continued to be viewed as a part of France. It was perceived as a French-speaking country (even though it does not take part in the *francophonie* summits, which it denounced as sheer neo-colonialism) whose polity was secular and in line with the times (claims for self-determination in the 1960s, for international restructuring in the 1970s and a shift to *infatah* economic policies the 1980s). The FIS vote demonstrated that if the Algerian elite had the same frame of mind as the French, not all Algerians saw France as a near kin. This very fact has been difficult to accept in France. Bonds of understanding and friendship between French and Algerian elites reinforced French hostility to the FIS both because the French political establishment sought to defend its peers across the Mediterranean and because a 'change of staff' in Algiers would question the way in which personal relations operated up until the present.

Notes

1. See e.g. E. Said (1991); M. Rodinson (1988); H. Jaït (1985).
2. Sheik Abdullah Djaballah (leader of the MNI), comment made during the conference on 'The Future of Maghrib' organized by the Geopolitics and International Boundaries Research Centre, 6–7 October 1994, Royal Institute of International Affairs, London.
3. F. Burgat (1995), pp. 39-40 who generalises the argument to most 'international observers' and J. Cesari (1994/95), pp. 177-9.
4. Speech to parliament, 11 October 1994 in MAE (September–October 1994), p. 204.
5. Press conference on 23 June 1994 in MAE (May–June 1994), p. 317.
6. In MAE (September–October 1994), p. 204. See also his press conference of 14 April 1994 in MAE (March–April 1994), p. 176.
7. Interview with the author, 21 April 1994. Claude Cheysson insisted for his part on the lack of socio-economic development (due, in part, to the legacy of French colonialism) and on the identity crisis of the Algerians (Interview with the author, 22 April 1994).
8. See e.g. C. Spencer (1994); M. Gilsnan (1992); A. Khelladi (1992); A. Lamchichi (1992); M. Al-Ahnaf *et. al.* (1991); L. Anderson (1991); F. Jeanson (1991); F. Burgat (1988a); H. Roberts (1988).
9. Quoted in P. Djité (1992), pp. 17-8. It was actually on the basis of Ben Badis's trilogy 'Arabic is my language, Algeria my country and Islam my religion' that the various pre-nationalist movements came to claim Independence from France.
10. B. Dillman (1992); J. Entelis (1992).
11. C. Spencer (1994); E. Hermassi and D. Vandewalle (1993); J. Tzschaschel (1993); A. Lamchichi (1992); J. Ruedy (1992); R. Mortimer (1991); T. Fabre (1990).

12. C. Spencer (1994); A. Lamchichi (1992); J. Ruedy (1992); T. Fabre (1990). For an account of the failed cultural synthesis in Algeria, see I. Zartman (1985). For an insight into the contradictory effects of Arabisation, see J. Entelis (1981). The themes of discredited regimes and of the crisis of identity are also found in the general literature on Islamism. See e.g. N. Ayubi (1991); J. Esposito (1988).

13. J. Ruedy (1992); L. Addi (1990); H. Roberts (1988). The view that, in authoritarian regimes, the mosque becomes the privileged channel of political protest is also developed in the literature dealing with Islamism. See e.g. S. Zubaida (1993) or L. Hadar (1993). On the development of 'free mosques' in Algeria, see A. Rouadjïa (1990).

14. B. Dillman (1992); D. Brumberg (1991).

15. B. Dillman (1992); F. Burgat also argued that the French media and the political class had contributed to undermine the credibility of the secular opposition forces by openly supporting them before the June 1990 elections (document given by the author, dated 24 June 1994). Because of the past relationship with Algeria, political credibility in Algeria derives from the capacity of a political party to dissociate itself from France (notably by anti-French rhetorics which the FLN also used).

16. Interview with Christophe Bigot, 21 April 1994. See also Juppé's claim that 'The only card we are left with today in order to avoid the destabilisation of that country [Algeria], with the domino effects that could follow from it, is the economic card' (in MAE (May–June 1994), p. 199).

17. For a critique of essentialism, see S. Zubaida (1993).

18. The European and/or Christian heritage bequeathed by the Carthaginians (1 100 – 147 BC), the Romans (146 BC – 432), the Vandals (432 – 533), the Byzantines (533 – 633), the short Spanish occupation in the late fifteenth century and French colonialism was wholly rejected. The Arab-Islamic dimension of Algeria's history, which began in the late seventh century with the ousting of the Byzantines by Muslim Arabs (755–1516) and which was reinforced in its Islamic aspect by the Ottoman Empire (1516–1830), was the sole to be retained. The Berber heritage was also simply negated (the Berbers, who peopled the area before these invasions and who constitute some 20% of the Algerian population today, were Arabised and Islamised in the early eighth century. Nevertheless, they constitute an ethnic group with its own language and customs).

19. H. Roberts (1993a), pp. 438-9 and 445.

20. H. Sanson (1983).

21. Until the promulgation of the 1984 Family Code, largely inspired by Islamic jurisprudence, several projects to regulate the personal status (family law, inheritance law and legal representation) had been proposed successively in 1966, 1973 and 1981. The polemic between the religious current and secular leftists around the issue of family and of women's rights did not allow the adoption of any of these projects. As a consequence, until 1984, this domain was regulated both by a colonial decree of 1959 and Islamic jurisprudence. In most cases, the *fiqu* and customary law were applied. See H. Dennouni (1986).

22. For details on the use of Islam by the state as a legitimising tool, see e.g. M. Tozy

(1993); A. Rouadjïa (1990).

23. A. Rouadjïa (1990), pp. 20-3.

24. L.W. Deheuvels (1991).

25. B. Guetta (1995), pp. 261-2.

26. F. Burgat (1995), p. 77.

27. See, in particular, the seminal work of F. Burgat (1995) and (1988a). N. Ayubi (1991) also sees Islamism as cultural nationalism. S. Zubaida (1993) shows that such international events as the Gulf War brought Islamism to be the voice of nationalism and of opposition to Western (political and military) hegemony. Other authors, without concluding that Islamism is nationalism, nevertheless identify it as a reaction to the Westernizing colonial legacy or simply to Westernization: J. Esposito (1992) and (1988); H. Hassan (1990).

28. This is my own formula to sum up the argument of G. Salamé (1993, pp. 22-6) according to which third-generation Islamists (the new wave of militants) would like to be viewed as the true anti-imperialist force.

29. B. Stora interviewed by *Jeune Afrique* (1539), 27 June–3 July 1990.

30. M. Gadant (1982, p. 31) whose book is enlightening about the dynamics between Islam and secularism at the time of the War of Independence.

31. Madani interviewed by S. Zéghidour (1990), p. 180. The brochure of the Algerian Brothers in Britain, 'Jihad in Algeria' (October 29, 1993) also develops the theme of the 'hijack of Algerian Independence by the leftists'. Several authors have underlined that, at any rate in the Algerian case, Islamism is not the repudiation of populist nationalism but its re-appropriation: H. Roberts (1993a) and (1993b); B. Stora (1993); R. Leveau (1992); R. Mortimer (1991); L. Addi (1990).

32. Quoted in *Le Monde*, 16 November 1995.

33. M. Azzam has rightly argued that the argument, according to which an Islamic system of government needed to be resisted because it was unlikely to be democratic, was weak in light of the fact that the vast majority of Arab regimes were undemocratic (1994, p. 92). The issue whether Islamist movements are prone to democratic practices or pathologically anti-democratic has been hotly debated. The view that Islamism and Islamist movements should no longer be treated as a monolith is, however, gaining ground. With it, it is recognized that whereas some movements or some factions within Islamist movements advocate an anti-democratic agenda, others participate to the democratic process and see no incompatibility between Western democratic principles and Islamic principles (*shura, ijma, mubaya* and institutionalized *ijtihad*). For a discussion over this issue see e.g. B. Korany (1994); J. Esposito (1992); J. Esposito and J. Piscatori (1991); J. Iqbal (1983).

34. On the *shari'a-fiqu* distinction, see N. Ayubi (1991), pp. 1-33.

35. L. Addi (1991), pp. 24-5.

36. Interview, 7 March 1994 in MAE (March–April 1994), p. 24.

37. Speech to parliament, 11 October 1994 in MAE (September–October 1994), p. 204.

38. One of the Algerian Islamists' favourite themes is the acculturation objective that France would be seeking in Algeria (see M. Al-Ahnaf *et. al.* (1991), pp. 267-88). It

will be noted that whereas Islamists denounce such an objective in terms of a crusader mentality, secular nationalists did so in terms of 'cultural imperialism' (see e.g. Moroccan B. El Mellouki Riffi's account of French policy towards the Maghreb since Independence (1989), pp. 62-84, 206-23, 249-60). However, both denounce this cultural neocolonialism which is seen as a means to maintain Algeria in a state of dependence.

39. Diversity and internal change are two themes that were particularly developed by F. Burgat (1995) and J. Esposito (1992). Note will be taken that, as of September 1994, Juppé recognized that the Islamist movement in Algeria was divided (see chapter two). Also, it is worth mentioning that, in April 1994, Cheysson argued that it was not possible to talk with the 'fundamentalists', but that dialogue could be established with the 'Islamists' such as Hamas (interview, April 22, 1994).

40. F. Burgat, *L'Islamisme au Maghreb. La voix du Sud*, Paris: Karthala, 1988.

41. J.R. Henry (1992).

42. B. Stora interviewed by *Jeune Afrique* (1539), 27 June–3 July 1990.

43. It is, for instance, the 'le Penist' reaction. Le Pen, who fought in Algeria and who was a sympathiser of the OAS' cause, created in 1960 the National Front for French Algeria (Front national pour l'Algérie française). The OAS (Armed Secret Organization) was a terrorist organization created in 1961 to rally French settlers in Algeria against Independence. General Salan who took part in the abortive *putsch* against de Gaulle's decolonisation scheme was a member of the OAS.

44. Interview with the author, 22 April 1994. A Franco-Algerian public body was created by the Evian Accords to overview the exploitation of oil in Algeria and the construction of infrastructures.

45. M. Bedayoun (1993).

Conclusion:
A Shifting Policy – Supporting
Democratization or Political Stability?

The central argument of this book has been that since the January 1992 coup d'état in Algiers, France's foreign policy towards Algeria has been shifting around the issue of conciliation / eradication *vis-à-vis* the Islamist opposition. In Algeria, the eradication strategy consisted in combating the violence perpetrated by the Islamist armed groups and in eliminating the political project of Islamism at least as it was conveyed by the FIS – the most popular (but also the most radical) political party of the Islamist opposition. In contrast, the conciliation option involved the reintegration of the banned FIS into the political game under commonly agreed conditions regarding, for instance, the respect of democratic rule, of freedom of expression, of human rights, etc. In front of the conciliation / eradication choice, a summary picture of French policy towards Algeria after the 1992 coup d'état until the November 1995 Algerian presidential election brings out a sequence of three shifts: (1) the January 1993 shift under the socialist government of Bérégovoy (April 1992 – March 93) – from promoting compromise with the Islamist mainstream to throwing France's weight behind the Algerian regime which refused such a compromise; (2) the September 1994 shift under the right-wing government of Balladur (March 1993 – May 95) – from buttressing eradication to advocating conciliation; and (3) the October 1995 shift under the Juppé government (May 1995 –) – from supporting the conciliation option only halfheartedly (despite the view that the eradication strategy led nowhere) to urging the Algerian authorities to democratize their political system, which involved conciliation.

The various French governments' foreign policy towards Algeria has been oscillating in this way because the policy principles behind conciliation or eradication were not what mattered to Paris. French policy-makers were concerned about how each of these two strategies affected political stability in Algeria and how their end-result might affect the stability of Franco-Algerian relations. Depending on political and security developments in Algeria, conciliation and eradication were both in turn seen in Paris as strategies preserving stability in Algeria and safeguarding the relationship between France and Algeria. In the last months of Bérégovoy's socialist government, the security situation in Algeria had become worse. A FIS take-over by guerrilla warfare was thought within the odds. This prospect led the Bérégovoy government to support the *status quo*, that is the Algerian regime in power with its eradication strategy. The *rapprochement* with Algiers in January 1993 derived from the French government's view that a FIS violent take-over would involve a significant degree of political instability in Algeria as well as throughout the Mediterranean (by domino and 'revolution export' effects). The prospect of the advent of an anti-Western Islamic state in Algeria was also perceived as threatening the stability of Franco-Algerian relations. Even though it was assumed in Paris that a potential FIS regime would probably not overhaul Algeria's economic ties with France, it was considered that a new regime might broaden its horizons away from France. To a certain extent, Paris was also disquieted about the prospect of a radical revolutionary Islamist regime which might be tempted by international terrorism. Most importantly, the FIS' coming to power was opposed by Paris because of its foreseen disturbing impact on France's socio-political system through the immigration problems it raised (risk of a massive influx of refugees from Algeria and risk of re-Islamisation within the Muslim community living in France).

This series of concerns equally led the Balladur government to support, at first, the Algerian regime in its eradication strategy. The policy of 'FIS containment' was backed under Balladur even after it was believed that the FIS could not take power by warfare. Indeed, the mere reintegration of the FIS within the political process was thought dangerous for political stability in Algeria and the Maghreb because political stability was, without question, equated with regime stability. Moreover, just like the Bérégovoy government, the Balladur government was also led to oppose conciliation because of the perceived risks that this option involved for France, particularly, in the area of immigration. Ideological differences as well as the 'emotional link' between France and Algeria reinforced French hostility to the FIS. From April 1993 to September 1994, the Balladur government, thus, fully backed eradication in Algeria. It provided the Algerian regime with economic aid and established a tight police and intelligence co-operation with Algiers. Some anti-guerrilla military hardware was also sold to the Algerian Army. Finally, France became Algeria's defender on the international scene.

If, at certain times, eradication was viewed in France as the appropriate strategy to preserve political stability in Algeria and to protect the *modus operandi* of Franco-Algerian relations, at other times, conciliation was seen as fulfilling the same goals. In the wake of the 1992 coup d'état, Cresson's socialist government (May 1991 – April 92) believed that force would not resolve the problem of Islamism in Algeria and that, as a result, a certain form of compromise needed to be struck with the Islamists. The Cresson government did not wish the FIS to come to power nor did it wish the FIS to be formally included in the government. It simply hoped that giving a greater weight to the Islamic trend of the state apparatus (and perhaps co-opting some Islamist personalities) would calm down the Islamists after the Algerian authorities' seizure of January 1992. Reaching such a compromise offered a double advantage for Paris. Without significantly changing the power structure and the polity orientations of the Algerian state, a compromise with the FIS back in early 1992 would have helped to maintain stability in the Algerian political arena by avoiding a repressive drift which eventually led to more violence – a cause for embarrassment in Paris later on. In addition, compromise with the FIS at that time would have ensured steadiness in Franco-Algerian relations. Algiers refused to consider France's proposal for conciliation and embarked upon eradicating its Islamist opponents. Without severing relations with Algeria, the Cresson and Bérégovoy governments maintained minimal contacts until January 1993.

Under Cresson and in the early months of the Bérégovoy government, a controlled inclusion of the Islamist movement within the Algerian political system was seen as the best guarantee to save Algeria from political chaos. Under Prime Minister Balladur (after the shift of September 1994) and under Prime Minister Juppé (particularly after October 1995), conciliation was understood as the best solution to get Algeria out of the now generalised political chaos. In September 1994, the Quai d'Orsay came to the conclusion that eradication had failed in its objectives since guerrilla warfare continued unabated. In addition, it was realised that force could not solve the political, economic and social problems on which Islamism thrived. Because Algeria was by then sinking in a devastating political deadlock, conciliation was seen as the only means to restore political stability there. Since the Islamist armed groups were no longer thought to be able to take power by violence and since the FIS had proved relatively flexible in its negotiations with the Algerian authorities, conciliation did not seem so risky an orientation. Other factors may also have led the Balladur government to switch to conciliation. The fact that France was increasingly isolated internationally in its strong support to Algiers may have been one. The Quai d'Orsay's September 1994 shift did not, however, translate into effective policy measures seeking, if not to force, at least to influence the reaching of a political settlement encompassing the FIS. The Balladur government did not directly intervene to bring pressure to bear on the Algerian regime because it considered that a conciliation imposed from abroad was not a viable long-term solution for stability in Algeria. In addition, an active conciliatory policy would have entailed risks of reprisal actions from Algerian eradicators in power.

A month prior to the Algerian presidential election (November 1995), the Juppé government also took a firm stand for conciliation. In the wake of domestic criticisms against President Chirac's policy towards Algeria and in the midst of GIA-sponsored terrorist attacks on French soil, the Juppé government argued that there would be no return to political stability in Algeria without democratization. Letting the FIS run in the presidential election was perceived as too risky. But, the Juppé government certainly thought that the FIS should be accepted back in the political game on the occasion of future parliamentary elections. It showed some firmness by breaking the taboo of politically conditioned economic aid. In view of Prime Minister Juppé's actions, the French government's actual determination to concretely push for conciliation in Algeria can be doubted. However, the move it made in October 1995 clearly showed that Paris believed that conciliation was the key to Algeria's political stability.

Whatever the governments in Matignon, political stability was France's guideline in defining its Algeria policy ever since the 1992 coup d'état. Democracy and human rights became principles of secondary importance. Certainly, when France was supporting a conciliatory solution to Algeria's political crisis, it was also supporting a democratic agenda. But France did not support conciliation because it, first and foremost, supported democratization. Rather, it favoured conciliation only when the Algerian domestic circumstances made it look as the best solution for political stability in Algeria and for stability in Franco-Algerian relations. The contention that the ideal of democracy was only an accessory in France's policy *vis-à-vis* Algeria is well illustrated by France's support of the Algerian authorities' undemocratic rule and by France's unconditional backing of the eradication strategy which involved wide-scale flouting of human rights. It is a tragic irony that Algeria's democratization experience of 1989 – 1991 ended up pushing aside the principle of democracy and convinced many world leaders that, in the Arab/Muslim world at any rate, opening the political system might prove too costly in terms of political stability.

Bibliography

Primary Sources

Interviews by the author
J. Audibert, French Ambassador to Algiers (1989–92); June 7, 1995, Marignane.

C. Bigot, Assistant-deputy to the head of the Maghreb-Mashreq department of the Quai d'Orsay; April 21, 1994, Paris.

S. Boussena, Algerian Minister for Mines and Industry (1989–91) and President of OPEC (1990–91); January 4, 1993; July 26, 1993; April 19, 1994, Grenoble.

J.P. Brevost, Total Company; December 9, 1993, Paris.

C. Cheysson, French Minister for Foreign Affairs (1981–84); April 22, 1994, Paris.

R. Dumas, French Minister for Foreign Affairs (1984–86; 1988–93); May 16, 1995, Paris.

G. Morin, Head of the Maghreb department of the International Secretariat of the Socialist Party; June 29, 1994, Paris.

L. Schmid, Centre d'analyses et de prévisions; July 18, 1995, Paris.

Speeches
MAE, *La Politique étrangère de la France. Textes et documents*. Paris: La Documentation française.

F. Mitterrand (1981), *Politique 2. 1977–1981*. Paris: Fayard.

Secondary Sources

Statistical series
BDF (1994a), *La Balance des paiements et la position extérieure de la France 1993*. Paris: BDF.

BDF (1994b), *Bulletin de la Banque de France. 4 trimestre 1994. Supplément étude*. Paris: BDF.

DREE (1995), *Les Echanges commerciaux de la France en 1994*. Paris: CFCE.

GDF (1994), *Annual Report 1993*. Paris: GDF.

IBRD (1992), *World Debt Tables 1991–1992*. Washington D.C.: IBRD.

IBRD (1994), *World Debt Tables 1994–1995*. Washington D.C.: IBRD.

IEA (1987), *Energy Statistics 1970–1985*. Paris: OECD.

IEA (1994a), *Energy Policies of IEA Countries. 1993 Review.* Paris: OECD.

IEA (1994b), *Oil and Gas Information 1993.* Paris: OECD.

IMF (1994), *Balance of Payments Statistics Yearbook 1994.* Washington D.C.: IMF.

OPEC (1994), *Annual Statistical Bulletin 1993.* Vienna: OPEC.

UN (1994), *International Trade Statistics Yearbook 1993.* New York: UN.

Books, articles and conference papers

B. Abdesselam (1990), *Le Gaz algérien. Stratégies et enjeux.* Alger: Bouchène.

R. Abdoun (1989), 'Le partenariat en Algérie' in *Mondes en développement*, 17 (67), pp. 109-116.

J. Adda and M.C. Smouts (1989), *La France face au Sud: le miroir brisé.* Paris: Karthala.

L. Addi (1990), 'Du FLN au FIS' in *Esprit*, 163 (7–8), pp. 127-8.

L. Addi (1991), 'L'opinion publique française et le FIS' in *Modern & Contemporary France*, 45, pp. 22-6.

M. Akacem (1993), 'Algeria: in Search of an Economic and Political Future' in *Middle East Policy*, 2 (2), pp. 50-60.

M. Al-Ahnaf, B. Botiveau and F. Frégosi (1991), *L'Algérie par ses islamistes.* Paris: Karthala.

R. Aliboni (1993), 'La sécurité militaire en Méditerranée occidentale: le point de vue européen' in A. Vasconcelos (dir.), *Européens et Maghrébins. Une solidarité obligée.* Paris: Karthala, pp. 47-64.

B. Allouche (1989), *Small States and International Mediation. The Case of Algeria.* Algiers: OPU.

L. Anderson (1991), 'Obligation and Accountability: Islamic Politics in North Africa' in *Daedalus*, 120 (3), pp. 93-112.

N. Ayubi (1991), *Political Islam: Religion and Politics in the Arab World.* London: Routledge.

M. Azzam (1994), 'Islam: Political Implications for Europe and the Middle East' in P. Ludlow (ed.), *Europe and the Mediterranean.* London: Brassey's, pp. 89-104.

P.R. Baduel (1994), 'L'impasse algérienne de la transition démocratique' in P.R. Baduel (dir.), *L'Algérie incertaine.* Paris: Edisud, pp. 5-22.

P. Balta (1986), 'French Policy in North Africa' in *The Middle East Journal*, 40 (2), pp. 238-51.

P. Balta (1991), *L'Islam dans le monde.* Paris: Le Monde Editions.

P. Balta and C. Rulleau (1973), *La Politique arabe de la France de De Gaulle à Pompidou.* Paris: Sindbad.

K. Basfao and J.R. Henry (dir.) (1992), *Le Maghreb, l'Europe et la France.* Paris: CNRS.

J.F. Bayart (1984), *La Politique africaine de François Mitterrand*. Paris: Karthala.

N. Beau (1995), *Paris, capitale arabe*. Paris: Le Seuil.

M. Bedayoun (1993), 'The Revival of Islam in Algeria' (lecture organised by the SOAS Islamic Society, November 4, 1993, SOAS, London).

L. Belaïd (1995), 'Les réactions des Algériens vivant en France' in G. Ignasse and E. Wallon (dir.), *Demain l'Algérie*. Paris: Syros, pp. 191-200.

M. Bennoune (1988), *The Making of Contemporary Algeria, 1830–1987. Colonial Upheavals and Post-Independence Development*. Cambridge: Cambridge University Press.

L. Blin and E. Gobe (1991), 'Chronique internationale' in *Annuaire de l'Afrique du Nord 1989*, 28, pp. 469-500.

M. Bonnefous (1992), 'Nouvelle approche en Méditerranée occidentale' in *Défense nationale*, 48 (6), pp. 79-85.

A. Boyer (1992), *L'Institut musulman de la mosquée de Paris*. Paris: CHEAM.

A. Brahimi (1991), *Stratégies de développement pour l'Algérie. Défis et enjeux*. Paris: Economica.

A. Brahimi (1994), 'Algeria now: Crisis and Mutations in Gestation' (seminar organised by the Geopolitics and International Boundaries Research Centre and the Society for Algerian Studies, June 2, 1994, SOAS, London).

I. Brandell (1981), *Les Rapports franco-algériens depuis 1962. Du Pétrole et des hommes*. Paris: L'Harmattan.

D. Brumberg (1991), 'Islam, Elections, and Reform in Algeria' in *Journal of Democracy*, 2 (1), pp. 58-71.

F. Burgat (1988a), 'Islamisme au Maghreb' in *Les Temps modernes*, 500, pp. 75-118.

F. Burgat (1988b), 'De la difficulté de nommer intégrisme, fondamentalisme, islamisme' in *Les Temps modernes*, 500, pp. 119-39.

F. Burgat (1994), 'Les islamistes au révélateur de la crise' in *Annuaire de l'Afrique du Nord 1992*, 31, pp. 201-13.

F. Burgat (1995), *L'Islamisme en face*. Paris: La Découverte.

J. Cesari (1994a), 'Chronique algérienne' in *Annuaire de l'Afrique du Nord 1992*, 31, pp. 615-83.

J. Cesari (1994b), *Etre Musulman en France. Associations, militants et mosquées*. Paris: Karthala-IREMAM.

J. Cesari (1994/95), 'France-Algérie: l'effet 'Airbus'' in *Les Cahiers de l'Orient*, 36/37, pp. 175-91.

Chambre de commerce et d'industrie de Paris (1993), *Répartition des exportateurs et importateurs français par secteurs d'activités à partir de firmexport/firmimport*. Paris: Chambre de commerce et d'industrie de Paris.

A. Charef (1994), *Algérie: le grand dérapage*. Paris: Editions de l'Aube.

D. Colard (1978), 'La politique Méditerranéenne et proche-orientale de Georges Pom' in *Politique étrangère*, 48 (2), pp. 283-306.

Commissariat général du plan (1993), *L'Europe, la France et la Méditerranée: vers de nouveaux partenariats*. Paris: La Documentation Française.

G. Corm (1993), 'La réforme économique algérienne: une réforme mal-aimée?' in *Monde arabe: Maghreb-Machrek*, 139, pp. 9-27.

S. Cornot-Gandolphe and M.F. Chabrelle (1995), *Le Gaz naturel dans le monde. Edition 1995*. CEDIGAZ: Paris.

J.P. Cot (1984), *A l'Epreuve du pouvoir. Le tiers-mondisme pour quoi faire?* Paris: Le Seuil.

J.F. Daguzan (1993/94), 'Les Rapports franco-algériens, 1962–1992. Réconciliation ou conciliation permanente?' in *Politique étrangère*, 58, pp. 885-96.

J. Damis (1984), 'French Foreign Policy' in A. Al-Marayati (ed.), *International Relations of the Middle East and North Africa*. Cambridge (Mass.): Schenkman Publishing Company, pp. 175-204.

J. Damis (1993), 'The Maghreb Arab Union and Regional Reconciliation' in G. Joffé (ed.) (1993a), *North Africa. State, Nation and Region*. London: Routledge, pp.288-96.

H. Davis (1992), 'Taking up Space in Tlemcen. The Islamist Occupation of Urban Algeria. An Interview with Rabia Bekkar' in *Middle East Report*, 179, pp.11-14.

L.W. Deheuvels (1991), *Islam et pensée contemporaine en Algérie. La revue al-asâla (1971–1981)*. Paris: CNRS.

H. Dennouni (1986), 'Les dispositions du code algérien de la famille' in *Annuaire de l'Afrique du Nord 1984*, 23, pp. 711-26.

P. Dévoluy and M. Duteil (1994), *La Poudrière algérienne. Histoire secrète d'une république sous influence*. Paris: Calmann-Levy.

B. Dillman (1992), 'Transition to Democracy in Algeria' in J. Entelis and P. Naylor (eds.), *State and Society in Algeria*. Boulder: Westview Press, pp. 31-51.

A. Djeghloul (1990), 'Le multipartisme à l'algérienne' in *Monde arabe: Maghreb-Machrek*, 127, pp. 194-210.

P. Djité (1992), 'The Arabization of Algeria: Linguistic and Sociopolitical Motivations' in *International Journal of the Sociology of Language*, 98, pp. 15-28.

K. Duran (1989), 'The Second Battle of Algiers' in *Orbis*, 33 (3), pp. 403-21.

M. Ecrement (1986), *Indépendance politique et libération économique. Un quart de siècle de développement de l'Algérie (1962–1985)*. Alger/Grenoble: ENAP-OPU/PUG.

B. El Mellouki Riffi (1989), *La Politique française de coopération avec les Etats du Maghreb (1955–1987)*. Paris/Casablanca: Publisud/Toubkal.

D. Engelis (1994), address on the European policy towards the Maghrib given at the conference on 'The Future of Maghrib' organised by the Geopolitics and International Boundaries Research Centre, 6–7 October 1994, Royal Institute of International Affairs, London.

J. Entelis (1981), 'Elite Political Culture and Socialization in Algeria: Tensions and Discontinuities' in *The Middle East Journal*, 25 (2), pp. 191-208.

J. Entelis (1986), *Algeria. The Revolution Institutionalized*. Boulder: Westview Press.

J. Entelis (1992), 'The Crisis of Authoritarianism in North Africa: the Case of Algeria' in *Problems of Communism*, XLI (3), pp. 71-81.

J. Entelis and L. Arone (1992), 'Algeria in Turmoil: Islam, Democracy and the State: in *Middle East Policy*, 1 (2), pp. 23-35.

J. Esposito (1988), *Islam. The Straight Path*. New York/Oxford: Oxford University Press.

J. Esposito (1992), *The Islamic Threat: Myth or Reality?* New York/Oxford: Oxford University Press.

J. Esposito and J. Piscatori (1991), 'Democratization and Islam' in *The Middle East Journal*, 45 (3), pp. 427-40.

P. Euzière (1994), 'Algérie: autopsie d'une tragédie annoncée' in *Cahiers du communisme*, 70 (9), pp. 68-75.

P. Eveno (1994), *L'Algérie*. Paris: Le Monde Editions.

T. Fabre (1990), 'L'Algérie. Islam et démocratie' in *Esprit*, 165 (10), pp. 113-22.

F. Faria (1994), 'The Portuguese View of the Maghreb' (address given at the conference 'The Future of the Maghrib', organised by the Geopolitics and International Boundaries Research Centre, 6–7 October 1994, Royal Institute of International Affairs, London).

F. Favier and M. Martin-Roland (1990), *La Décennie Mitterrand. Les Ruptures (1981–1984)*. Volume I. Paris: Le Seuil.

M. Gadant (1982), *Islam et nationalisme en Algérie d'après 'El Moudjahid' organe central du FLN de 1956 à 1962*. Paris: L'Harmattan.

GDF (1990), *Technologie et progrès*. Paris: GDF.

M. Gilsnan (1992), *Recognising Islam. Religion and Society in the Modern Middle East*. London: I. B. Tauris & Co. Ltd.

P. Golub (1994/95), 'Etats-Unis-Algérie: les ambiguïtés d'une politique' in *Les Cahiers de l'Orient*, 36/37, pp. 193-203.

P.M. Gorce (de la) (1993), 'Paris et Washington face à la crise' in *Le Monde Diplomatique*, 473, pp. 6–7.

N. Grimaud (1984a), *La Politique extérieure de l'Algérie (1962–1978)*. Paris: Karthala.

N. Grimaud (1984b), 'Nouvelles orientations des relations entre la France et l'Algérie' in *Monde arabe: Maghreb-Machrek*, 103, pp. 96-106.

N. Grimaud (1986), 'Algeria and Socialist France' in *The Middle East Journal*, 40 (2), pp. 252-66.

N. Grimaud (1991), 'Prolongements externes des élections algériennes' in *Les Cahiers de l'Orient*, 23, pp. 29-40.

N. Grimaud (1993), 'La diplomatie sous Chadli ou la politique du possible' in *Annuaire de l'Afrique du Nord 1991*, 30, pp. 401-35. Paris: CNRS.

B. Guetta (1995), *Géopolitique*. Paris: Editions de l'Olivier.

L. Hadar (1993), 'What Green Peril?' in *Foreign Affairs*, 72 (2), pp. 27-42.

F. Halliday (1993), address on the theme of '*L'Islam, l'islamisme et nous*' at the conference '*Un péril islamiste?*', 4 *Carrefour de la pensée*, December 9–10, 1993, Le Mans.

A. Hargreaves (1994), 'The Algerian Community in France' (lecture organised by the Society for Algerian Studies, May 23, 1994, SOAS, London).

A. Hargreaves and T. Stenhouse (1991), 'Islamic Beliefs among Youths of Immigrant Origin in France' in *Modern & Contemporary France*, 45, pp. 27-35.

H. Hassan (1990), 'Islamic Revivalism and its Impact on the Middle East and the Superpowers' in J. Chay (ed.), *Culture and International Relations*. New York/London: Praeger, pp. 207-20.

Haut conseil à l'intégration (1992), *Conditions juridiques et culturelles de l'intégration*. Paris: La Documentation Française.

J.R. Henry (1992), 'L'univers mental des rapports franco-algériens', in K. Basfao and J.R. Henry (dir.), *Le Maghreb, l'Europe et la France*. Paris: CNRS, pp. 369-77.

E. Hermassi and D. Vandewalle (1993), 'The Second Stage of State Building' in I. Zartman and D. Habeeb (eds.), *Polity and Society in Contemporary North Africa*. Boulder: Westview Press, pp. 19-41.

M. Hernando de Larramendi (1993), 'Chronique internationale' in *Annuaire de l'Afrique du Nord 1991*, 30, pp. 477-548.

A. Hirèche (1989), *Algérie: l'après-pétrole. Quelles stratégies pour 1995 et 2005?* Paris: L'Harmattan.

J. Iqbal (1983), 'Democracy and the Modern Islamic State' in J. Esposito (1983), *Voices of Resurgent Islam*. New York/Oxford: Oxford University Press, pp. 252-60.

H. Jaït (1985), *Europe and Islam*. Berkeley: University of California Press.

A. Jazouli (1992), *Les Années banlieues*. Paris: Le Seuil.

F. Jeanson (1991), *Algéries. De Retour en retour*. Paris: Le Seuil.

C. Jelen (1991), *Ils feront de bons Français. Enquête sur l'assimilation des Maghrébins*. Paris: R. Laffont.

G. Joffé (1993b), 'The Development of the UMA and Integration in the Western Arab World' in G. Nonneman (ed.), *The Middle East and Europe. The Search for Stability and Integration*. London: Federal Trust for Education and Research (second edition), pp. 203-18.

G. Joffé (1994a), 'Algeria: the Failure of Dialogue' in Europa Publications, *The Middle East and North Africa 1995*. London: Europa Publications Ltd. (41th edition), pp. 3-14.

G. Joffé (1994b), 'Conditionality and European Aid to the Maghrib' (address given at the conference 'The Future of the Maghrib', organised by the Geopolitics and International Boundaries Research Centre, 6–7 October 1994, Royal Institute of International Affairs, London).

A. Kapil (1992), 'L'évolution du régime autoritaire en Algérie: le 5 octobre et les réformes politiques de 1988–89' in *Annuaire de l'Afrique du Nord 1990*, 29, pp. 417-57.

G. Kepel (1991), *Les Banlieues de l'Islam. Naissance d'une religion en France*. Paris: Le Seuil (second edition).

G. Kepel (1994b), *A l'Ouest d'Allah*. Paris: Le Seuil.

B. Khader (1992), *Le grand Maghreb et l'Europe. Enjeux et perspectives*. Paris: Publisud.

A. Khelladi (1992), *Algérie: les islamistes face au pouvoir*. Alger: Alfa.

E. Kolodziej (1974), *French International Policy under De Gaulle and Pompidou: the Politics of Grandeur*. Ithaca: Cornell University Press.

B. Korany (1991), 'From Revolution to Domestication: the Foreign Policy of Algeria' in B. Korany and A. Hillal Dessouki (eds.), *The Foreign Policies of Arab States: the Challenge of Change*. Boulder: Westview Press, pp. 103-55.

B. Korany (1994), 'Arab Democratization: a Poor Cousin?' in *Political Science & Politics*, 27 (3), pp. 511-13.

A. Krieger-Krynicki (1988), 'The Children of Muslim Immigrants in France' in T. Gerholm and Y. Lithman (eds.), *The New Islamic Presence in Western Europe*. London: Mansell, pp. 123-32.

L'Algérie au cœur (1994), *L'Algérie au cœur*, 1, mai–juin 1994.

S. Labat (1994), 'Islamismes et islamistes en Algérie. Un nouveau militantisme' in G. Kepel (dir.) (1994a), *Exils et Royaumes. Les appartenances au monde arabo-musulman aujourd'hui*. Paris: FNSP, pp. 41-67.

S. Labat (1995a), *Les islamistes algériens. Entre les urnes et le maquis*. Paris: Le Seuil.

S. Labat (1995b), 'Le FIS à l'épreuve de la lutte armée' in R. Leveau (dir.), *L'Algérie dans la guerre*. Bruxelles: Editions Complexe, pp. 87-110.

A. Lamchichi (1992), *L'Islamisme en Algérie*. Paris: L'Harmattan.

A. Lassassi (1988), *Non-Alignment and Algerian Foreign Policy*. Avebury: Aldershot.

J.J. Lavenue (1993), *Algérie: la démocratie interdite*. Paris: L'Harmattan.

R. Lawless (1984), 'Algeria: the Contradictions of Rapid Industrialisation' in R. Lawless and A. Findlay (eds.), *North Africa: Contemporary Politics and Economic Development*. London: Croom Helm, pp. 153-90.

A. Lebon (1992), *Aspects de l'immigration et de la présence étrangère en France, 1991–1992*. Paris: La Documentation Française.

A. Lebon (1994), *Situation de l'immigration et présence étrangère en France, 1993–1994*. Paris: La Documentation Française.

Les Amis d'Alger Républicain en France, *Bulletin n° 2*.

R. Leveau (1988), 'The Islamic Presence in France' in T. Gerholm and Y. Lithman (eds.), *The New Islamic Presence in Western Europe*. London: Mansell, pp. 107-22.

R. Leveau (1992), 'Algeria: Adversaries in Search of Uncertain Compromises', in *Chaillot Papers*, 4, pp. 1-29.

R. Leveau (1995), 'Derrière la violence, la négociation' in R. Leveau (dir.), *L'Algérie dans la guerre*. Bruxelles: Editions Complexe, pp. 111-34.

D. Levy (1987), 'Foreign Policy: Business as Usual?' in S. Mazey and M. Newman (eds.), *Mitterrand's France*. London: Croom Helm, pp. 166-91.

D. MacShane (1982), *François Mitterrand: a Political Odyssey*. London: Quartet Books.

Maison Lazard et Compagnie, Lehman Brothers, S.G. Warburg & Co. Ltd. (1993), *Algeria. Economic Information Memorandum*.

L. Martinez (1995), 'L'enivrement de la violence: 'djihad' dans la banlieue d'Alger' in R. Leveau (dir.) (1995), *L'Algérie dans la guerre*. Bruxelles: Editions Complexe, pp. 39-70.

C. Moore (1994), 'The Islamic Challenge and Contemporary US Policy' (address given at the conference 'The Future of the Maghrib', organised by the Geopolitics and International Boundaries Research Centre, 6–7 October 1994, Royal Institute of International Affairs, London).

R. Mortimer (1984), *The Third World Coalition in International Politics*. Boulder: Westview Press.

R. Mortimer (1991), 'Islam and Multiparty Politics in Algeria' in *The Middle East Journal*, 45 (4), pp. 575-93.

R. Mortimer (1992), 'Algerian Foreign Policy in Transition' in J. Entelis and P. Naylor (eds.), *State and Society in Algeria*. Boulder: Westview Press, pp. 241-66.

S. Mouhoubi (1989), *La Politique de coopération algéro-française. Bilan et perspective*. Paris/Alger: Publisud/OPU.

M. Naudy (1993), *Un Crime d'Etats. L'affaire Mécili*. Paris: Albin Michel.

P. Naylor (1992), 'French-Algerian Relations, 1980–1990' in J. Entelis and P. Naylor (eds.), *State and Society in Algeria*. Boulder: Westview Press, pp. 217-40.

T. Niblock (1993), 'Towards a Conference on Security and Cooperation in the Mediterranean and the Middle East (CSCM)' in G. Nonneman (ed.), *The Middle East and Europe. The Search for Stability and Integration*. London: Federal Trust for Education and Research (second edition), pp. 251-5.

Notes de la fondation Saint-Simon (1995), *Comprendre l'Algérie*, 73. Paris: Saint-Simon.

M. Ortega (1993), 'Structures pour la sécurité et la coopération en Méditerranée occidentale' in *Etudes internationales*, 49 (4), pp. 70-103.

C. Pellegrini (1992), *Le FIS en France, mythe ou réalité?* Paris: Edition 1.

R. Pelletreau, D. Pipes and J. Esposito (1994), 'Symposium: Resurgent Islam in the Middle East' in *Middle East Policy*, 3 (2), pp. 1-21.

V. Perthes (1994), 'The German View of the Maghreb' (address given at the conference 'The Future of the Maghrib', organised by the Geopolitics and International Boundaries Research Centre, 6–7 October 1994, Royal Institute of International Affairs, London).

K. Pfeifer (1992), 'Economic Liberalization in the 1980s: Algeria in Comparative Perspective' in J. Entelis and P. Naylor (eds.), *State and Society in Algeria*. Boulder: Westview Press, pp. 97-116.

H. Roberts (1988), 'Radical Islamism and the Dilemma of Algerian Nationalism: the Embattled Arians of Algiers' in *Third World Quarterly*, 10 (2), pp. 556-89.

H. Roberts (1993a), 'The Algerian State and the Challenge of Democracy' in *Government and Opposition*, 27 (4), pp. 433-54.

H. Roberts (1993b), 'The FLN. French Conceptions, Algerian Realities' in G. Joffé (ed.) (1993a), *North Africa. State, Nation and Region*. London: Routledge, pp. 111-41.

H. Roberts (1994), 'Algeria between Eradicators and Conciliators' in *Middle East Report*, 189, pp. 24-7.

M. Rodinson (1988), *Europe and the Mystique of Islam*. London: I.B. Tauris & Co. Ltd.

A. Rouadjïa (1990), *Les Frères et la mosquée. Enquête sur le mouvement islamiste en Algérie*. Paris: Karthala.

A. Rouadjïa (1995), 'Corruption: le pillage légalisé' in *Croissance*, 379, pp. 36-8.

F. Rouziek (1989), 'Chroniques intérieures. Algérie' in *Annuaire de l'Afrique du Nord 1987*, 26, pp. 549-81.

F. Rouziek (1990), 'Chronique algérienne' in *Annuaire de l'Afrique du Nord 1988*, 27, pp. 575-627.

F. Rouziek (1991), 'Chronique algérienne' in *Annuaire de l'Afrique du Nord 1989*, 28, pp. 533-88.

F. Rouziek (1992), 'Chronique algérienne' in *Annuaire de l'Afrique du Nord 1990*,

29, pp. 635-75.

F. Rouziek (1993), 'Chronique algérienne' in *Annuaire de l'Afrique du Nord 1991*, 30, pp. 597-643.

J. Ruedy (1992), *Modern Algeria. The Origins and Development of a Nation.* Bloomington: Indiana University Press.

C. Rulleau (1989), 'La nouvelle Constitution algérienne: une volte-face complète' in *Les Cahiers de l'Orient*, 14, pp. 157-69.

L. Rummel (1992), 'Privatization and Democratization in Algeria' in J. Entelis and P. Naylor (eds.), *State and Society in Algeria*. Boulder: Westview Press, pp. 53-71.

S. Sadi (1992), *Plate-forme pour l'Algérie républicaine. Réinventer novembre.*

E. Said (1991), *Orientalism. Western Conceptions of the Orient.* London: Penguin Books (third edition).

G. Salamé (1993), 'Islam and the West' in *Foreign Policy*, 90, pp. 22-37.

H. Sanson (1983), *Laïcité islamique en Algérie.* Paris: CNRS.

D. Schnapper (1994), 'The Debate on Immigration and the Crisis of National Identity' in *West European Politics*, 17 (2), pp. 127-39.

C. Silberzahn (1995), *Au Cœur du secret. 1500 jours aux commandes de la DGSE. 1989–1993.* Paris: Fayard.

C. Spencer (1993), *The Maghreb in the 1990s. Political and Economic Developments in Algeria, Morocco and Tunisia (Adelphi Paper, 274).* London: IISS/Brassey's.

C. Spencer (1994), 'Algeria in Crisis' in *Survival*, 36 (2), pp. 149-63.

B. Stora (1993), 'L'Islamisme algérien' in *Esprit*, 196, pp. 163-7.

A. Sydnes (1989), *The Franco-Algerian Affair: Love and Hate in Natural Gas Trade.* Lysaker: The Fridtjof Narsen Institute.

L. Tahla (1993), 'Relations Europe-Maghreb. La question des investissements directs' in *Revue Tiers-Monde*, 34, pp. 927-35.

H. Terrel (1994), 'L'enclave islamique de la rue Jean-Pierre Timbaud' in G. Kepel (dir.) (1994a), *Exils et Royaumes. Les appartenances au monde arabo-musulman aujourd'hui.* Paris: FNSP, pp. 347-63.

M. Tozy (1993), 'Islam and the State' in I. Zartman and W. Habeeb (eds.), *Polity and Society in Contemporary North Africa.* Boulder: Westview Press, pp. 102-22.

Y. Troquet (le) (1994), 'Maghreb. Chronique internationale' in *Annuaire de l'Afrique du Nord 1992*, 31, pp. 475-523.

J. Tzschaschel (1993), 'Algeria Torn between Fundamentalism and Democracy' in *Aussenpolitik*, 44 (1), pp. 23-34.

C. Wauthier (1995), *Quatre Présidents et l'Afrique. De Gaulle, Pompidou, Giscard d'Estaing, Mitterrand.* Paris: Le Seuil, 1995.

P. Weil and J. Crowley (1994), 'Integration in Theory and Practice: A Comparison of France and Britain' in *West European Politics*, 17 (2), pp. 110-26.

C. Withol de Wenden (1991), 'Les beurs et la guerre' in *Esprit*, 172, pp. 102-7.

C. Withol de Wenden (1992a), 'L'immigration maghrébine, entre une représentation figée du passé et une perception fantasmatique du présent' in K. Basfao and J.R. Henry (dir.), *Le Maghreb, l'Europe et la France*. Paris: CNRS, pp. 391-400.

C. Withol de Wenden (1992b), 'Immigration et imaginaire' in E. Rude-Antoine (dir.), *L'Immigration face aux lois de la République*. Paris: Karthala, pp. 69-81.

I. Zartman (1985), 'Political Dynamics of the Maghrib: the Cultural Dialectic' in H. Barakat (ed.), *Contemporary North Africa. Issues of Development and Integration*. London: Croom Helm, pp. 20-36.

I. Zartman and A. Bassani (1987), *The Algerian Gas Negotiations*. Washington D.C.: Foreign Policy Institute.

S. Zéghidour (1990), 'Pour un nouvelle légalité islamique. Entretien avec Abbassi Madani' in *Politique internationale*, 49, pp. 177-92.

A. Zerouali (1994), 'The People's Choice' in *Index on Censorship*, 23 (4/5), pp. 163-5.

R. Zouaimia (1991), 'Le régime de l'investissement international en Algérie' in *Revue algérienne des sciences juridiques, économiques et politiques*, 29 (3), pp. 403-32.

S. Zubaida (1993), *Islam, the People and the State. Essays on Political Ideas and Movements in the Middle East*. London: I. B. Tauris & Co. Ltd. (second edition).

The Press

Algerian press: Press cuts of the Centre Culturel de la République Algérienne, Paris.

French press: Press cuts of the Institut d'Etudes Politiques, Grenoble.

Personal press reviews: *Europe Daily Bulletin*

Le Monde

MEED

MEI

Index